dance **to the piper**

The Highland Bagpipe in Nova Scotia

Barry W. Shears

Cape Breton University Press
Sydney, Nova Scotia

Cape Breton University Press recognizes the support of the Province of Nova Scotia, through the Department of Tourism, Culture and Heritage and the support received for it publishing program from the Canada Council's Block Grants Program. We are pleased to work in partnership with these bodies to develop and promote our cultural resources.

NOVA SCOTIA
Tourism, Culture and Heritage

Canada Council   Conseil des Arts
for the Arts   du Canada

Cover Design: Cathy MacLean, Pleasant Bay, NS
Layout: Gail Jones, Sydney, NS
Printing in Canada by Transcontinental Printing/Book Division.

Library and Archives Canada Cataloguing in Publication

Shears, Barry, 1956-
    Dance to the piper : the Highland bagpipe in Nova Scotia / Barry W. Shears.

ISBN 978-1-897009-33-8.--.SBN 1-897009-33-X

    1. Bagpipe--Social aspects--Nova Scotia. 2. Bagpipe--Nova Scotia--History. 3. Bagpipers--Nova Scotia--Biography. I. Title.

ML980.S539 2008   788.4'909716   C2008-902874-0

Cape Breton University Press
PO Box 5300
Sydney, NS B1P 6L2 Canada

"The bagpipe and the spinning wheel are still heard discoursing sweet music within their dwellings." [1]

Fig. 1. *"Big" Farquhar and Margory MacKinnon, East Lake Ainslie, ca. 1910. East Lake Ainslie Historical Society.*

---

1. Spedan, *Rambles Among the Bluenoses*, 197.

Acknowledgements

In 1968, at the age of twelve and at my father's urging, I began to learn to play the Highland Bagpipe. My first piping instructor was Angus MacIntyre, an elderly piper and retired coal miner then living in Glace Bay. I don't remember what first attracted me to the instrument but over the years it has become a passionate interest indeed, first as a competitor and later as a part-time researcher of pipers and pipe music in Nova Scotia.

I fondly remember those Friday afternoons after school sitting in his sun porch going over my weekly lessons, the air heavy with the smell of pipe tobacco. Of particular interest to me were the stories of pipers, both in Cape Breton and in Scotland, which were occasionally inserted between explanations of grace notes and quarter notes, strathspeys and reels. In essence, the seeds for this book were sown in Glace Bay almost forty years ago.

This project could never have reached fruition without the contributions and support of several people. I would like to take this opportunity to thank my late father, Angus MacLean Shears, whose knowledge and passion for history continues to be an inspiration; Ron Caplan, John Gibson and the late Paddy MacIntyre, for their advice and encouragement; the dozen or so individuals, most of who have passed on, who kindly shared memories and music. A special thanks to the Helen Creighton Folklore Society for their generous financial support and permission to include a portion of Helen's field recordings in the accompanying recording; the staff at the Nova Scotia Archives and Records Management for their assistance. This book would seem naked without the numerous photographs which put a human face on this particular aspect of Gaelic culture and so I would like to thank the following people and organizations for allowing me to use photographs in their possession: Ron Caplan, Donnie Campbell, Kerry Delorey, Janice Ferguson, Hazel MacIntyre, Roddy MacLennan, Margaret Gillis, John Gibson, the late Alex Holmes, the late Paddy MacIntyre, and Allister MacGillivray, Donald D. Munro, Eugene Quigley, James O. Ross, Randy Smith, Ian Gillies, The Beaton Institute, The National Library of Scotland and the Nova Scotia Archives and Records Management.

Additional material was generously provided by Jim Watson, Iona, Effie Rankin, Mabou; Stan Chapman, Antigonish; Keith Sanger, Edinburgh; John Pearson, Brian and Kathleen Stinson and Colin MacRae, Seattle.

This book is the result of more than twenty-five years of research into the piping traditions of Nova Scotia. I am indebted to Saint Mary's University, Halifax, and the university's Atlantic Canada Studies Program for allowing me the opportunity to present my research in a contextual format which resulted in the completion of my Master of Arts degree in 2005 and to Mike Hunter, Editor, Cape Breton University Press, for his suggestions and advice. Thanks also to professors: Heather MacLeod, Peter Twohig, Richard Twomey, Margaret Harry, all of Saint Mary's University, for their invaluable advice and encouragement, and Professor Jamie MacDonald who travelled from Antigonish to sit on the examiners panel in addition to making several helpful suggestions. A special thank you to my thesis supervisor Professor John G. Reid for his interest in the topic, and his advice on what in the beginning was an enormous amount of research. Dr. Reid helped pilot the research through the shoals of verbosity and repetition. Any glaring errors or omissions are the sole responsibility of the author.

My family has always been very encouraging of my endeavours. A special thank you to my wife, Margaret, and two daughters, Alison and Siobhan for their continued love and support. My wife Margaret has always been extremely supportive of my research and musical interests. Many of our family vacations were often interrupted by temporary detours in order for me to visit and record the old-style pipers, and I am forever indebted for my family's understanding and patience in this regard.

B.W.S.

Editor's note: Except where otherwise noted, images are from the author's personal collection.

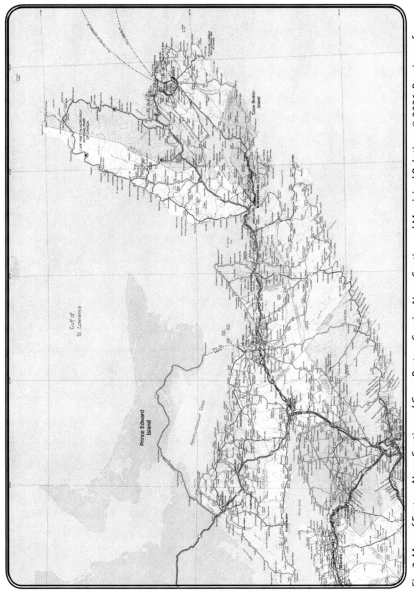

Fig. 2. Map of Eastern Nova Scotia and Cape Breton. Service Nova Scotia and Municipal Relations © 2006. Province of Nova Scotia. All rights reserved.

Table of Contents

U.S. and U.K. purchasers may download accompanying music by going to:
www.cbupress.ca/piper.
See Appendix G, page 218.

Barry W. Shears

Introduction

Soulful Music for a Soulful People

The music of the bagpipes, like every other kind of music, cannot be understood or appreciated unless it is heard in its proper and natural setting. It is not the music of the music hall, although it has been played there, and when you confine it within walls and a ceiling it is like chaining a lion to a tree or caging an eagle. The pibroch is the music of the glens and lakes, of the woods and the mountains, of the campfire and the dark night, of marching men and the battlefield. It is heroic music. It can also be bright or sad, the music of the stirring dance and the dirge for the fallen hero. It is a soulful music for a soulful people.[1]

In recent years academics have increasingly devoted some of their energies to a variety of subjects dealing with cultural history, in which music plays an important role. In particular, the Scottish Highland bagpipe is now attracting the attention of several academics with an interest in its evolution, music and traditions.

The Highland bagpipe has evolved from an ethnic instrument associated mainly with Scotland to one of international stature, and bagpipe music was an integral component of Highland society in both Scotland and Nova Scotia. More recently bagpiping in Nova Scotia has become a cultural icon and, as a result, is sometimes the subject of stereotyping and misconceptions; subsequently, many inaccuracies have emerged surrounding the role of pipers in Highland society. This is a step in reversing the romanticized ideal of the Highland piper; a re-evaluation of erroneous cultural stereotypes of the Scottish Gael in Nova Scotia introduced in the early 20th century and permeating much of its second half.

Dance to the Piper is a study of the arrival and evolution of Highland bag-piping in Nova Scotia, the history and exodus of Gaelic-speaking pipers from Scotland to Nova Scotia, beginning in 1773, and the cultural status and di-minishing social role of these musicians within their evolving communities. The book describes Nova Scotia's rich and authentic traditional Gaelic piping style which survived in the province much longer than in Scotland. It provides historical background and analysis as to why this cultural reality endured in Nova Scotia and reviews the many social, economic and cultural developments which, along with world events, altered the status, role and perception of the community piper within Nova Scotia society.

This book should be of interest to anyone with an interest in Gaelic language, music and culture, not only in Nova Scotia, but wherever bagpipes are played. In a broader context this study could be augmented by research into the musi-cal traditions of other immigrant groups to Nova Scotia such as, African Nova Scotians, Germans, French, Irish and United Empire Loyalists, as well as Aboriginal peoples. Considering that these ethnic groups retained and devel-oped their musical traditions in Nova Scotia, a comprehensive evaluation of these traditions seems to be wanting.

The story of the bagpipe in Scotland has been well documented by such schol-arly treatments as *The Highland Bagpipe* by Francis Collinson,[2] *The Bagpipe and its Music* by Roderick Cannon,[3] *The Highland Bagpipe and Scottish Society, 1750-1950* by William Donaldson[4] and *A Piper in Peace and War* by C. A. Malcolm.[5] There is, however, a deficiency in the amount of material deal-ing with the tradition of bagpiping outside Scotland. This void is gradually being filled by some recent studies such as: *The Piobaireachd of Simon Fraser* by Barrie Orme,[6] *Traditional Gaelic Bagpiping, 1745-1945*[7] and *Old and New World Highland Bagpiping*[8] by John G. Gibson.

For pipers, and those interested in Scottish history, this recent academic in-terest has been well received since, as William Donaldson, a Scottish piper and social historian points out, Highland piping has become a world-wide phenomenon:

> Nowadays piping is a worldwide culture with many thousands of per-formers, composers, teachers and learners, not only in Scotland but in Canada and the U.S.A., Australia, New Zealand and Ireland; there are devotees of the Highland pipe in continental Europe as well, particularly in Brittany. It supports an extensive manufacturing and retail base, involving bagpipe and reed makers, drum manufactur-ers, makers of kilts and uniforms for bands; a complex web of teach-ing and regulatory institutions such as the Piobaireachd Society, the Army School of Bagpipe Music, and the Royal Scottish Pipe Band Association; systems of grading and certification of performers, net-works of local, national and international competitions for solo play-ers and for bands, and a specialist media including magazines, radio broadcasts and commercial recordings.[9]

In Nova Scotia, piping is a cultural icon and its history, development and traditions have had an economic, social and cultural impact on the Province. Organizations such as the Atlantic Canada Pipe Band Association, formerly the Nova Scotia Pipers and Pipe Band Association, draw on more than four hundred members across the region.[10] The Association sponsors competitions, grades performers, and judges and organizes workshops. In addition, institutions such as the Nova Scotia Gaelic College of Arts and Crafts at St. Ann's, and the College of Piping and Celtic Performing Arts, Summerside, Prince Edward Island, conduct classes in Scottish performing arts which attract tens of thousands of visitors each year to the region. The image of a kilted Highland piper has been displayed prominently on various tourist brochures and maps, marketing Nova Scotia's "Scottish-ness" for the past several decades. Surprisingly, few people know much about the history of the bagpipe in Nova Scotia—its Gaelic origins, music and traditions, or about the hundreds of players who played an important role maintaining this musical heritage. This work is not an attempt to name all the people in Nova Scotia who have played the bagpipe. Rather, it attempts to set out the context in which piping survived as cultural pastime in Nova Scotia, as well as the study of musical performance in a social environment.

There are several difficulties associated with the study of music and musical performance as a form of recreation. In the case of Gaelic instrumental music, several samples of immigrant bagpipes and fiddles survive in Nova Scotia, but less tangible features of both musical traditions are the actual tunes or melodies associated with each instrument. This is because most pipers and fiddlers in 19th-century Nova Scotia were unable to read or write music, learning their tunes aurally from older musicians in the community. In addition, by the beginning of the 20th century an increasing number of pipers were becoming musically literate, and improved access to printed musical collections from Scotland no doubt displaced many of the older tunes.

Written primary sources dealing specifically with pipers in Nova Scotia are few. The New World Gaels were largely illiterate and those who could read had limited access to journals written in their own language.[11] In order to fill the void, several sources were examined. Local community histories and provincial censuses offer tantalizing leads regarding pipers and piping families in Nova Scotia. These have been cross-referenced with personal interviews with tradition-bearers conducted over the past twenty-five years to compile the lists of pipers and pipe-makers with a Nova Scotia connection. It soon became evident from available research that these musicians were not "random, backwoods skirlers," but well-trained tradition bearers who represented a very old and unique style of bagpipe playing. Unfortunately, by the early 20th century only a handful of pipers continued to be trained to fulfill traditional roles in Gaelic society—roles which by the mid-20th century were for the most part no longer required.

Research indicates that in the 19th and early 20th centuries, bagpipe playing in Nova Scotia was closely aligned with the strength and vibrancy of the Gaelic language and culture. In Nova Scotia the term "traditional piper" refers to a person raised in a Gaelic-speaking, or bilingual (Gaelic-English) environment, who originally learned by ear and who, for the most part, was unacquainted with written music. Judging from the following quotation from a source associated with the Nova Scotia Highland Brigade serving in Europe during the First World War, the bagpipe appears to have had a large following among the Gaels of Nova Scotia:

> The pipers of the 85th (Nova Scotia) Battalion belonged to a province where pipe music was the favourite form of entertainment, "the people preferring it to all other kinds of music." So spoke an officer of the battalion.[12]

Despite the opinion expressed by this unnamed officer, the music of the bagpipe may not have been entirely appreciated by some members of Nova Scotia society, even in areas of significant Scottish settlement. For example, on New Year's night in 1884, a new ice-rink was opened at Stellarton, Pictou County. Within a month of the official opening the bylaws had been revised, singling out a local piper who, under the amended rules, was prohibited from playing his bagpipe at the rink.[13] This may mean nothing more than the fact that in piping, as in all musical disciplines, there have always been good and bad performers.

The relative contradiction of these two sources, however, highlights how widespread piping was in the areas of Gaelic settlement in Nova Scotia. Comparing census information on population growth in the Nova Scotia *Gaidhealtachd* (Gaelic-speaking area) with a list of second- and third-generation pipers (Appendix B) does indicate a healthy musical tradition. Appendix B also alludes to the extent of the transmission of musical skill within certain families and communities. Families like the MacIntyres, Jamiesons, Beatons and several others, preserved and passed on musical traditions within their families until well into the 20th century. These musical traditions included regional playing techniques and repertoire. As many of the pipers mentioned in this work were bards as well as fiddlers, some references to poems in both English and Gaelic have been included to further illustrate the cultural bond between language and instrument. The Gaelic material contained herein was taken directly from a variety of 19th and 20th century sources referenced in the footnotes.

In addition, several of the musicians studied in this work shared a common surname and Christian name and this can, at times, be confusing. A constant problem with any research regarding people of Scottish descent in the New World is the predominance of sobriquets or nicknames.[14] Geopolitics also presents a difficulty in a work of this nature. Under the British, from the founding of Sydney in 1784, Cape Breton had been a separate colony until

1820 when it was repatriated to the Nova Scotia mainland.[15] The province of New Brunswick was considered part of Nova Scotia until 1784.[16] For the purpose of simplicity, this work deals with Nova Scotia as it is defined by its current geographical boundaries.

Common nicknames in Gaelic or English might denote a particular physical characteristic of an individual, i.e. "Little" Hughie, Donald *Mòr* or Big Donald, Donald *Ban* or Fair-haired Donald. The trade or particular skill associated with an individual family or family member can also be used. Piper and pipe maker Duncan Gillis of Grand Mira was not known as such but was referred to as Duncan "Tailor," most likely a reference to his father's profession. Equally confusing is a family of MacNeils from Piper's Cove, descendants of the Laird of Barra's piper, Rory MacNeil. They were known as the "The Pipers" even though very few of them actually played the bagpipe. For others a place name or area would be sufficient to distinguish a particular family, as was the case with the "Ridge" MacDonalds of Mabou Ridge, Inverness County, who later settled at South Lower South River, Antigonish County.

Dance to the Piper is not a treatise on Gaelic instrumental music but rather offers an overview of the development of Highland bagpipe music and traditions in Nova Scotia over a 225-year period—from the first significant arrival of Scottish immigrants to Nova Scotia in 1773 to the bicentenary celebrations of the landing of the ship *Hector* in 1973. It ends with the death, in 1997, of Alex Currie, Frenchvale, Cape Breton, one of the last of the old-style pipers. This time frame is important because it covers the arrival, decline and eventual dissolution of a Gaelic-flavoured bagpiping tradition.

In an effort to present a contextual interpretation on the subject of Highland bagpiping in Nova Scotia, the study begins with a detailed chapter on the development of the bagpipe and its traditions in Scotland. Chapter one, "The Highland Bagpipe in Scotland," comments on several aspects of the changing role of the Highland piper. It describes the origins of the bagpipe in Scotland, the structure and eventual collapse of the Clan system and piping in the army. This chapter provides cross-case analysis of the changes that affected pipers in Nova Scotia, especially with regard to the development of the Scottish tourist trade in the early 19th century. Nova Scotia's piping traditions remained unique since many of these musical developments in Scotland occurred after widespread Highland immigration to Nova Scotia had ceased. Nova Scotia's relative geographical isolation for much of the 19th century limited external influences and provided the ideal environment for the continuity of tradition in Gaelic language, music and dance.

The extended time frame may seem unwieldy, but it is made more manageable by dividing the stages of development into three sections. There is, of course, overlap between these stages of musical development. For instance, cultural isolation in several rural areas of Nova Scotia allowed an essentially 19th-century style of piping to survive and coexist for a time with the modern 20th-century style. It is the existence of this older piping tradition that has attracted the recent interest of a handful of folklorists, historians and amateur musicologists from Canada, the United States and Scotland.

Chapters two and three cover the first and longest stage, the period between the years 1773-1890. This period saw the arrival of tens of thousands of Scottish Gaels, beginning with arrival of the ship *Hector* to Pictou in 1773, and their second- and third-generation descendants. The arrival of dozens of professional and semi-professional musicians (Appendix A), who accompanied this large migration, represented a particularly rich vein of piping and assured the presence of pipers in Nova Scotia communities.

Fig. 3. Roderick MacLean, ca. 1870, an immigrant piper from Barra. Washabuck, Cape Breton County.

Chapter two details two distinct periods of Highland immigration to Nova Scotia and explains early settlement patterns among Scottish Gaels to the province during the first of these periods. It describes the establishment of Highland communities in Nova Scotia, the development of a limited economic base dependent on farming, fishing, lumbering and the kelp industry, and the fate of several of the middle-class piping families who immigrated to Nova Scotia (Appendix A). During the second period, the fecundity of many Highland families resulted in increased numbers of Gaelic-speaking Nova Scotians and increased demands on limited agricultural resources.

Improvements in transportation and communication made it easier for large segments of the population to relocate to the United States. The industrialization of Nova Scotia in the late 19th century encouraged relocation of many of the remaining Scottish Gaels, as well as other ethnic groups, from rural areas to newly established urban centres. Education also played a significant role in cultural change.

Fig. 4. Stephen B. MacNeil, ca. 1880, Gillis Point, Cape Breton County.

Chapter three describes the role of female pipers in Nova Scotia, the multi-faceted role of the piper in 19th-century Nova Scotia and the development of a small pipe-making industry. The substantial increase in the number of Gaelic-speaking Nova Scotians during the 19th century was accompanied by a corresponding increase in the number of pipers in the province (Appendix B). Since bagpipes were expensive and difficult to obtain from Scotland, a market for homemade instruments emerged and several pipe makers began supplying the increasing demand for locally produced bagpipes (Appendix C). Chapter three also describes early bagpipe making in Scotland and compares it to the development of a small musical instrument "cottage industry" in Nova Scotia. The role of Highland piper in Nova Scotia during much of the 19th century was still one of community musician. The responsibility of these pipers, whether female or male, was to provide music for social dancing, weddings and funerals.

Fig. 5. "Big" Colin Chisholm, ca. 1885, Antigonish County.

Chapter four, "Tradition in Transition, 1895-1930," covers the period of large-scale industrialization in Nova Scotia, improvements in transportation, the First World War and a general decline in the number of Gaelic speakers in Nova Scotia (30,000 in 1931 down from an estimated 100,000 in 1891). This chapter opens by drawing parallels to the oral transmission of instrumental music, songs and storytelling. It describes the continued decline of Gaelic language use in the province aided, in part, by the demographic shift which accompanied further industrial development and outward migration. The period 1895-1930 also witnessed the arrival of several Scottish-trained immigrant pipers to Nova Scotia (Appendix E) and the increased influence of the army on piping. The modern "Scottish" pipers who came to Nova Scotia during this period included Pipe Major MacKenzie Baillie and his wife Catherine, and George Dey. These musicians and others like them, were well versed in contemporary piping styles and their influence coincided with the development of the first civilian pipe bands in the Province. In addition, chapter four examines the careers of a few "champion" pipers from Nova Scotia whose lives straddled both the 19th and 20th centuries. The changing perception of a piper's role in society, to one of a kilted pipe band musician, was reinforced by the army's involvement in recruiting and retraining pipers during the First World War.

Chapter five notes that the military's influence on piping in rural Gaelic-speaking communities was keenly felt in the 20th century, however, and gives a brief account of several Highland regiments stationed in Nova Scotia during

Fig. 6. Standing: Donald Andrew MacLellan (left) and Angus MacFarlane. Seated: Archie A. MacLellan (left) and Sandy MacDonnell. Courtesy Janice Ferguson.

the period from the Seven Years war until the 19th century (1765-1800). This chapter also examines the Highland military tradition in Nova Scotia after Canadian confederation (1867) and focuses on one unit in particular, the 94th Regiment, Victoria Battalion. Despite a shrinking Gaelic population by the outbreak of the First World War, more than 75 per cent of the officers and men of the 94th Regiment were Gaelic speakers, the only such unit in the Canadian army at that time. This chapter also covers the period from the First World War to the Second and the postwar years. A full examination of military piping would require a separate study.

Chapter six discusses the third stage of development, 1930-1997, which contributed to the elimination of traditional piping styles and function in Nova Scotia. Influences included the founding of the Gaelic College in 1938, the Second World War, a further decrease in the number of Gaelic speakers in the province (less than 7,000 by 1951), the opening of the Canso Causeway in 1955, the increased use of kilted figures in tourist literature and the bicentenary celebrations of the landing of the ship *Hector* in 1973.

The number of traditionally trained pipers was at an all time low by the 1960s and entertainment preferences had changed to reflect modern forms of social dancing. It would appear that the descendants of the first urban Gaels opted for a more tenuous attachment to their culture.[17] Often this was manifest as a denial of their cultural heritage and an increasing willingness to accept the cultural stereotypes reinforced after the Second World War by institutions such as the Gaelic College at St Ann's, Cape Breton, and the Nova Scotia Department of Tourism. The training of pipers by the army during the Second World War continued to promote modern concepts of piping and the Scottish instructors teaching at the Gaelic College in the late 1950s dismissed local piping traditions as all but worthless.[18] By the 1980s the number of pipe bands in Nova Scotia had almost doubled and much of the colourful history of 19th-century Gaelic musical tradition had been largely ignored or forgotten.

Chapter seven and the appendices provide an interpretation of the material presented in the previous chapters and illustrate how the playing of the bagpipe managed to survive and find a niche in 20th-century society. The development of the Scottish tourist trade in 19th-century Scotland had significant similarities with the expansion of Nova Scotia's modern Scottish identity in mid-20th century. In both cases, Highland culture was redefined and transformed into a commodity.

Appendix F includes notes aimed at pipers who may wish to explore some of the finer points of musical expression and technique used by traditional pipers in the Nova Scotia and complements the recording found at the back of this book.

Bagpipe Construction

The great Highland bagpipe consists of fifteen separate sections and can be accurately described as a collection of wooden tubes. Each section is mounted at its weaker points with any one of a variety of materials, from horn and animal bone, to silver and ivory and currently plastic, depending on the cost of the instrument. The pieces are assembled together and attached to a bag (air reservoir) to form three drones (one bass and two tenor which sound a continuous note, one octave apart, producing rudimentary harmony), a chanter (melody pipe capable of sounding nine notes) and a blowpipe and mouthpiece with a one-way valve to allow air to enter the bag. The air reservoir, which is made from animal hide, allows the performer to take a breath without interrupting the continuous sound of the bagpipe. The instrument plays four reeds simultaneously in three octaves. Single reeds are used for the drones and double reeds, consisting of two pieces of cane lashed to a copper tube, used for the pipe chanter.[19] Because the chanter produces only nine melody notes, the types of music which can be played on it is very limited.

The great Highland bagpipe, when played, emits a continuous sound. It cannot play a note louder or softer, and so does not possess the dynamics of other instruments such as the violin or piano and, over relatively short periods of time, the drones must be retuned. To differentiate between notes of the same pitch, and to "colour" or embellish the melody or tune, a very sophisticated system of grace noting (quick notes to embellish the primary score) was developed. With the advent of printed music for the bagpipe in 19th-century Scotland, embellishments have become standardized and today they are accepted universally by the piping community. Several of the older 19th-century embellishments were discarded by Scottish players in the early 20th century. By the late 20th century, remnants of these ancient fingering techniques survived only in the remote areas of the Scottish Gaelic diaspora such as Cape Breton and the west coast of Newfoundland.[20]

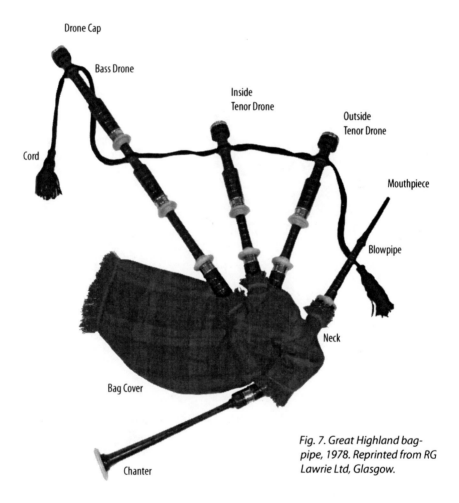

Fig. 7. Great Highland bagpipe, 1978. Reprinted from RG Lawrie Ltd, Glasgow.

Fig. 8. An immigrant bagpipe, belonging to Angus Ban MacDougall.

Fig. 9. The single drone Menzie bagpipe. Reprinted from D.P. Menzies.

Barry W. Shears

Early Piping in Scotland

Oral tradition suggests that the Highland bagpipe usurped the harp as the favoured court instrument, largely due to the patronage of Alasdair "Crotach" MacLeod, 8th Chief of Dunvegan in the late 15th century.[21] By the 18th century the harp was a rarity in the Highlands of Scotland and the office of harper had almost disappeared.[22] Although the bagpipe was a relative newcomer to Highland society, its increasing prestige among clan chiefs did not go unnoticed by those who felt threatened by the piper's increasing importance as an exponent of Gaelic instrumental music:

> The rise of the Highland bagpipe to prominence did not go unchallenged. There is a considerable corpus of satirical poetry in Gaelic by the antagonists and protagonists of the Highland bagpipe. The di-moladh and moladh, "dispraise" and "praise," of pipes and pipers, are recurrent notes in 17th-century poetry and song. For example, the 17th-century poet, Niall MacMhuirich, contemptuously denounced the music of the pipes as harsh and barbaric in a vicious satire Seanchas na Pìob o Thus (History of the Pipe from the Beginning of Time) and did not spare the player from his vituperation.[23]

Despite the condemnation of bards such as MacMhuirich, schools or colleges were established to help pipers perfect their chosen profession. These colleges were apparently patterned after similar piping schools in Ireland. Some traditions have the length of instruction from six months to an extraordinary eleven years, but to date little is known of the day-to-day functions or duration of these piping schools.[24]

Some of the piping colleges were originally established and directed by a few of the more successful middle-class clan pipers. The MacCrimmons, pipers to MacLeod of Dunvegan, had a college at Boreraig, on Skye.[25] The MacArthurs, pipers to MacDonald of the Isles maintained a college at Hungladder, also on the Isle of Skye.[26] The Rankins, pipers to MacLean of Duart, had a school for piping on the Isle of Mull.[27] The MacRaes established a school for piping in Kintail during the late 18th century.[28] The MacDougalls, pipers to MacDougall of Dunollie, supervised a school for piping at Kilbride, and a family of MacGregors taught piping in Perthshire.[29]

The early existence of piping "colleges" and "hereditary" pipers was documented by both Thomas Pennant and Boswell and Johnson, after their respective tours of the Highlands in 1772 and 1773. Recent research by John Gibson in *Old and New World Highland Bagpiping* attributes the longevity of some piping families, not so much to any superior musical skill, but rather to the fact that during the 17th and 18th century, as in most trades, most sons learned their father's trade.[30] Significant documentary evidence exists to prove that during the 17th and 18th centuries pipers were sent from all over the Highlands to further their education with recognized masters of the instrument.[31] The education probably consisted of learning new tunes orally, studying methods of composition and possibly peculiar grace-noting techniques.[32] Whether or not this education fulfils our modern concept of schools or colleges is still open for debate. Recent evidence suggests that once educated in their chosen profession, pipers were not restricted to serving one particular family. Then as now, skilled individuals moved around from place to place, taking advantage of the most rewarding positions. These colleges continued for several generations. After the collapse of the clan system in the Highlands of Scotland following the Battle of Culloden in 1746 and changing rental agreements which displaced many middle-class Gaels, they were all eventually closed.

The MacCrimmons of Skye

The MacCrimmons were hereditary pipers to the MacLeods of Dunvegan on the Isle of Skye, and their place in piping lore has achieved almost supernatural status. The origins of the family are obscure and speculation range from the family having Italian roots in Cremona, Italy, to originally having coming from Ireland.

The family was established in Skye from the early 17th century. Tradition states that members of the family were principals of the most famous college of piping in the Highlands. At the time no piper was considered perfected until he received at least some instruction from them.[33]

Finlay of the White Plaid (ca. 1500) is believed to have been the first MacCrimmon piper to Macleod of Dunvegan.[34] According to 19th-century oral tradition, his descendants held the position in perpetuity until the 1820s. They held lands rent free in exchange for their piping services. The MacCrimmon College was eventually disbanded in 1772 when one of these celebrated pipers immigrated to North America, eventually settling in Nova Scotia.

Donald "Ruadh" MacCrimmon was a member of the tacksman or middle class. The time-honored custom of letting a farm from the clan chief in exchange for piping services was abrogated as the value of land rose considerably in the mid-18th century and like many middle-class Gaels, he chose emigration to North America as an alternative. In an effort to maintain a relatively high standard of living compared to the subtenants, he and his family immigrated to the Cape Fear district of North Carolina. During the American Revolution, Donald served as an officer with Tarleton's British Legion. After Britain's defeat, his lands were confiscated.[35] He eventually relocated to East Jordan, Shelburne County, Nova Scotia, as part of the Loyalist migration. In 1786 he was granted permission to operate a ferry service across the Jordan River where he had a farm on Lot No. 2.[36] He eventually returned to Scotland but one daughter married and remained in Nova Scotia.

Several other well-known and prominent piping families had Maritime connections. These included the MacKays of Gairloch, pipers to MacKenzie of Gairloch; the MacIntyres of Rannoch, pipers to Menzies of Weem; the MacNeils, pipers to the Laird of Barra; Kenneth Chisholm, piper to Chisholm of Strathglas; John MacGillivray, piper and bard to MacDonald of Glenaladale; Conndullie Rankin, piper to the MacLeans of Mull; and Duncan MacIntyre, piper to MacDonald of Clanranald. These piping families were middle class and following the collapse of the clan system in Scotland, they, or their descendants, immigrated to what is now Maritime Canada in the late-18th and early-19th centuries. An assessment of the impact on the musical traditions of Highland society after the emigration of so many excellent musicians has never been undertaken. There is little doubt that this "brain drain" of talent was one of the main causes for the eventual decline of "traditional" bagpipe music in Scotland.

Bagpipe Music

One of the most obvious changes in piping in 19th-century Scotland was the spread of musical literacy. The transmission of the music and art of playing the bagpipe had always been passed on orally and by example in a student-teacher relationship. Over a relatively brief period in history different styles developed in various parts of Scotland, and it was these regional styles which were brought to the New World with the immigrant Gaels. The impetus for a literate class of musicians came first from the Highland Society of London, which attempted to commit to paper many of the tunes and traditions surrounding the Highland bagpipe in Scotland.

The Highland Society of London was founded in 1778 and had as one of its aims "to take appropriate steps to preserve the poetry, music and language of the Highlands."[37] The Highland Society was well connected, both politically and socially. By the early 1800s its membership boasted landlords, Dukes and the Prince of Wales, later King George IV. To achieve its mandate regarding music, the Highland Society sponsored piping competitions beginning in 1781 and, from the early 19th century, offered special prizes for the writing of pipe music in staff notation. One of the first recipients of the award was Donald MacDonald of Edinburgh, in 1806. MacDonald was not the first to attempt writing pipe music in staff notation, but his method proved to be one of the most popular and resilient.

The first collection of bagpipe music, MacDonald's *Vocal Airs*, was a small folio containing 186 melodies published around 1794 by Patrick MacDonald, a piper and fiddler from Durness, Sutherlandshire. This was followed in 1818 by Captain Robert Menzie's *The Bagpipe Preceptor*, Donald MacDonald's *A Collection of the Ancient Martial Music of Caledonia* (1822) and *A Collection of Quicksteps, Strathspeys, Reels and Jigs* (1828).

Donald MacDonald was an Edinburgh pipe maker who is credited with standardizing written music for the bagpipe. MacDonald's acquaintance with numerous classical musicians no doubt influenced his revolutionary and now universal method of writing pipe music. By his own admission he found fault with the way the bagpipe was being played in the more remote regions of Scotland and with the variety of styles, many of which had already been brought to North America by emigrant Gaels. MacDonald introduced several innovations in writing pipe music and in the preface to his 1828 collection he explained his decision for writing music the way he did:

> The different modes of playing the bagpipe, adopted by the northern Highlanders and those inhabiting the Western Isles, must convince all that it would have been highly improper to use either, as the sphere of the Publisher's utility would thus be circumscribed. He has therefore, followed the example of Robert Burns' Ghost, and "ta' en the gate that pleased himself." The experience of fifty years, devoted principally to the bagpipe, and a tolerable acquaintance with other kinds of music, embolden him to recommend the following Tunes as played by himself. [38]

As the 19th century progressed in time, additional collections of music were published by Angus MacKay, Queen Victoria's piper from 1843-1854, William MacKay (no relation), William Gunn, William Ross, Queen Victoria's piper from 1854 until his death in 1891, and David Glen.[39] Some of the collections were printed only once but the more popular collections were updated, expanded and reprinted many times over during the 19th century. Roderick Cannon points out in his exhaustive work, *The Literature of the Bagpipe*:

> By 1900 there had been a total of 25 music books published for the Highland bagpipe, most of them in the last quarter of the 19th century, and the tradition of the instrument had undergone a total and irreversible change. As late as 1850, according to one observer who was well qualified to know, few pipers could even read written music, but by 1900 the tradition inaugurated by Donald MacDonald had taken a firm hold and for the vast majority of pipers the printed page had become the principal means of dissemination of new music.[40]

During the late Victorian period bagpipe music was subdivided into three categories: big music (ceòl mór), middling music (ceòl meadhonach) and little music (ceòl beag). Prior to this, all music performed on the bagpipe was known in Gaelic as pìobaireachd (pìob is Gaelic for bagpipe, pìobair is a piper and pìobaireachd is what a piper does with his bagpipe).[41] The Gaelic terms ceòl beag and ceòl mór are believed to be 19th-century creations making their first appearance in printed literature dealing with bagpipe music in 1875.[42] These classifications of Highland bagpipe music probably owe their existence to the Victorian interpretation of "high" and "low" culture rather than to any common usage by pipers at the time.

Pìobaireachd (pibroch in English) is often referred to as the classical music of the bagpipe and it is held in very high esteem by most pipers. This form of music commences with a basic theme, followed by a series of variations increasing in complexity, finishing with a repeat of the theme. This melody construction has been compared to the Italian rondo and has led some early

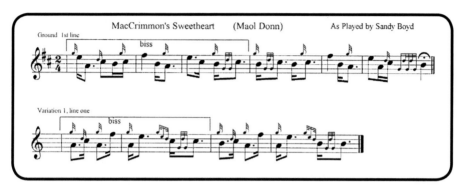

Fig. 10. MacCrimmons Sweetheart.

researchers to assume a continental European musical influence. Many of these grand, and at times lengthy, compositions appear to have been composed between the 17th and 19th century. Their classification can be further subdivided into laments, marches, and gathering or rallying tunes and many tunes are associated with specific clans, chiefs and battles which may indicate a close relationship between the bardic poems and songs and instrumental music. There are approximately three hundred such tunes in existence today and it is believed that there were more than five hundred tunes in the repertoire during its heyday. An essential feature of the Scottish *ceòl mór* tradition is that it "was handed down by a small number of leading professional players to present day."[43] Many Scottish pipers pride themselves on their "piping pedigree," modern pipers going to great lengths to trace their musical roots for generations, through successive pupil/teacher relationships of the past masters of the instrument in order to justify and add credence to a particular style or method of playing. Many top performers on the bagpipe today claim to be able to trace their knowledge of *ceòl mór* back to the famous MacCrimmon family and, during the Victorian Age, the oral transmission of music from the MacCrimmons to 19th-century pipers achieved almost apostolic status. (See p. 26.)

Middle or middling music (*ceòl meadhonach*) encompassed slow airs, Gaelic airs and assorted folk tunes, but now comes under the broader heading of little or light music. Little music (*ceòl beag*) now includes all music which is essentially not ceòl mór. Airs, marches, strathspeys, reels, hornpipes, jigs, clogs and waltzes, all of a variety of written musical time signatures, comprise this category, and a conservative estimate of the present number of *ceòl beag* tunes is in the tens of thousands. Individual melodies composed for the bagpipe are named by their composers after people, places, objects and events and, in essence, represent a form of commemoration and local history.

Although *ceòl mór* playing declined in Nova Scotia, dance music played on the bagpipes thrived. There was a paucity of piping competitions and associated Highland Games in Nova Scotia until the latter decades of the 19th century. The effects of musical literacy, which played such a prominent role in the development of bagpipe music in 19th-century Scotland, were mitigated by the fact that very few of the immigrant pipers to Nova Scotia could read or write music, let alone afford printed books of music. All of these factors protected the survival of a more traditional and social piping culture.

In Scotland a break with the step-dance tradition and an increasing emphasis on competitions helped transform functional pipe music into art music. In the first few decades of the 20th century this piping "renaissance" was sweeping Scotland and it was further refined after the Second World War. As Seumas MacNeill, Principal of the College of Piping in Glasgow, pointed out in 1968, competition strathspeys and reels bore little resemblance to their 19th-century counterparts:

> The situation is somewhat different nowadays, with the immense popularity among pipers of what are termed "competition-type" marches, strathspeys and reels. These are marches to which no one is expected to march (in the accepted sense of the term), strathspeys to which no one dances, and reels whose only link with dance tunes of the same nominal category lies in their time signature.[44]

The arrival of the bagpipe in Scotland around the 15th century displaced the music of the harp in the Highlands and Islands. The volume of the instrument and its mobility appealed to the Scottish Gaels and during the next three hundred years the piper became an increasingly important figure in clan society, and this rise to prominence was accompanied by very sophisticated developments in music. In Scotland, the music and culture of the bagpipe has changed dramatically, especially over the last hundred and fifty years. The impetus for change came from a variety of sources: competitions, patronage, musical literacy and the army. Piping competitions established a means whereby the playing ability of pipers could be assessed, usually by a panel of aristocratic judges with little or no experience in piping. The major prize winners of these competitions could find relatively secure employment on estates. By providing employment opportunities for these musicians the landlords could retain an increasingly popular but tenuous relationship to the fast disappearing 18th-century culture of the Gael. Immigration to the cities, the attraction of army (and later civilian) pipe bands allowed the instrument to move from its traditional rural roots in Gaelic Scotland to an increasingly urban-based society.

Chapter One

The Highland Bagpipe in Scotland

The Piper was also one of the great officers of the chief, and he paid no rent for his farm: this office was often hereditary in the same family. There were in the Isle of Sky, two famous schools where the candidates for this place learned to play on the bagpipe. One of the privileges attached to the office of Piper was to accompany the eldest son of the Laird in his travels. The Piper was required to know all appropriate airs; to play when the chief was at table, and when he sailed in a boat on the sea, or on the lakes; he accompanied him also to battle, and his music was heard at the funerals; for the bagpipe, the national instrument of the Gaels, was heard in all the principal scenes of life, whether in rousing the courage of warriors, or enlivening the festivals, or lastly, in honouring the memory of the dead, and mingling its plaintive sounds in the funeral ceremonies with the mournful airs of the Coronach.[1]

One of the most recognizable icons of Scottish culture is the Great Highland Bagpipe. It consists of a very limited, almost primitive, musical scale when compared with modern musical instruments. Nevertheless, for those who play the instrument or enjoy its music, it is capable of evoking a wide range of emotions. From the introduction of the instrument to Scotland, sometime in the 15th century, to its current international appeal, bagpipes and pipers have been called upon to fill a variety of roles in Scottish society. The bagpipe provided courtly music and martial airs during the halcyon days of the now defunct Highland clan system of the Gaels. In Scotland, the piper found a place not only on the battlefield, where the sheer volume of the instrument rendered it a perfect form of open-air communication clearly heard above the clatter of 16th-to 8th-century warfare, but also as a purveyor of dance music. In addition, rowers and harvesters were often accompanied by the music of the bagpipe.[2]

By the mid-19th century, pipers were well established in the Highland regiments of the British army. The combination of pipers and drummers in the British army led to the first formally recognized pipe bands around 1854.[3] The lead (and usually more experienced) player in the band was appointed Pipe Major. This basic organization has been the template, with only minor changes, for every military and civilian pipe band in existence today. From the mid-19th to the early 20th century, the music of the bagpipe made a transition from a largely oral tradition to a written one. This change was accompanied by changing roles for the piper in Scottish society.

Despite the importance of the bagpipe to the culture and social relationships of the Scottish Gaels it has received little critical analysis in Scotland. Even less attention has been paid to the areas settled by Scottish emigrant pipers. Much of the available literature devoted to the bagpipe has been restricted to a handful of books published in and around the first and last decades of the 20th century.[4]

While the three-droned or great Highland bagpipe is mostly associated with Scotland, many authorities agree the bagpipe began its life as a simple reed pipe in ancient Egypt about 2500 BCE.[5] Later a bag (air reservoir) and blow-pipe were added to allow the pipe to produce a constant sound. This early form of the bagpipe was used in Roman society in the first century CE and there are some claims that the Roman Emperor, Nero, played a form of bagpipe.[6] Successive alterations to the instrument over the next 1600 years included the addition of one or more drones, offering a rudimentary harmony for the melody pipe or chanter, and in some areas the addition of a bellows to replace the mouth-blown method of bag inflation.

A lack of historical records makes it impossible to ascertain with any accuracy when the bagpipe reached Scotland. Some historians claim the bagpipe was introduced to Scotland by the Roman legions, while others maintain it came from Ireland. Whatever the origins, the bagpipe appears to have been further developed in Europe after the 12th century, reaching England about 1200 CE. [7] By the 15th century it was adopted by the Gaelic-speaking peoples of Scotland and Ireland. In both countries it was used as an incitement to battle and for lamenting the dead.[8]

There are several forms of bagpipes played throughout Europe today whose origins can be traced to the 12th century, as Hugh Cheape explains:

> The 12th century has been characterized as a period of "renaissance" in European history when the arts, science and literature flourished in a way in which they had clearly not in the preceding centuries. Identifiable phenomena such as the growth of towns, the Crusading

Barry W. Shears

movement and the collision and exchange with Islam provided fertile ground for the spread of music and song. The years from 1099 to about 1291 experienced a complex of social, economic and cultural interaction between Muslims and Crusaders, and new instruments of science and music were imported into Europe from the richer cultures of the Middle East. In this period the bagpipe seems to have traveled fast and far and to have developed into the universal musical instrument of medieval Europe. Its presence in a vigorous folk tradition in Eastern Europe is as likely to be attributed to the same renaissance as breathed life into it in Western Europe. Poland, Czechoslovakia, Ukraine, Yugoslavia, Romania, Bulgaria and Macedonia all have remarkable bagpipes with their own histories.[9]

However, it is the Scottish form of bagpipe which can be found in many parts of the world. This is due, in large part, to the numerous emigrants who left Scotland for one reason or another and eventually colonized parts of North America, Australia and New Zealand, and to the various Highland regiments (all of which retained numerous pipers and pipe bands) recruited and dispatched around the globe to help secure and protect Britain's military and economic interests. As a result, the Highland bagpipe today is played in many countries around the world.

The Clan System

From medieval times there existed in the Highlands of Scotland a social system based on filial relationships, a clan system of large tribal districts which flourished until the middle of the 18th century. At its root lay kinship, the common bond of blood relationship.[10] Among the smaller clans, this socio-political system was essentially self-government, but in the larger clans or federations of clans, like the Lordship of the Isles, it resembled a full and formal parliament. [11] A highly parochial society, the clan system was abundant in regional warfare, cattle raiding and a rich and varied tradition of folklore.

This system was patriarchal in structure and feudal in nature. The clan chief maintained a paternal interest in his people and their welfare. At its pyramidal head was the clan chief, whose position was quasi-royal and who had the power to wage war on enemies of the clan, mediate disputes among his people and, in some cases, decide on matters of life and death.[12] This position resembled a hereditary monarchy of sorts, founded on custom and regulated by laws and family tradition.[13] The power of the clan chief, however, was far from absolute. He ruled with the assistance of a clan or tribal council consisting of the heads of various prominent families within the group.[14]

The clan chief kept a retinue of bodyguards (known as henchmen), consisting usually of close relatives, as well as poets and chroniclers, whose job it was to record in song and verse the history of the clan. The clan chief patronized the arts and employed several court musicians such as harpers and, later, pipers and fiddlers.[15] Many of these positions were passed on from father to son in perpetuity, and some families became famous for their musical and bardic skills. In exchange for their piping services, the chiefs were responsible for outfitting the piper with clothes and accessories. In some cases this also extended to purchasing instruments.[16]

The layer of clan structure below the clan chief and his family was the tacksman class. Usually more distant relatives of the clan chief, the tacksman class sublet farms, or tacks, to tenants and in turn paid a portion of the profits to the head of the clan.[17] The tacksman occupied the position of middle class and also acted as military lieutenants for the clan chief in times of war.

The bottom and largest part of the social order consisted of tenants and subtenants. The tenants controlled larger farms or a part of a larger farm. The subtenants were essentially "land-less labourers" who lived on small parcels of land. They were subject to rental terms which provided little opportunity for them to accumulate wealth or assets in the form of livestock or land.[18]

In some cases members of the clan were exempt from rent in exchange for a particular service or circumstance. The MacCrimmons of Skye, as middleclass hereditary pipers to MacLeod of Dunvegan, held their farm at Boreraig rent-free until the late 18th century.[19] In addition, every able-bodied man was required to fulfill his military obligations and in so doing provided the clan chief with a formidable standing army.

The social infrastructure of the clan system in Scotland received a major setback shortly after the English-speaking James VI became monarch over both England and Scotland in 1603 as James I. The linguistic and cultural differences of the Gaels took on a political dimension. The language was perceived by Lowland Scots and the English court as the basis for everything wrong with Gaelic society, from uncivilized barbarism to cattle reiving and a proclivity for war. In an effort to persuade the Gaels to abandon their own language and learn English language and customs, James signed the Statutes of Iona in 1609, the official beginning of linguistic discrimination against the Gaelic language and culture. The Statutes of Iona were designed to break the power of the clan chiefs and extend the hegemony of the Scottish Lowlands over the Highlands and Islands. By the time the Gaels began immigrating to North America (1750-1850) the English language and its broader culture was already making serious inroads on the Scottish mainland. Efforts to detach the Gael from his culture started at the end of the 15th century when a Scottish education act obliged barons and freeholders to send their children to school to learn Latin. In the 17th century the national government sought to replace Gaelic with English.[20]

> The Preface to the 1609 Statutes of Iona, enacted by the Scottish Parliament under military pressure from the English, was later legitimized and ratified by the Scottish Privy Council in the Education Act of 1616. It stated that the "Inglishe toung be universaille plantit" and the Gaelic language, which was "one of the chief and princpall causis

of the continewance of barbaritie and incivilitie amongis the inhabitants of the Isles and Heylandis be abolisheit and removit."[21]

Among other things clan chiefs were now required to send their eldest sons to
the Lowlands to be educated in English and to expel the bards, whose Gaelic
poetry preserved the history and distinctiveness of each clan. The effects of
the Statutes of Iona had long-term ramifications for the Scottish Highlander.
By moving the heirs to chieftainships out of the Highlands, and educating
them in the language and customs of England, paternal attachments to their
kinsmen were significantly diminished. The break with traditional values and
language made the transition from Highland chief to profit-driven landlord
much easier in the late 18th and 19th century.

Piping in the Army

After the inglorious and deciding defeat of the Jacobite rebellion under Bonnie
Prince Charlie at Culloden in 1746 and his eventual flight back to France,
England was left to ponder the possibilities of future uprisings in Scotland.
William Pitt proposed a scheme to recruit regiments from the Highlands of
Scotland and to have them commanded by English or "Loyal" Scottish offi-
cers. This idea had first been proposed by Lord Duncan Forbes of Culloden in
a letter sent to Lord Milton, the Lord Justice Clerk, in 1738:

> I propose that the Government should raise four or five regiments of
> Highlanders, appointing an English or Scottish officer of undoubted
> loyalty to be Colonel of each regiment, and naming the lieutenant-col-
> onels, majors, and captains and subalterns from this list in my hand,
> which comprehends all the chiefs and chieftains of the disaffected
> clans, who are the very persons whom France and Spain will call upon
> in case of war to take up arms for the Pretender. If the Government
> pre-engages the Highlanders in the manner I propose, they will not
> only serve well against the enemy abroad, but will be hostages for the
> good behavior of their relatives at home, and I am persuaded it will be
> absolutely impossible to raise a rebellion in the Highlands.[22]

The immediate benefits to the English of such a plan would be twofold. First,
it would provide additional soldiers to expand ever increasing and diverse
mercantile interests abroad, especially ongoing wars with France for control
of North America. Second, it would reduce the numbers of Highlanders available for any future attempt at an armed rebellion and, with the proper incen-
tives, might persuade them to settle in the colonies. This scheme was accepted
by Sir Robert Walpole, but was later vetoed by Cabinet. Despite widespread
opposition to the plan, one pro-government regiment, the Black Watch, was
successfully established in 1739 for home defense.[23]

The recruitment scheme was later revisited during Britain's struggle for control of North America in the mid-18th century and several additional Highland

regiments were raised for military service. The Fraser Highlanders and Montgomery's Highlanders were raised in Scotland during the Seven Years War but quickly disbanded once hostilities had subsided. When peace came, many of these soldiers and their families were given land grants in North America. Several officers in these regiments were sons of many prominent clan chiefs and, keeping with long established custom, they were accompanied abroad by their personal pipers.[24] These pipers were often close relatives of the clan chiefs and in return for pay and upkeep, they sometimes acted as attendants or servants. The financial burden of paying for the maintenance of these pipers was shouldered by the officers themselves rather than government coffers.[25] Although there were large numbers of pipers in the army they did not form a part of the recognized British military establishment until the mid-19th century.[26]

The necessity of pipe music to the well-being of the Highland soldier in these regiments was well known at the time.[27] Whether on the field of battle as company piper or providing social dance music by the camp fires, the piper was continuously in demand. Unlike armies of today, the armies of the 18th and 19th century had numerous camp followers and, when not billeted in local communities, their encampments resembled small, portable villages. The camp followers consisted of soldier's wives and children, cooks, butchers and laundresses. The composition of these military encampments provided ample opportunity for social interaction and afforded the piper plenty of occasions to fulfill the role as a purveyor of dance music. By the beginning of the 19th century there were only two ways of making a living as a full-time piper in Scotland. One was as a piper to the aristocracy,[28] provided the estate owner or laird had sufficient interest and funds to maintain such a position; the other was as a piper in the army.

Following the success of the three Highland regiments engaged in service in North America during the Seven Years War, the British government continued to recruit Highlanders into the army. Four Highland regiments participated in the Napoleonic Wars and several Fencible Regiments, a form of militia used for training full-time soldiers, were raised in Scotland. Pipers were indispensable to these regiments and although not officially recognized by the War Office, their music was often used as a recruiting tool.[29]

Development of the Scottish Tourist Industry

Once the ban on wearing Highland dress, imposed in 1747 by the Act of Proscription after Culloden, was rescinded in 1782, and after Prince Charles Edward Stewart died in 1788 without an heir, there was a revival, albeit skewed, of all things Scottish. The Highland Scots, who had been demonized during the last Jacobite rebellion of 1745, now represented a form of "Noble Barbarism."[30] This transformation can be attributed to the writings of James MacPherson, Sir Walter Scott and, to a lesser extent, James Logan.

James MacPherson was born in 1736. As a member of the tacksman or middle class he was afforded a modest education, studying at both King's and Marischal Colleges in Aberdeen. He was capable of reading and writing in Gaelic, and collected and edited several ancient folk tales from various informants in the Highlands. In 1760 his *Fragments of Ancient Poetry* was published, followed in 1765 by *The Works of Ossian*. This later work was a collection of several epic poems dealing with the mythical life of Fingal, the ancient Caledonian warrior and leader of a race of giants. According to legend these poems were originally composed by Ossian, the blind son of Fingal and last representative of the race of giants. These works were an immediate success throughout Europe and were eventually translated into several languages. Napoleon Bonaparte carried an Italian translation of the work with him during his campaigns. It became the inspiration for countless other poems, novels, plays and paintings and secured for MacPherson a certain degree of fame and fortune.[31]

Sir Walter Scott was born in 1771 in Edinburgh, Scotland. He popularized Scottish culture with such works as *Rob Roy* (1817), one of the first historical novels ever written, and *The Heart of Midlothian* (1819), a tale of two early Jacobite insurrections. These works created a positive and romantic impression of the Gaels among English and European readers. Even the music was the focus of renewed interest and some of the first printed collections of Highland pipe music were published at this time. "Many of the [musical] traditions were connected to Jacobitism, which, with its political force safely spent, had become respectable again under the influence of Sir Walter Scott."[32]

There is an ironic twist to the romantic writings of MacPherson in the late 18th century, and Scott in the early 19th century. These authors were reaching an unprecedented European market and they accrued substantial recognition and financial reward. At the same time in history the Highlands and Islands of Scotland were being depopulated and, in later instances, people forced from the region and replaced with sheep. Two decades after the appearance of MacPherson's *The Works of Ossian*, thousands of Highland Scots had already immigrated to places such as Georgia, North Carolina, Prince Edward Island and Nova Scotia. Sir Walter Scott's romantic depiction of the Scottish Gael coincided with large-scale evictions throughout the Highlands and Islands, the victims of which were finding new homes in the area now known as Maritime Canada.

James MacPherson had succeeded in drawing European attention to the Scottish Highlands and Sir Walter Scott, through his romantic depictions of Scottish life, is credited with single-handedly creating the Scottish tourist trade.[33] The work of these two men would be augmented by another Scot, James Logan, whose written contributions to Scottish culture in the 19th century influenced a generation of writers and performers.

James Logan was born at Aberdeen in the early 1790s. The son of a merchant, he was educated at the city's Grammar School and although he was intended for a career in Law or Medicine, he achieved neither.[34] Logan lived for a time in

London, spending long hours at the British Museum and, at some point during his career, found time to learn to play the bagpipe. In 1826 he travelled to the north of Scotland to gather material for his book on the customs and habits of the Scottish Gaels.[35] In 1831 James Logan's *The Scottish Gael* was published in London in two volumes. Logan's observations on playing the instrument and his historical notes on several of the "hereditary" pipers meshed perfectly with the emerging attitudes of Victorian Britain toward Scottish culture.[36] Both Scott and Logan solidified the association of a primitive and noble instrument with a primitive and noble people.

Logan also wrote the "Historical Accounts of Hereditary Pipers" and "Historical and Traditional Notes on the Pìobaireachds" included in Angus MacKay's *Collection of Ancient Pìobaireachd* (1838).[37] In addition, Logan wrote *The Clans of the Scottish Highlands*, complete with illustrations of various tartans and figures supplied by a local artist, R. R. McIan. This was also published in London in 1845-1847.

These works contained some wild exaggerations of fact, especially in matters of Highland dress. As William Donaldson points out:

> Logan's enthusiasm for costume was typical of his opportunistic approach to Highland culture. "The fact that the so-called 'clan' tartans often bore but slender resemblance to more traditional patterns and that they had little traceable existence before the second decade of the nineteenth century did not constitute a problem."[38]

To a large extent both *The Scottish Gael* and *The Clans of the Scottish Highlands* misrepresented the culture of the Gael to an expanding European market. With the political power of the Gaels diminished, the culture and costume (particularly the kilt) associated with the Gael was being defined more and more by Lowland and English perceptions and economic interests.

The great kilt, the versatile and common garb of the Highlander, was abolished from use under the terms of the Act of Proscription (1747). It was essentially a large tartan blanket (approx. 2 m (6 ft) in length), gathered together and secured with a belt around the waist and a brooch at the shoulder. The top portion of the kilt could be drawn over the head and shoulders in inclement weather. In the early 18th century it was eventually modified, by a Lancashire merchant no less, to become a small kilt,[39] shortened in length to extend from the mid-knee to just above the waist, with the eventual addition of permanent pleats sewn in the back. The individual plaid patterns or septs were also distorted, growing from a handful of district tartans, to a vast selection of family or clan tartans. These tartan offerings would eventually include not only the major clan names, but a host of other small, distantly related cadet branches of the same family, subdivided even further into "hunting" and "dress" patterns. The development of this vast array of family tartans from a handful of traditional patterns developed towards the end of the 18th century and can be attributed to a large extent to the Sobieski brothers of Europe.[40]

John and Charles Edward Sobieski claimed to be relatives of Bonnie Prince Charlie on his mother's side (Bonnie Prince Charlie's mother's maiden name was Sobieski). They were well connected in high society and made unsubstantiated claims that every clan had one or more distinctive tartans associated with them. In 1829 they produced *Vestiarium Scoticum*. This book consisted of 55 septs of tartans and was, apparently, more fantasy than fact:[41]

> The Highlands became Britain's Alps, a stage for romanticism and healthy sport. When Lord Brougham introduced the fashion of tartan trousers to London, ordering bolts of every sett from Mr. MacDougall the draper at Inverness, English Society went a` L'Ecosse in a fanatic way that lasted until the death of Victoria seventy years later. Those picaresque confidence tricksters, John and Charles Sobieski Stuart, charmed everybody with their claims to be the grandsons of Bonnie Prince Charlie, by a legitimate son no less. They handsomely refused to press their right to the Throne, grew their black hair down to their shoulders, painted their own portraits in Highland dress, lived with musical-comedy splendour on an island given to them by Lord Lovat, and fed public credulity with their *Vestiarium Scoticum*, a treatise on the tartan based on three ancient manuscripts which they said they possessed but which nobody else ever saw.[42]

The dubious authenticity of many of these tartans did not matter and what followed was an entrepreneur's dream. As more areas of the Highlands were cleared of its inhabitants and replaced with sheep runs there was an abundance of wool, especially after the end of the Napoleonic Wars. It would appear that the owners of the woolen mills, many of which were located in the Lowlands, were more than eager to participate in the manufacture of tartans supplying kilts and other articles of "Highland costume" to meet the demands of a public fascinated with Scottish/Gaelic culture.[43] The demand for tartan began with the kilted regiments of the British army and members of the Scottish aristocracy but it would later spread to North America and beyond. The wool produced by flocks of Cheviot sheep, which were introduced to the Highlands in the mid-18th century, was in turn manufactured into, among other things, tartan cloth and sold to descendants of the very Highlanders who were evicted to make way for sheep runs in the first place.

So effective was the revisionism of Gaelic culture in the 19nth century that, in 1822, the Hanoverian King George IV landed at Leith Walk in Edinburgh outfitted from head to foot in "traditional" Highland attire.[44] This visit had been organized by The Celtic Society of Scotland whose then president was Sir Walter Scott. Later, Queen Victoria established the position of Sovereign's Piper, a position which required the appointed musician to divide his time between the Royal family's residences at both Balmoral Castle and London. It is important to note that two of the pipers who fulfilled the position of Sovereign's Piper in the 19th century were also at the forefront of musical literacy. The appointment of a Sovereign's Piper has continued to the present day, although with Scotland moving towards greater political independence, the position might be in jeopardy.

Several members of the aristocracy mimicked the Royal household's patronage of court musicians in the early 19th century and, in turn, provided employment for pipers on estates throughout Britain. These opportunities, coupled with positions in the army, provided pipers with a welcome alternative to permanent emigration from Scotland to Britain's overseas colonies. These factors helped to inject a new vigor and musical direction into the playing of the bagpipe in 19th-century Scotland. The manufacture and wearing of tartan began to symbolize the Scottish identity to the world and during the 19th century the role of the piper changed significantly in Scottish society. After four hundred years of history in Scotland, the bagpipe—adopted by Highland Gaels—found a function that would guarantee its survival through the following decades of social and economic upheaval.

Conclusion

The tens of thousands of Gaels who came to the region later known as the Canadian Maritimes left Scotland before this piping evolution occurred. As a result, a form of traditional Highland bagpipe music survived in this area far longer than in Scotland. The immigrant Gaels sought to escape the effects of the collapse of the clan system and its inevitable economic and social upheavals. There were no clan chiefs in Nova Scotia and therefore no patronage for piping or any of the other Gaelic cultural arts.

Widespread use of the kilt as a form of formal wear in the 19th century was absent in Nova Scotia, particularly in rural areas. The family or "hereditary" pipers and ex-military pipers who emigrated to Nova Scotia during the period 1773-1830 may have brought such articles of clothing from Scotland with them, but a lack of primary sources precludes much more than a passing comment on the subject.[45] There is evidence to suggest that some articles of Highland costume, particularly tartan, were manufactured in Prince Edward Island in the mid-19th century[46] and tintype photographs of pipers (Fig. 11-13) taken in Nova Scotia in the late 1880s demonstrates at least a local interest in the Victorian portrayal of the Scottish Highlander. As for the military, it would be almost one hundred years before the army was involved in any meaningful role in the change and development of pipe music in Nova Scotia.

Barry W. Shears

Three pipers from Pictou County, ca. 1885:

Fig. 11. Donald Murray (1830-1899) ca.1885, Rogers Hill, NS. Courtesy Donald D. Munro.

Fig. 12. William Ross (1826-1915), ca. 1885, Cummings Mountain, NS. Courtesy James O. Ross.

Fig. 13. J. J. Chisholm, ca. 1885, Pictou, NS, formerly from Marydale, Antigonish County.

Chapter Two

Immigration, Settlement and Industrialization

Whether the mischiefs of emigration were immediately perceived, may be justly questioned. They who went first, were probably such as could best be spared; but the accounts sent by the earliest adventurers, whether true or false, inclined many to follow them; and whole neighbourhoods formed parties for removal; so that departure from their native country is no longer exile. He that goes thus accompanied carries with him all that makes life pleasant. He sits down in a better climate, surrounded by his kindred and his friends: they carry with them their language, their opinions, their popular songs, and hereditary merriment: they change nothing but the place of their abode; and of that change they perceive the benefit. This is the real effect of emigration, if those that go away together settle on the same spot, and preserve their ancient union.[1]

It has been more than two hundred years since Scottish Gaels began emigrating to the area now known as the Maritime Provinces of Canada. The Gaelic name for Nova Scotia (Latin for New Scotland) is Alba Nuadh, and the descendants of these Scottish settlers comprise one of the largest ethnic groups in the province. Scottish heritage is evident in the duplication of Scottish place names in Nova Scotia such as Bervie (near Truro), Inverness, Portree, Knoydart, Iona, Beauly, Boisdale and several communities called Glencoe, to name a few. In addition, several place names associated with the Highland pipers include Piper's Cove, Cape Breton County; Piper's Glen, Inverness County; Piper's Clearing and Piper's Brook, Victoria County; and Piper's Pond, Hants County. Gaelic immigrants brought with them not only one of the oldest languages in the world but a largely oral culture rich in poetry, song, instrumental music and dance. Far from being members of a larger cohesive political structure in the 17th century, however, Scottish Gaels were a fragmented tribal society whose allegiance was based on kinship and regionalism. This clannish, or parochial nature, was also part of the immigrant culture of the Gael and probably contributed to the inability of New World Gaels to resist the constant pressures of assimilation into a dominant English society.

King James I established the Order of the Knights Baronets of Scotland in 1624-1625 to encourage settlement in the colonies. Sir William Alexander, then Royal Secretary for Scotland, was an early promoter of colonization and the first attempts at Scottish settlement included Charles Fort, Port Royal, on mainland Nova Scotia, and Baleine, Cape Breton in 1629.[2] These settlements were short-lived. The French, who also laid claim to various parts of North America, captured Baleine and forced the inhabitants to help build the French fort at St. Ann's, Cape Breton. Later, most of the Scots were returned to Scotland. In 1632, the area known as Nova Scotia was ceded by treaty to France.

Later Scottish colonization included disbanded Highland soldiers after the Seven Years War and the American Revolution, a portion of Loyalist resettlement, Gaelic middle-class immigrants (1772-1815), and lastly tenant and subtenant farmers, victims of the infamous Highland clearances (1815-1848).

Land grants (totalling approximately 32,000 hectares (80,000 acres) on the north shore of St. John Island (PEI) were set aside for disbanded soldiers of the Fraser Highlanders after the Peace of Paris in 1763. Veterans of the Black Watch were also granted land along areas of the St. John River in what is now the province of New Brunswick. A large group of United Empire Loyalists who were settled in Shelburne County after the American Revolution were drawn from the areas of earlier Highland settlement in North America such as North Carolina.[3]

There is a dearth of complete and reliable records for the actual number of Scottish immigrants to the Maritimes during the late 18th and early 19th centuries. Many ship's passenger lists have not survived and, due to the implementation of a head tax on immigrants by the colonial government, it is widely believed that many Scottish immigrants entered the region without the knowledge of either the colonial or imperial governments. A common perception of these transatlantic migrations is that all of the immigrants were poor, uneducated clansmen, betrayed by uncaring clan chiefs, and forced *en masse* to emigrate. Although there were certainly recorded cases of extreme force and brutality in removing people from the land, especially after the end of Napoleonic War, every indication is that many of the first emigrant Gaels to North America were not necessarily impoverished or physically forced to leave.[4] For instance, John Roy MacKay, who held the middle-class position of piper and gamekeeper for Alexander MacKenzie of Gairloch, made a conscious decision to immigrate to Pictou in 1805. MacKay was able to pay the passage for his wife and ten children, and all their belongings.

Causes of Emigration

There were several complex reasons for the mass emigrations from Scotland, including political, religious and economic.

As mentioned previously the feudal clan system, which had been the foundation of Highland Gaelic society for centuries, was in accelerated decline after the final Jacobite Rebellion of 1745. The first segment of the population to feel the effects of economic restructuring was the educated middle class known as tacksmen. Historically, the tacksman class occupied positions in Highland society such as clerics, teachers, military officers, physicians, poets and musicians. Toward the end of the 18th century, the value of land rose dramatically in the Highlands and Islands of Scotland accompanied by a massive reorganization of the local economy:

> The value of land had previously been its ability to support a large, robust community. In the new socio-economic regime, it was transformed solely into a commercial commodity designed to provide maximum profit for those at the very top of the social structure—the land holding and increasingly anglicized clan chiefs.[5]

The Gaelic middle class, who for generations held farms in hereditary succession (which they in turn leased to tenants), were marginalized by their respective clan chiefs. In the closing decades of the 18th century many clan chiefs lost any paternal interest in their kinsmen, resulting in the confiscation of land, raised rents and a rupture of long-established roles, customs, rights and obligations.[6] The chiefs simply became land proprieters. The tacksman class was faced with ever decreasing political influence and increasing financial demands. In an effort to maintain a relatively high standard of living, many members of the tacksman class who could afford to chose emigration. North Carolina, New York and Georgia were popular destinations, but following the American Revolution, immigrant Gaels increasingly turned their attention to British North America.[7]

The areas now known as Nova Scotia, Prince Edward Island and New Brunswick rapidly became a collection basin for displaced Gaels. Because Scottish immigration to the Maritimes occurred over several decades, it is best viewed in two stages. The first period, from 1772 to 1815, followed the continental wars between Britain and France; the second includes the post-Napoleonic period from 1815 to 1850. Many early emigration schemes during the period 1772-1815 were conceived and coordinated by several members of an increasingly frustrated middle class; the second period was characterized by wholesale evictions, especially in the Hebrides.

One of the earliest Highland settlements in the Maritimes was at Malpeque Bay in Prince Edward Island in 1772. This settlement consisted of immigrants from South Uist and part of the adjacent Scottish mainland, and the migration was largely religious in its motivation:

> [The migration] had its origin both in religious persecution of Roman Catholics and economic pressures upon the tacksman class. The religious troubles began in 1769 when Colin MacDonald of Boisdale began to try to force his Roman Catholic tenants to convert to Presbyterianism. The leaders of the Roman Catholic Church in Scotland—reduced to only 13,000 adherents in the Highland region- responded to this action with a decision to relieve their people by removing them to America, a move which might simultaneously prevent the spread of the Protestant faith to other lairds by threatening a general depopulation of their estates.[8]

This endeavor was led by John MacDonald of Glenaladale, a Catholic member of the tacksman class. It was financially supported by the Catholic Church and it proved a highly successful settlement.[9]

Despite the religious differences in Scotland at the time of emigration the number of Catholic and Protestant pipers who came to Nova Scotia during the early immigration period was almost evenly split and this was particularly true from 1773 to about 1817. An evangelical form of Protestantism had spread to several of the islands from the Scottish mainland during this period of time and with it came repressive attitudes towards music and dance.

Angus Morrison, Isle of Harris

One piper who adopted the stricter tenants of Protestantism, to the detriment of his musical talents, was the Isle of Harris born piper, Angus Morrison. Angus Morrison was a direct descendant of the hereditary judges of Lewis.[10] He was born at Stroud, Harris, in 1792, and immigrated to St. Ann's, Cape Breton in the 1820s. A brief account of his early life published in a genealogical study of the Morrison family in 1880 in the United States illustrates the effects of religion on some forms of entertainment in Scotland:

> In his youth he was an accomplished player of the Highland bagpipes, but at the age of twenty-six he became religiously inclined, and gave up playing on his favorite instrument, for the reason, he remarked that he found it "tended to lead him into temptation." Some years later, when a handsome sum was offered for his bagpipes, he refused the money, neither would he give the

instrument as a gift, stating that he found it an injury to himself, and what was an injury to him he would not "place in the hands of another." He then took it, tied a stone to it, and threw it into the sea.[11]

Angus may have given up playing the bagpipe but his love for the Gaelic language never waned. Angus' youngest son, John A. (b. 1833) was a staunch supporter of the Gaelic language in Nova Scotia. From 1850-1872 he was employed as a school teacher and in 1878 he was elected to the Nova Scotia House of Assembly representing Victoria County. The following year he made the now famous speech, entirely in Gaelic, in the House of Assembly demanding the teaching of the language in the Province's school system.[12] This was reputed to have been the first Gaelic speech ever delivered in the provincial legislature. Despite his best efforts no further action was taken to provide either educational or institutional support for the language. In the 1890s the family eventually abandoned the farm in Cape Breton and moved to Moosomin, Saskatchewan.

Serious emigration from Scotland to Nova Scotia began in 1773 with the arrival of the ship *Hector* at Pictou. The town of Pictou soon became one of the most important ports of entry for many Scottish immigrants between 1773 and 1815. Between 1773 and 1805 Pictou County, Antigonish County and the western side of Cape Breton Island became common destinations for Scottish exiles. Other Highland immigrants entered the province via the port of Sydney, while hundreds more, evading a government head tax on immigrants, were simply put ashore at isolated coves.[13]

Rise and Fall of the Kelp Industry

The Napoleonic Wars (1793-1815) substantially reduced the number of people leaving Scotland and increased the dependence of the Hebridean economy on the harvesting and processing of kelp.[14] With the outbreak of hostilities in Europe, England's supply of substances used in the manufacture of soap and glass (such as barilla) was greatly reduced as France had placed an embargo on Spanish barilla. Kelp proved to be a viable alternative, and the Outer Hebrides was rich in this type of seaweed. The industry was labour-intensive with men, women and children all taking part in harvesting and processing. The population of the Isle of Skye and the outer islands, including North and South Uist, Barra, Lewis and Harris, increased from 19,000 in 1750 to 33,000 in 1811.[15] This population increase of more than 75 per cent does not factor in the substantial emigration from these areas which was already taking place to destinations such as Cape Breton and Prince Edward Island.

During the Napoleonic War, kelp had become an integral part of the Hebridean economy. Edward Daniel Clarke, chemist and professor of mineralogy at

Cambridge University, described the process of kelp manufacture after his 1797 tour of the Hebrides as follows:

> The manufacture of kelp is conducted by the following process: the sea-weed is first collected and dried. The usual mode is to cut a portion of the kelp annually from the rocks, taking it from the same place only once in three years. After the kelp has been dried it is burned in a kiln ... of stones loosely piled together.... After it is consumed, and the fire is extinguished, a long pole pointed with iron is plunged into it and it is stirred about; the result of the burning being, by this time, a thick glutinous liquid, which runs from the kelp in burning. As soon as this liquid cools, it hardens and the operation is at an end. The usual expense of manufacturing the kelp is about two guineas a ton for the labour; if it is sold on the shore, which is generally the case, and estimating of the kelp only at eight guineas a ton, the proprietor clears six.[16]

Understandably, with the demand for kelp at an all time high, the clan chiefs were worried about a loss of cheap labour if emigration remained unchecked. Immigration to the colonies was also curbed in an effort to keep men at home for military service on the continent. From the early 18th century the war-like nature of the Gael had been channelled into numerous Highland regiments. These units had experienced significant military successes both in North America and Europe and with the threat of Napoleon still looming, the availability of new recruits was a major concern. To restrict overseas emigration, the Highland lairds called on government to enact the *Ships Passenger Act* of 1803, and to provide subsidies for the fisheries, road and canal building, and manufacturing to help lessen unemployment.[17] The *Ships' Passengers Act* was ostensibly intended to improve the conditions of the emigrants on board ship, but these conditions were rarely enforced and in the years after it was enacted, the cost of emigration doubled.[18] These measures, and a renewed conflict with France, reduced legal emigration to the colonies to a trickle, but a perusal of land grant applications held in the Public Archives of Nova Scotia for the years 1803-1843 indicates that numerous Gaels left Scotland during this period of government intervention and eventually ended up in Cape Breton seeking land.[19]

In the years following the war in Europe, cheaper ingredients for soap and glass were found on the Continent. For a Highland west-coast economy almost totally dependent on cattle and kelp, any downward trend in the price of kelp was devastating. The bottom fell out of the kelp market almost over night and what followed in the Western Isles was widespread poverty and destitution. The population boom, which had accompanied the introduction of the potato in the mid-18th century, and the rise of the kelp industry in the latter part of the 18th century, resulted in too many people chasing too few resources, compounding the downturn in the economy. This situation was further complicated by returning Highland soldiers who had fought for

Barry W. Shears

Britain against Napoleon. Upon their return the disbanded soldiers found that entire communities had been displaced.[20] Much of the population was now considered surplus, and various methods of removal were implemented. The Highland landlords must have found the disbanding of trained soldiers, fresh from their victories on the Continent, more than a little distressing and the presence of veteran soldiers may have been a deterrent to even more violent forms of evicting tenants. In the end, rents were raised well above the ability of tenant farmers to pay and families were eventually driven from their small farms. Many more were forced to settle on the coastal areas of the west coast of Scotland, where the land was not conducive to agriculture. For most Gaels, immigration, either to the colonies or to large cities in Scotland, was the only avenue of survival open to them. What followed was a transatlantic exodus from the Hebrides to Canada.

Despite the *Ships' Passenger Act* (1803), overcrowding and the spread of disease on board immigrant vessels had changed very little since the *Hector* landed at Pictou thirty years earlier. During the eleven-week voyage of the Hector in 1773, eighteen children on board died from smallpox and dysentery. The ship was so rotten in places that passengers claimed to be able to pick out splinters from the vessel's hull when they were below deck. In 1827 crossings were still dangerous as Dr. John Whyte noted in his correspondence to R. D. George of Sydney:

> I find that the brig *Stephen Wright*, of Newcastle, which performed Quarantine in this port during the past season had on board 170 passengers More than one third of whom were afflicted with Small Pox, and many now with Dysentery and other diseases—that during the passage 3 deaths occurred, while in port 10, and 2 after landing ... the ship *Harmony* of Whitehaven also arrived at a neighbouring port in August last having taken on board at Leith & Stornoway above 200 Emigrants, 13 of whom died on the passage—5 were dead on board & 22 were cut off after landing on an uninhabited Spot by Measles—Dysentery, and Starvation. The Cause of such dire fatality, can, I imagine, be readily traced to the confined, crowded & filthy state of the vessels—the quantity & quality of food in the case of one of them at least the scarcity of water. It was stated here by the Captains of the Vessels that a very extensive emigration was contemplated in the ensuing Spring and that 10 to 15 vessels belonging to the Owners of the *Stephen Wright* had been chartered to convey these poor Creatures from the Highlands and Islands of Scotland to meet famine, disease and death on the shores of Cape Breton.[21]

In the following year the *Universe* left Stornoway with 464 passengers and such was the overcrowding on board that "six families were obliged to live in the long boat during the whole voyage."[22] Such accounts of overcrowding and disease clearly show that the *Ships Passenger Act* was rarely enforced. Despite the hazards of the voyage, Cape Breton remained the preferred destination for many Scottish Gaels. By the 1820s Scottish Highlanders were opting for settlement in Cape Breton rather than mainland Nova Scotia. This did not go unnoticed by government officials; in 1826 it was noted that almost 500 Scots from the Western Islands had come to Cape Breton at their own expense and once they landed, they "immediately disappeared in search of their friends and unoccupied land."[23]

Patterns of Settlement

The following map shows the extent of Gaelic settlement in Nova Scotia and Prince Edward Island.[24]

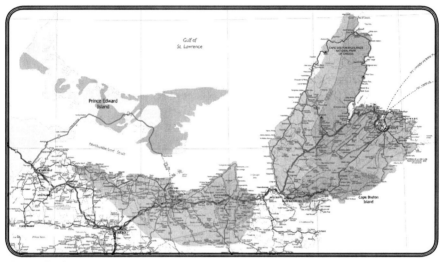

Fig. 14. Settlement map.

For these early immigrants, proximity to relatives, religious denomination and dialect determined to a large extent where they would settle.[25] This preserved the continuity of communities from the old country to the new. These settlements became miniature replicas of the Highland areas or localities which had been left behind in Scotland. This type of immigration is referred to as "chain migration," and many family clusters were multi-generational, consisting of parents, children and one or more grandparents.[26]

Pictou County was settled to a large extent by people from Sutherlandshire. Colchester County received immigrants from Sutherland and Ross, victims of the brutal Sutherland Clearances, as well as significant numbers of Ulster Scots.[27] Antigonish County became the new home for Gaels from areas of the Scottish mainland such as Morar, Moidart, Strathglas and Lochaber.

Cape Breton Island was the last area of substantial Scottish settlement in North America. It is estimated that more than thirty thousand Gaels settled in Cape Breton during the 19th century.[28] Cape Breton was not the first choice, but because of its geographical position in relation to Scotland, it proved to be the cheapest. People from North and South Uist, Benbecula and Morar inhabited the Mira River area; immigrants from Barra settled at Iona, Grand Narrows and Washabuck. Gaelic-speaking Highlanders from Lewis, Harris and Scalpay settled at St Ann's Bay, Little Narrows and along the North Shore of Cape Breton. Gaels from the islands of Mull, Tiree, Colonsay, Rum, Muck, Skye and mainland areas such as Lochaber, Moidart, Knoydart and Morar settled in small enclaves throughout the counties of Inverness and Cape Breton.[29] In addition, several Scottish Gaels moved to Cape Breton from neighbouring Prince Edward Island (where it was much harder to obtain land grants) to take advantage of land availability and to be closer to friends and relatives.

Coastal and waterfront areas were those most sought after for settlement: the Northumberland Strait, the Atlantic Ocean, the Bras d'Or Lake or any one of the numerous river valleys in Atlantic Canada provided settlers with basic means of transportation and supplies of fresh seafood. Many of the Highlanders who came to Nova Scotia were unprepared for life in the so-called new world. Coming from small farming or crofting communities, many of the immigrants from the largely treeless Outer Hebrides were confronted with dense forests on their arrival. For many in the first year of settlement, a crude lean-to provided the only shelter from a long, cold winter. Contrary to the glowing reports of cleared farmland from the immigrant agents, the new settlers were faced with the daunting task of felling large trees, some of which grew down to the water's edge. Many of the immigrant Gaels were unaccustomed to using an axe and the methods of clearing the forest for cultivation were primitive, time consuming and dangerous.[30] Fatal accidents and debilitating injuries from clearing land were not uncommon during settlement, especially in areas where lumbering proved to be an important source of income. Despite these difficulties the early Scottish immigrants managed to become quite proficient at clearing the land and there eventually developed a thriving timber trade with Britain:

> The [timber] trade forged new shipping routes from Scotland to the timber-producing areas of the eastern Maritimes. Being the earliest major group of immigrants to arrive in eastern Nova Scotia and Cape Breton, emigrant [sic] Scots found the most favourable locations close to the timber collecting bays and along the rivers which flowed into them. They felled the timber and cleared the land along these coastal and river frontages, creating distinct pockets of settlement. Thus the timber trade and colonization were not separate developments but were inextricably linked.[31]

Despite the successful adaptation of many of these settlers to their new environment, at least two immigrant pipers, Neil MacVicar and Kenneth Chisholm, were injured while clearing land in the early 19th century.

"Big Red-haired" Neil MacVicar (*Niall Ruadh Mòr*) was a bard, fiddler and veteran piper of the Napoleonic Wars. He came to Cape Breton in 1829 from Vallay, a small island just off North Uist, and upon arrival spent a miserable winter in Sydney at the hands of an unscrupulous landlady named Ahearn, an ordeal he later commemorated in the Gaelic song "*Mo Mhallachd-sa gu Siorruidh air Cailleach 'Hearn*" (My Curse Forever on the Ahearn Hag). The following summer he moved with his family to live with relatives and friends at Catalone. Neil MacVicar, who was described as "a huge and powerful man [who] died ca. 1850, some years after having suffered a terrible injury working in the woods cutting timber."[32] His surviving works include an elegy on the death of two of his sons by drowning, and three satirical pieces "*Oran nam Bodach*" (Song of the Old Men), "*Oran na Rhodan*" (Song of the Rats), and *Oran nan Cat* (Song of the Cats), a sardonic song about a ceilidh in North Uist.[33]

~

Kenneth Chisholm was the last family piper to Chisholm of Strathglas before he emigrated to Antigonish County around 1801. As family piper it was quite likely Kenneth Chisholm who played a "rant of triumph"[34] on his bagpipe after Alexander Chisholm, the twenty-third chief, refused to evict his people and replace them with sheep. Alexander Chisholm died in 1793 and was succeeded by his half-brother William, who wasted little time in clearing the people from Strathglas. Between the years 1801-1803 more than five thousand Highlanders were evicted from Strathglas with most of these settling in Antigonish County. Kenneth Chisholm was reputed to be a piping student of John "Beag" MacRae and was in all probability a product of the MacRae piping college at Kintail, Scotland, in the late 18th century.[35] Kenneth Chisholm was killed by a falling tree several years after his arrival in Nova Scotia and it is unknown if he taught any local pipers.

Most of the early settlers had been crofters in Scotland, making a living from subsistence farming, raising cattle and fishing. Early settlement in some areas of Cape Breton quickly claimed the best agricultural and water-frontage areas of land. Successive waves of Highland immigrants were forced further inland, where subsistence farming and hunting were to become their only means of survival. In these "rear" or "backland" areas there was very little agricultural opportunity, with much of the land described as being "wretchedly bad."[36] By mid-century these areas were home to most of the island's population.[37]

Despite the availability of waterways for transportation, poor roads and a scarcity of bridges isolated many Gaelic communities throughout Nova Scotia until the 20th century.[38] Comparative isolation was good for the maintenance of culture, but bad for economic development:

> Farming for most Highlanders in Cape Breton was a matter of trial and error. Few Highlanders possessed a practical knowledge of crop rotation, soil exhaustion and field drainage. They deliberately eschewed scientific procedures and clung to primitive ancestral practices, considering it an act of presumption and audacity, to make any improvement or alteration in the practices of their ancestors.[39]

As Nova Scotia's industrial base began to develop, feudal farming techniques and occasional crop failures made the prospect of steady wages in industrialized centres increasingly attractive to many hard-pressed rural residents.

Industrialization, Urbanization and Education

By the 1890s, industrialization had affected many predominantly Gaelic-speaking areas of Nova Scotia. Coal mining, small manufacturing industries and, later, steel-making all provided economic opportunities not available in rural agricultural areas. By the late 19th century, coal mining in Nova Scotia already had a long history. The French, fulfilling the fuel requirements of the nearby Fortress of Louisburg, were the first to mine coal in the area in the early 1700s.[40] During the early to mid-19th century small mines sprang up in many areas adjacent to Highland settlements. In Inverness County there were coal mines at Mabou and Inverness town;[41] Pictou County had substantial mine workings at Westville and Stellarton and small coal mines dotted the coast between Sydney Mines, New Waterford, Glace Bay and Donkin.[42] There were also small coal mines at Joggins and River Hebert in Cumberland County, a modest steel plant at Londonderry and much larger steel-making facility at Sydney. Industrialization in Nova Scotia was accompanied by urbanization and both of these developments would eventually have a negative impact on the language and musical culture of the Gael. The availability of English education, first in the urban centres and later in rural areas, reinforced the ability of the language of the school to displace the language of the home.

Until this time Gaelic permeated much of the day to day lives of Nova Scotians. During the 19th century, Highland settlements had grown and stabilized. This growth eventually resulted in a large *Gaidhealtachd* (Gaelic-speaking) region stretching from parts of Colchester County east to Pictou and Antigonish County, and continuing on to the northern tip of Cape Breton. As the Gaels adapted to their new surroundings and established a linguistically secure environment, various cultural art forms such as piping, fiddling, dancing and poetry flourished.[43] During this period, knowledge of the Gaelic language was almost indispensable for everything from commercial transactions to education. In the 1850s, English residents living in Colchester County adjacent to

Gaelic settlements complained that they could not "well transact business with the inhabitants of Earltown as it is generally done in the Gaelic language."[44] In Cape Breton, teachers complained that instruction without Gaelic-speaking teachers was almost useless since "the children were utterly unacquainted with English.[45]

Cultural Decline

There were several contributing factors in the decline of Gaelic culture in Nova Scotia. First, there was a major decline in rural population starting in about the 1880s. The agricultural capacity of the land to support growing communities and sustain a swelling population simply did not exist. Secondly, the growth of larger urban centres which accompanied the industrialization of Nova Scotia successfully eroded any form of cultural solidarity the rural Gaels may have had. The expansion of coal mining in Inverness, Cape Breton, Cumberland and Pictou counties and a new steel mill in Sydney provided the impetus for migration from the farms and fishing villages to the growing centres of steel and coal production. These urban areas were attracting not only rural Gaels but other linguistic and cultural groups as well. Over time these new urban centres became effective cultural "melting pots" fuelled by a predominantly English-language educational system. Although the Gaels represented a majority of these 20th-century urbanites, they lacked any uniform approach to language retention or institutional support. After a few generations the Gaels, like several other urbanized immigrant groups, were absorbed into the dominant English culture:

> The populations of these mining towns were not exclusively made up of these old comers (ie: the Scots). There was a continuing trickle of new immigrants from Great Britain and at about the turn of the century, of middle Europeans. But the old comers were the main component of the emerging workforce and controlled the character of the towns that were formed around the maelstrom that became the mining town of the twentieth century.[46]

Thirdly, improvements in transportation, including roads, bridges and railways, opened up new economic opportunities in the United States; many Gaels left Nova Scotia to improve their financial situations. The "Boston States" proved to be a favourite destination[47] and while many of those who left the Province married and raised families in the United Sates, others did return home to settle. Unfortunately, many Gaels suffered ridicule from non-Gaelic speakers during their time in the United States and upon their return—whether permanently or for summer visits—many Gaels continued to carry with them a prejudice against their mother tongue.

Charles Dunn, in his book, *Highland Settler*, found that many Gaels who experienced life in the United States, eventually began to associate the Gaelic language and culture with scarcity and want.

Fig. 15. Pipers gathered at the Gaelic Society Night in Boston, 1927 (detail). Beaton Institute. 79-1021-4001.

To explain the growth of this fierce contempt for the mother tongue, amateur sociologists among the Gaels point out that the young people who grew up in the pioneering communities unwittingly tended to associate the Gaelic language which they had heard at the time with the incessant toil, hardship and scarcity peculiar to primitive conditions. When they went to the city, the universal language was English, while Gaelic was unknown; the standard of living there was inconceivably superior to what they had known. Hence Gaelic came to be considered the language of poverty and ignorance and was therefore despised, while English was regarded as the language of refinement and culture and therefore cherished.[48]

Hereditary or Family Pipers

It is impossible to ascertain precisely how many immigrant Gaels to the Maritimes were pipers. However, by carefully examining the primary sources in Scotland and comparing them to the local histories compiled in Nova Scotia, a fairly accurate picture emerges.[49] The historical notes compiled by James Logan and published in Angus MacKay's *A Collection of Ancient Pìobaireachd, or Pipe Music*, emphasize the importance of these "hereditary" piping families and their role as tradition bearers in Scotland. All too often, however, these published family sketches fall short with the simple phrase "he went to America." There appears to have been little concern or interest, from a Scottish perspective, as to the fate of these musicians after they left Scotland and what if any of the tradition survived in Nova Scotia, or anywhere else in the New World. The Highland Society of London had already established branches in the Maritimes in the early 19th century, and there was certainly communication between Gaels on both sides of the Atlantic, but no evidence has surfaced to date to indicate that the Highland Society had anything but a passing interest in what was probably considered the periphery of Gaelic culture. The preoccupation with the hereditary or family pipers, which came to prominence during the Victorian era, has eclipsed the importance of the lesser known piping families who came to Atlantic Canada. This is probably because, as members of the Gaelic middle class, the hereditary pipers were deemed to be of greater importance in the preservation, performance and transmission of *ceòl mór*. Published local histories supply the bulk of the information on several immigrant pipers, both tenant and tacksman. The list of known immigrant pipers can, for the most part, be split into these two distinct classes (Appendix A).

The MacKays of Gairloch, Chisholms of Strathglas, John MacGillivray of Glenaladale, Robert MacIntyre of Rannoch, the MacNeils of Barra and the Rankins of Mull were all middle-class musicians who left Scotland for the Maritimes in the late 1700s- early 1800s.[50] These families were known to have trained pipers, and one family in particular, the Rankins, is reputed to have rivalled the fame of the MacCrimmons of Skye as teachers of pipe music.[51] These families dominated perceptions of Highland bagpipe culture for most of the 19th century in Scotland and there is considerably more information available concerning their lives and family history.

The MacKays of Gairloch

The piping dynasty of the Gairloch MacKay family began with Rory MacKay (ca. 1592-1689). The MacKay family of Gairloch supplied four generations of pipers to the MacKenzie Lairds. At age sixty, Rory is believed to have married a daughter of Donald Doughal MacKay, which would have placed him high on the social ladder, and his son John (ca. 1656-1754) succeeded him in his position as family piper. John MacKay was known in Gaelic as Am Piobair Dall (the Blind Piper) or sometimes as Iain Dall (Blind John). Blind John was a gifted piper and poet. He lost his eyesight to smallpox at age seven and this appeared to have enhanced his other senses. He learned piping first from his father, and at age eighteen was sent to the MacCrimmon college at Boreraig, Skye. He studied with one of the more famous members of this piping dynasty, Patrick "Og" MacCrimmon, for approximately seven years and was considered by many, to be his best pupil. According to tradition, his playing abilities proved far superior to the other students attending the college, and several stories of jealousy and even attempted murder form part of piping folklore.[52]

Blind John MacKay was, like his father, in his sixties when he married. He had two sons, John and Angus, both of whom were pipers. Angus (b. 1725) succeeded his father as piper to MacKenzie of Gairloch. The young Laird, Sir Kenneth MacKenzie, and Angus MacKay were very good friends. They travelled a great deal together and both men died at a comparably young age. According to Angus MacKay's *Collection*, Blind John's son, John MacKay, emigrated to North America around 1770. As the younger son he would have had little claim on the farm after his father passed away and his older brother, Angus, became established as the family piper. Keeping in mind the trends in immigration patterns at the time, there is a very good chance that this John MacKay was the piper on the immigrant ship *Hector* when it sailed for Pictou from Loch Broom in 1773.

Angus's son, John Roy MacKay (b. 1753) became the last family piper to MacKenzie of Gairloch. John Roy, like his father, also had a favourable relationship with the clan chief, so much so that after John Roy immigrated to Pictou in 1805 on the *Sir Sidney Smith*, Sir Hector MacKenzie said he would never care to hear pipe music again and he never kept another piper.[53]

One story about the family's departure from Scotland concerns a tune which John Roy MacKay is said to have been playing while being rowed out to the *Sir Sidney Smith*. Oral tradition states that the tune was called *The Departure of Piping from Scotland* and that it was a new composition by John Roy himself.[54] Whatever the origins of the tune, it has been lost. In fact much of the musical legacy of the Gairloch MacKays, including specific tunes and techniques brought to Nova Scotia, has been forgotten. One of the few glimpses of the Gairloch MacKay's life in Nova Scotia comes from Alexander MacKenzie, the editor of the *Celtic Magazine*.

The *Celtic Magazine* was a Scottish journal dealing with Scottish history and folklore. Alexander MacKenzie made a visit to Canada in 1879 and spent some time with John Roy's youngest son, Squire John MacKay, a stipendiary judge at New Glasgow. He published an account of his visit and some excerpts shed light on the MacKay family in the New World and contain one of the few and all-too-brief descriptions of piping among this particular class of musician:

> But more interesting to me than all my discoveries as yet on this continent, was finding a representative of the famous pipers and poets of Gairloch, in the person of John MacKay, who occupies the most honourable and prominent position in this thriving town—that of Stipendary [*sic*] Magistrate.... His great grandfather was the celebrated Blind Piper of Gairloch.... About four years ago a paragraph appeared in the *Celtic Magazine* making inquiries to whether any of this distinguished family were yet alive.... The only thing known about them was that one of them, the grandson of the famous Pìobair Dall, and the last male representative of the race in Gairloch, emigrated to some part of America in 1805, and carried with him more Ceol Mor or Piobaireachd than he left behind among all the pipers of Scotland. [Squire John's] father continued to play the national instrument all his life, and died

a very old man. His elder brother Angus, also played marches, reels and strathspeys, but piobaireachd not being appreciated in the land of his adoption, he practiced the higher form of music but little and was not, therefore, up to the family standard of excellence in that department.... [H]e died a few years ago when nearly one hundred. John himself also learned to play, but at the age of eighteen he finally gave it up.[55]

It is regrettable that Alexander MacKenzie did not gather and publish more information on the piping styles and tunes associated with the Gairloch MacKays. Squire John had given up piping but must have remembered some points of his early tuition. It may be possible, too, that Squire John, having achieved a certain amount of prominence and respectability in Pictou County, may have wanted to perpetuate Scottish myths regarding the fame of the Gairloch MacKays as pipers. Not everyone shared the sentiments of Alexander MacKenzie regarding the reputation of the Gairloch MacKays. In 1770 Dr. John MacLean wrote a letter to a Captain John Grant regarding the playing ability of the MacKay pipers at the time. The circumstances surrounding the letter concerned the decision to send a young Cummings piper to Skye instead of Gairloch for instruction and describes the Gairloch family of pipers in unflattering terms saying the "arrival of Cumming the young piper: will make the best bargain for him; knows that the Gerloch [sic] pipers were good but have degenerated; thinks recipient made the right decision in sending the lad to Skye." This reference may not be a scathing assessment of John Roy's playing ability, but more of a condemnation of John Roy's previous efforts to learn dance music instead of concentrating on ceòl mór.[56] Certainly the reputation of the MacKays of Gairloch was sufficient for Malcolm MacLeod, Fear Aire, to send the young John MacKay of Raasay to Gairloch for further piping tutelage.

No definitive reason for John Roy MacKay's departure from Scotland to Nova Scotia has yet been uncovered,[57] although it is quite possible that relations with Sir Hector MacKenzie were strained after the laird started removing tenants from some of his lands in 1790.[58] John Roy was comparatively well educated and in addition to being "the recognized and paid piper of the Gairloch family, he was also Game-Keeper, being in charge of the woods and forests of the estate."[59] His position afforded him a better lifestyle when compared to the numerous victims of the later Highland clearances. Perhaps it was the increasing frustration felt by many of the Gaelic middle class when faced with a loss of political influence and prestige which prompted them to seek a new life in a new land, or as John Lorne Campbell suggests in his Songs Remembered in Exile, "the hopes born in the 'Common Man' by the success of the American [and French] Revolution with its spirit of independence and egalitarianism."[60] In any case, John Roy MacKay seems to stand in the midst of social and political change. When the MacKay family came to Pictou in 1805 they brought with them a pipe chanter said to have once belonged to Blind John MacKay. The chanter, which dates to about the 1690s, is perhaps one of, if not the oldest, European woodwind artifact in North America. This interesting relic was photographed in 1934 by another Nova Scotian piper, Fred Calder.

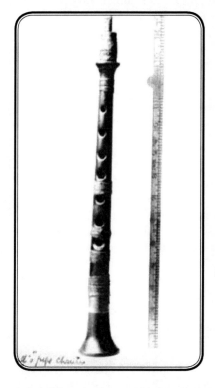

Fig. 16. The Blind Piper's chanter, photograph taken by Fred Calder in 1934.

Fred Calder was born at West Bay, Cape Breton in 1868 and learned his piping from the local players in the district. He studied law at Dalhousie University in Halifax and in 1900 moved with his family first to Dawson City, and then Cache Creek, British Columbia.[61] While visiting his Cape Breton home in 1934 he made a detour to New Glasgow to photograph and measure the Blind Piper's chanter. Later that year he forwarded copies of the photograph to George I. Campbell, Honorary Secretary and Treasurer of the Piobaireachd Society in Scotland. Campbell in turn sent a copy of the photograph to the *Oban Times*, in January of 1935, where it aroused immediate curiosity. The old chanter has been the subject of several articles.[62]

The Gairloch MacKays continued to teach piping after their arrival in Nova Scotia, but curiously enough not among their own descendants. The music was perpetuated by a few second- and third-generation pipers, but eventually the Gairloch MacKay style of playing, technique and repertoire died out in Pictou County. They did pass on some of their particular style and tune repertory to a few pipers in Pictou County, but by the beginning of the 20th century their influence appears to have been wiped from the musical map of Nova Scotia.

Also on the *Sir Sidney Smith* in 1805 was the family of Donald MacPherson. The MacKay and MacPherson families had been friends in the old country and they continued their friendship in the New World. Squire John's older brother Angus instructed Donald MacPherson's son John to play the bagpipe, and after becoming proficient he was in constant demand as a performer at all the local weddings, parties and fairs.

John MacPherson in turn taught three of his neighbour's sons to play the bagpipe, William, Hector and Donald MacKenzie. Donald MacKenzie became so well known for his piping that he was considered by many to be the best piper in the Maritime Provinces. An article in the records of the Church of Scotland on the Gairloch MacKays seems to support this claim:

> [Donald MacKenzie's] services were sought after on all gala occasions, not only in this Province, but in New Brunswick and Prince Edward Island. His last performance was at the Orange Walk in Shubenacadie. He came home sick from over-exertion and never rallied. Many middle-aged men and women will recall with delight the stirring strains of Donald MacKenzie's reels and marches. He taught his nephew, George MacKenzie, son of William, to play. After Donald MacKenzie and John MacPherson, the next best player was George MacKenzie. He died at an early age and of all the MacKenzie pipers there are now none left who can play but Alexander MacKenzie (William's son) and we believe Alexander MacKenzie, merchant of Westville.[63]

This quotation and the previous reference by Squire John MacKay that his brother, Angus, played mostly "marches, reels and strathspeys" indicates that dance music was still very common in Pictou County and the surrounding area in the closing decades of the 19th century. While Squire John's brother Angus continued to play and teach bagpipe music among the Gaelic communities of Pictou County for the remainder of his life, other middle-class pipers such as John MacGillivray, Robert MacIntyre, Condullie Rankin and Hector Johnston chose very different ways of making a living.

Barry W. Shears

John MacGillivray

John MacGillivray (1774-1862), was piper and bard to MacDonald of Glenaladale before he immigrated to Prince Edward Island, eventually settling on the Gulf Shore of Antigonish County. An article written by his grandson, A. T. MacDonald, which was published in the Antigonish *Casket* April 17, 1913, offers a brief glimpse of his career in Scotland:

John MacGillivray, Iain Pìobaire, of Highfield, Maryvale, Antigonish County, was poet of more than ordinary sweetness and energy, and such of his songs that have been published are read and sung everywhere the Gaelic language is spoken. He studied music with the celebrated MacKay of Skye, whose son Angus was afterwards piper to her Majesty, the late Queen Victoria. Before coming to America he was for years musician for the family of Glenaladale. It is he who is mentioned by Alexander MacKinnon, the martial poet of the Highlands in his *Dubh-Gleannach: Dh'aith-nich mi meoir ghrinn a Bhrataich* (I recognize the sweet fingering of MacGillivray).[64]

Fig. 17. John MacGillivray, from a portrait in the National Library of Scotland, listed incorrectly as John MacDonald, piper to Glenaladale. National Museum of Scotland. 22145-1.

Shortly before emigrating to Nova Scotia John MacGillivray, MacDonald of Glenaladale's piper and poet, married Margaret MacIain, one of the MacDonalds of Glencoe. "It seems that her people, like the MacDonald of the Strand were of a military disposition as sixteen of her cousins served in one regiment, the Scots Greys. All sixteen fell at Waterloo."[65] He continued to compose Gaelic songs after leaving Scotland and one of these surviving works, *Oran do Gaidheil Alba*, celebrated the contributions of the Gael in the Napoleonic Wars of the 19th century.[66]

In addition to farming, John MacGillivray taught school after his arrival in Nova Scotia. Unfortunately several of his new compositions were lost in a house fire a few years after his death, along with the bagpipe that MacDonald of Glenaladale had purchased for him before he left Scotland. He taught one son, John, to play the bagpipes and his eldest son, Alexander, was the author of *Companach an Oganaich, no An Comhairliche Taitneach* (The Youth's Companion, or The Friendly Counsellor,) the first Gaelic book written and published in British North America.[67]

The MacIntyres of Perthshire

Robert MacIntyre (1769-1833) also augmented his farming income by teaching school at Port Hood, Inverness County, after he arrived with his family around 1813.[68] Robert MacIntyre was descended from a long line of pipers in Perthshire, a few of whom were family pipers to Menzies of Weem. Robert was piper to John MacDonald of Clanranald until Clanranald's death in 1792 (or 1794). According to the notes in MacKay's *Collection*, Robert MacIntyre placed third in the Highland Society competitions in 1787, second in 1788 and earned first prize in 1790. His piping ability was commemorated in a Gaelic poem or *rann* by Alexander MacDonald, a lesser known North Uist bard, known locally as the Dall Mor. The poem, entitled "*Oran do Rob Domhnullach Mac-An-T-Saoir, Piobaire Mhic-Ic-Ailein*," was published in *The Uist Collection: The Poems and Songs of John MacCodrum, Archibald MacDonald and some of the Minor Uist Bards* (Glasgow: Archibald Sinclair, 1894).[69]

"Oran do Rob Mac-an-t-saoir, Piobair Mhic'ic Ailein" by Dall Mor

Oidhche domh 's mi ann am chadal,
Chuala mi sgal pioba mòire,
Dh' erich mi ealamh a' m' sheasamh,
Dh' aithnich mi 'm fleasgach a bhual i.

> One night when I was asleep.
> I heard the skirl of a great pipe,
> I quickly rose and stood up,
> I recognized the youth who had struck up the pipe.

Bha da leomhain orr' a' beadradh
Claidheamh 'us sleagh air an cruachain,
Bha fear dhuibh o 'n Chaisteal Thioram
Grunn de na dh' imich mu 'n cuairt d'a.

There were lions there playing
With sword and spear on their hips,
One of them was from Castle Tirrim
A crowd of those who had departed gathered round him.

Mac a Mhor-fhear a Duntuilm,
Gu' n d' labhair suilbhearra suairc,
Druidibh ri 'cheile 'Chlann Dòmhnuill,
Leanaibh a chòir mar bu dual duibh.

The son of the Lord of Duntulm
spoke cheerfully in polite tones
"Close ranks Clan Donald
Uphold the right of your linage."

Rob Mac Dhòmhnuill Bhàin a Raineach,
Boinead is breacan an cuaich air:
Bha sùil leomhain 's i 'na aodan,
Coltas caonnaig 'dol san ruaig air

Rob, son of fair-haired Donald from Rannoch,
wearing bonnet and plaited tartan,
Had the eye of a lion in his face
Turning a fight into a rout

Cluich e "corr-bhein" air a' mhaighdinn
(Ceol a's coaimhneil' chaidh ri m' chluasan)
Nach iarr biadh, no deoch, no éideadh,
Ach aon léine chur mu 'n cuairt dhi.

He played "corr-bhein' on the maiden [the bagpipe]
(The sweetest music to come to my ears)
Who would not ask for food, nor drink, nor clothing
But for one shirt to put around her.

Chluich e air maighdinn Chlann Raoghnuill,
Rob a leannan gràidh 'g a' pògadh,
Meal do mheodhair, meal do mheòirean;
Meal do chuimhne 's do glòir shìobhalt'.

He played on the maiden of Clanranald
Rob her beloved darling kissing her
Here's to your memory, here's to your fingers
Here's to your remembrance and your fine glory.

Meal do phiob-mhor, 's meal do Ghàilig;
Do mhaighistair dh' fhàg an rìoghachd.
Iain Muideartach mòr nam bratach;
Raoghnull a mhac thogas ìre.

> Here's to your great pipe and here's to your Gaelic
> Your master who left the kingdom,
> Big John of Moydart of the banners,
> Ranald his son will lift our condition.

'S coma leam co ghabhas anntlachd,
'S e Rob maighstir gach pìobair'
Bha 'n urram greis an siol Leòid ac';
'N uair 'bha 'n òinseach aig na daoin' ud.

> I care not who is displeased with what I say
> T'is Rob the master of every piper
> The seed of Leod once had their honour
> When the bagpipe was with those people.

Bha i 'n sin aig Clann Mhic Artuir
Pìobair sgairteach na caonnaig,
Tha i 'nis 's a' Chaisteal-Thioram,
'S ait leis an fhinne so 'faotainn.

> Then the Clan MacArthur had it-
> the shrieking piper of the skirmish,
> It is now in Castle Tirrim,
> The place that is obtaining this beautiful woman.

Fhad 's a dh' fhanas Rob 'na bheò-shlaint'
Gleidhidh Clann Dòmhnuill an Fhraoich i

> So long as Rob remains alive and well,
> Clan Donald of the Heather shall retain it.

The author of this poem, Dall Mor, was a large powerful man who had
been blinded as a small child by smallpox. He was born at Baleshare,
North Uist, ca. 1750 and despite his handicap he developed a prodigious
memory and was able to recite large sections of the Bible from memory
in addition to some of the shorter catechisms and psalms. The poem was
composed sometime prior to 1792 while John MacDonald of Clanranald
was in residence at Nunton, Benbecula. Unfortunately, there is no precise
date for its composition. The poem describes Robert MacIntyre as a
"handsome youth" and places his piping abilities third behind that of
MacCrimmon and MacArthur, not unlike the famed Gaelic poet John
MacCodrum's comparison of Conndullie Rankin with MacCrimmon and

Charles MacArthur. It might well have been composed in celebration of Robert's success at gaining first prize in 1790 although there is no mention of the competition within its verses. Still, the description of Rob, "dressed in plaid and turning a fight into a rout" may be a metaphor for his success at gaining first prize in the Highland Society piping competition. According to recent research Robert MacIntyre applied to Clanranald for a tack (i.e., a farm) in South Uist in 1804 after serving some amount of time as piper to MacNeil of Barra. This reference indicates that Robert MacIntyre was still living and piping in Scotland a decade after John MacDonald of Clanranald's death in 1792.

Robert MacIntyre next appears in the service of Lieutenant Colonel Robertson MacDonald of Kinlochmoidart. This becomes confusing when one considers that Lt. Col. Robertson MacDonald was actually Lt. Col. David Robertson, the youngest son of the "celebrated historian and Very Reverend William Robertson, principal of the University of Edinburgh and Historiographer Royal for Scotland."[70] In 1799, David Robertson married Margaritta MacDonald in Edinburgh and when her older brother, Donald MacDonald of Kinlochmoidart died in 1804, Margaritta inherited the title. Subsequently, Lt. Col. Robertson added the name MacDonald to his own and was subsequently known as Lt. Col. Robertson MacDonald of Kinlochmoidart. This relationship may have been the basis for Seton Gordon's comment that "the hereditary pipers to MacDonald of Clanranald were MacIntyres who lived at Uldary, at the head of the Moidart River."[71]

Despite the lack of local records concerning Robert MacIntyre's life in Inverness County there is a tantalizing reference in a Gaelic song which might link the piping of the MacIntyre pipers of Rannoch to local society in early 19th-century Cape Breton.

The song, entitled "*Òran a'Ghìogain*" (The Thistle Song), was composed by Donald MacLellan in the early 19th century and was published by his son, multi-instrumentalist and poet Vincent MacLellan, in *Failte Cheap Breatuinn* ca. 1898. It describes a community attack on an overgrown field of thistles in Inverness County in which "the people are led by the sweet fingered piper playing "*Fàilte Phrionnsa*" (The Prince's Salute).[72] "*Fàilte Phrionnsa*" was reputed to have been composed by John MacIntyre of Rannoch in the 18th century. John MacIntyre was Robert's great-grandfather so it might be a reference to the playing of one Robert's sons or pupils.

Recent oral history from a descendent of Robert MacIntyre on the west coast of the United States provides additional information on the MacIntyre family in North America. According to family lore, Robert MacIntyre had a son David, who was also a piper. Naming his son David might indicate Robert's continued respect for his former benefactor,

Lt. Col. David Robertson MacDonald. After Robert's death, the family eventually moved to Ontario and when the Canadian west opened up for settlement in the late 19th century, some of Robert's descendents moved again, this time to Saskatchewan. Piping continued in the MacIntyre family for several more generations and a bagpipe reputed to have been played at the Battle of Culloden (1746) remains in the family's possession. According to one descendant, David had five sons and two daughters all of whom danced, piped or did both. They were Davie Junior, Andrew, Hugh, Charlie, John, Jean and Maggie; the descendants of this family can be found throughout the United States and Western Canada.[73]

The MacIntyre Pipers of Perthshire[74]

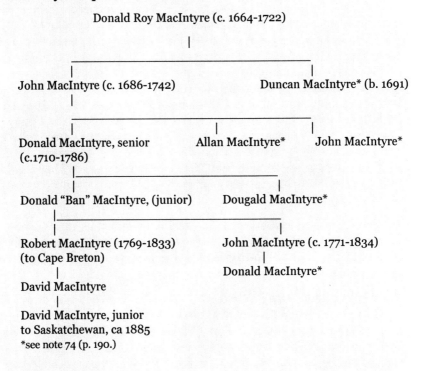

Donald Roy MacIntyre (c. 1664-1722)

John MacIntyre (c. 1686-1742)   Duncan MacIntyre* (b. 1691)

Donald MacIntyre, senior   Allan MacIntyre*   John MacIntyre*
(c.1710-1786)

Donald "Ban" MacIntyre, (junior)   Dougald MacIntyre*

Robert MacIntyre (1769-1833)   John MacIntyre (c. 1771-1834)
(to Cape Breton)   Donald MacIntyre*

David MacIntyre

David MacIntyre, junior
to Saskatchewan, ca 1885
*see note 74 (p. 190.)

The Rankins of Mull

Condullie Rankin (1774-1852) was descended from a long line of pipers to MacLean of Duart, on the Isle of Mull, and later on the Isle of Coll. According to tradition, the first piper to MacLean of Duart was the 17th-century piper Cu-duiligh mac Raing[75] (Condullie). He had been trained to play the pipes in Ireland and upon his return to Mull he established a piping school at Kilbrennan. The college eventually closed ca. 1760. It is ironic that this particular piping dynasty, which spanned five generations, began and ended with a Condullie Rankin. An interesting story is preserved in the *Transactions of the Gaelic Society of Inverness* concerning Condullie Rankin and the diminishing importance of piping to middle-class Highland society in the late 18th century:

> Condullie began learning to play in order to follow his father as piper to the Laird of Coll. One day he was playing his chanter in Breacachaidh Castle when the bailiff of Freaslan, the sheriff of the Coll estate, came by. The bailiff, who noticed how the piper's station was gradually being diminished, said, "Put that (i.e., the pipes) away, when others are keeping company with the nobility you will be with the dogs."[76]

The Condullie Rankin who eventually settled in Prince Edward Island took the bailiff's advice and soon after joined the army.[77] According to the *Transactions* article, Condullie Rankin accompanied Lord Hobart to Grenada in 1803, won great renown in the War of 1812, went to Scotland in 1817 and returned to Prince Edward Island with his brother, Hector, and several immigrants from Coll the same year. In 1831 he was in London bidding unsuccessfully to become Governor of Prince Edward Island.[78] During the 19th century, the Rankin family continued to play a role in Prince Edward Island affairs. Condullie Rankin was president of the local Highland Society in 1846[79] and his son, Neil Rankin, was Mayor of Charlottetown in the mid-19th century.[80] Condullie Rankin died in 1852 and is believed to have been the last piper in that family.

Hector Johnson

Another important link to the piping traditions of 19th-century Scotland and Nova Scotia was the "celebrated piper of Coll," Hector Johnston (1797-1869). Johnston was taught to play the bagpipe by Duncan MacMaster, piper to the Laird of Coll. Duncan MacMaster won first prize in the 1805 competition in Edinburgh and was reputed to have been taught by the last of the MacCrimmons of Skye.

Johnston left Scotland in 1819 and settled first at River John, Nova Scotia, and later moved to the Brudenell River area of Prince Edward Island around 1840.[81] Hector Johnston was a literate piper (meaning he could read and write music), a skill which immediately sets him apart from other immigrant pipers of his generation. He taught school in both Nova Scotia and Prince Edward Island and was a Deacon in the Baptist church.[82]

Conclusion

For many of the middle-class pipers such as MacKay, MacIntyre, MacGillivray, Rankin and Johnston who immigrated to the Maritimes in the first half of the 19th century, piping played a diminishing role in the community and wider

Maritimes society. While a few of these prominent pipers continued to teach music after their arrival, there were no clan chiefs on this side of the Atlantic to offer patronage to full-time musicians. There was little need to retain music which celebrated Highland lairds or clan chiefs. If these middle-class Gaels were to succeed in colonial society, they needed to occupy alternative roles, often in addition to their occupation as farmers. This usually meant relegating bagpipe playing to "hobby" status, if it was kept up at all.

To date, very little in the form of written records concerning the middle-class piping families has been uncovered in either Nova Scotia or Prince Edward Island. Squire John MacKay, Iain Dall's great-grandson, left a manuscript of his life in Scotland and Nova Scotia, but references to piping are brief. Condullie Rankin appears to have been literate, yet nothing has surfaced in the form of a memoir or written account of his family's piping history. Hector Johnson, the musically literate Coll piper, may have left a manuscript of *ceòl mór*, but to date such a collection (if it was ever compiled) or his bagpipe, a relic of Culloden, have ever been found. The Johnson family brought several previously unknown pieces of *ceòl mór* to Canada when they immigrated, a few of which were recovered by John Johnson of Coll and later published in the David Glen's *The Music of Clan MacLean*. One tune composed by the Rankins and which has apparently been either forgotten or identified by another name is the tune *Lament for the Noblemen of the Meeting*. It commemorates the slaying of a visiting Irish nobleman and his piper by one of the Lairds of Duart.[83] Perhaps one day it will resurface.

The social and economic standing of many of these families enabled them to integrate into Nova Scotia society more easily than their tenant counterparts. Career successes as school teachers, army officers, lay preachers and magistrates provided the main sources of income and social stability. By the turn of the 20th century, and with Gaelic in decline in some areas of the region, there appeared less and less interest in maintaining and preserving the music and folklore associated with the Highland bagpipe, especially in urban areas. *Ceòl mór* playing almost completely disappeared in Nova Scotia by the end of the 19th century. Dance piping, on the other hand, more reflective of the regional performance styles which had been brought from Scotland, retained its strength in rural Nova Scotia, where most areas maintained their community pipers, fiddlers and bards. Outward migration beginning in the 1880s, large-scale industrialization a decade and a half later, and urbanization all combined to realign large segments of Gaelic society in Nova Scotia.[84]

The growing number and size of urban centres in Nova Scotia did not bode well for the survival of either the Gaelic language or piping. Both the language and the musical traditions of the Gael flourished during the last half of the 19th century and would continue to find strength in rural areas away from the influence of towns and cities.

Chapter Three
The Piping Tradition in Nova Scotia

'S ann a bha mi air banais, an Ceap Mabou nan gallan, Ann an coibhneas 's an cai-dreabh mo chàirdean...

Far'n robh mir' agus beadradh, Ceòl theud agus fheadan Agus luinneagan eireach-dail bhàrdaibh...

Ruidhle h-ochnar 's gach oisinn; Fir a' falbh le'n cuid bhotol; 'S mnathan àlainn a' coiteach oirinn càise...

I attended a wedding in Mabou of the handsome youths, enjoying the hospitality and the fellowship of my friends...

Where there was mirth and flirting, music of stringed instruments and bagpipe chanters, and the beautiful songs of bards...

An eight-handed reel being danced in every corner: men moving around with their bottles, and handsome women pressing us to take some cheese...*

Music and the oral tradition were critically important to the New World Gaels of Nova Scotia. The original tunes, songs and stories which these early settlers brought with them were maintained virtually unchanged for several generations. The repertoires of the local musicians and singers were enlarged with new compositions, proving that the genius of the Gael was not mute in the new world. The role of the piper in Gaelic society in Nova Scotia was one of community musician. The cultural persistence of these roles in rural society reflected such essential components of community as

---

*"Òran na Bainnse" (The Wedding Song) by Donald MacLellan, Grand Mira, Cape Breton, in Creighton and MacLeod, eds. *Gaelic Songs in Nova Scotia*, 99. This song dates from the late 19th century.

biological succession, social organization, economics and cultural beliefs and values.[1] Isolation preserved the characteristics of many of these communities for much of the 19th century and it wasn't until the early 20th century that external forces related to demographics, economic expansion and world events would reduce and eventually change the role of the community piper. Despite external influences such as significant outward migration to the United States and to western Canada, relocation from rural areas to industrialized centres and an anglo-centric system of education, some characteristics of early 19th-century piping survived through the late 20th century in parts of Cape Breton Island. This anomaly was not confined to bagpipe music. Gaelic language researchers such as John Shaw and the late John Lorne Campbell discovered several archaic features in the song and storytelling traditions of new world Gaels in the second half of the 20th century. As Shaw points out:

> The striking degree of cultural conservatism among Cape Breton Gaels is certainly a result of geographical isolation. Cape Breton is the most recent and far-flung outpost of the Scottish *Gàidhealtachd* (Gaelic-speaking region), and it is a well-documented phenomenon that archaic survivals of social and cultural institutions are most likely to be found at the periphery of a given cultural area.[2]

In 1957, John Lorne Campbell was surprised to discover fragments of Fenian tales preserved in a song format in Nova Scotia long after they were lost in Scotland.[3] In the last thirty years similar research has unearthed anachronistic forms of Gaelic instrumental music such as violin and bagpipe playing. This is not to say that all styles of piping found in areas of Nova Scotia and Cape Breton in the last decades of the 20th century were strictly early 19th century, for they were not. For much of the 20th century a parallel piping cultural existed. Modern playing technique and repertory coexisted with regional styles of piping which had been brought from Scotland, but evolved largely outside Scotland's sphere of influence.

Piper, Fiddlers and Bards

During the 19th century the Nova Scotia *Gàidhealtachd* was far from being a moribund culture. During this period it produced numerous Gaelic bards, fiddlers, pipers, step dancers and storytellers. New material in the form of Gaelic songs and poems, and fiddle and pipe tunes took their places along side a wealth of traditional and contemporary material brought from Scotland by several leading exponents of Gaelic culture. These tradition bearers included several of the hereditary or family pipers as well as dozens of prominent Gaelic bards including John MacGillivray, piper and bard to MacDonald of Glenaladale, John MacLean, the Tiree Bard, Angus Campbell, Benbecula, Allan MacDonald, Bohuntin, and descendants of Niall MacMhurich, or Neil Currie of South Uist, known as the last of the bards.[4]

Barry W. Shears

One of the best known early Mabou bards, Alexander "The Ridge" MacDonald,[5] went so far as to claim that "all the best bards had immigrated to Cape Breton in the 19th century."[6] He was certainly in a position to comment on such matters; he was a recognized authority especially on the Bohuntin Keppoch MacDonalds. He would later supply much of the genealogical information for Keith N. MacDonald's book *MacDonald Bards from Medieval Times*.[7] Recent research has identified 168 Gaelic bards in communities throughout Nova Scotia,[8] which proves the observation of one song collector in the 20th century that *"Cha'n eil clachan's am bheil Gaidhlig air a labhairt nach do thog bard no dha"* (There's not a hamlet where Gaelic is spoken that did not produce a poet or two).[9] The same was true of community pipers.

Since a majority of the population which comprised the Nova Scotia *Gàidhealtachd* was unable to read or write in Gaelic (or musical staff notation for that matter), many of these new compositions were lost. In the case of instrumental music there were no active collectors, and publishers like Donald MacDonald, Angus MacKay, William Gunn or David Glen, who in 19th-century Scotland led the way in collecting, editing, standardizing and publishing collections of bagpipe music. The number of pipers in late 19th-century Nova Scotia could be counted in the hundreds and because few pipers could even read music, any potential market for such a collection would have been quite small or non-existent. If music collectors like Angus MacKay or David Glen had been active in the Nova Scotia *Gàidhealtachd* during the late 19th to early 20th centuries, there is no doubt that a significant amount of material might have been collected.[10] The late Alex Currie of Frenchvale, Cape Breton, claimed that he learned more than six hundred tunes aurally from several sources within his extended family. It is said that the late Joe Hughie MacIntyre, a member of the French Road piping family, had a repertoire of more than twelve hundred tunes. These two examples alone indicate a healthy and expanding tradition. *Piobaireachd* playing, which survived in Scotland due largely to various forms of patronage and competition, eventually died out among Nova Scotian pipers by the third and fourth generation, while dance music flourished and expanded with the composition of new melodies and additional variations added to existing tunes.[11]

The number of pipers was large in the first three or four generations of Gaelic settlement in Nova Scotia and Cape Breton, and this gave the tradition added vigor and resistance to change.[12] In the early 1800s, the east coast of Canada was unsurpassed in the quality of its pipers, having probably one of the largest concentrations outside Scotland at that time.[13] Much has been lost, but what did survive points to a vibrant musical way of life. The piping tradition in rural Nova Scotia was largely unaffected by changes among pipers in Scotland.

Women and Piping

For much of the 19th century, pipers in Nova Scotia continued the role of community minstrel established in Scotland in the second half of the 18th century. A little acknowledged aspect of the piping tradition in Nova Scotia, as in Scotland, is the importance of women in the process of learning, performing and subsequently transmitting pipe music within their families and communities. Much of the history of the bagpipe has focused on male pipers and all-male pipe bands. A male-dominated society and military establishment has reinforced these values—so much so that female pipers have been largely overlooked for their contributions to the art.

In 1896 an anonymous writer to the Antigonish *Casket,* the local newspaper, informed its readers that there were "two or three young ladies in the parish [Margaree] who could play very sweetly on both the violin and bagpipes."[14] In Cape Breton County there were several excellent female pipers.

Annie MacMullin was a piper from Mira who married John MacMillan (born ca. 1828) and settled at Glen Morrison. Both she and her husband were descended from immigrant families who came to Cape Breton from South Uist, Scotland. She played light music and *ceòl mór* and she taught seven of her children to play the bagpipes. She could sing from start to finish several pieces of *ceòl mór* including the tune known as "The Finger Lock."

Another splendid performer was "Little" Kate MacCormick, piper, who was born ca. 1872. Little Kate's father and grandfather had immigrated to Cape Breton around 1840 from either South Uist or Benbecula.[15] She was known in Gaelic as Ceatag Dhomhnuill Neill (Kate, daughter of Donald, son of Neil) and her many attributes were celebrated in a song composed by one of the local bards:

> Ceatag Dhòmhnuill Neìll,
> Tha i math gu seinn na pìoban,
> Tha i math da rireadh gu dannsadh;
> 'S iomadh rud a nì i
> Nach dean a h-aon 's an tìr seo;
> 'S e sin a chuir mi fhin ann an geall oirr.[16]

> > Katie, daughter of Donald, son of Niall,
> > She is good at the playing of the pipes
> > She is good indeed at dancing;
> > 'Tis many a thing that she does
> > That no one else in this land does;
> > It is because of that I am pledged to her.[17]

The late Alex Currie remembered as a young man seeing Kate MacCormick seated in a chair and playing for dancers at a local picnic and described her style of playing as being "the same as his."[18] Kate MacCormick's brother, Duncan, also played the bagpipe.

Appendix B lists almost three hundred second- and third-generation pipers in Nova Scotia. It includes the names of several female pipers and chanter players in 19th-century Cape Breton which indicates that, in Cape Breton at least, the instrument was not necessarily gender specific.

Traditional piping has always had close associations with the Gaelic language. Although these traditions weakened during Gaelic's long and near complete decline in the province, what remained of the tradition in the second half of the 20th century offers a rare glimpse into piping traditions in rural Nova Scotia and, by extension, early 19th-century Scotland.

Relative isolation for long periods of time until the mid-1900s enabled some areas of Highland settlement in Nova Scotia to maintain regional differences in Gaelic dialect and music, differences brought to the province by the first Scottish settlers. That is not to say that musicians did not intermingle, but the frequency was restricted by remoteness of location and methods of transportation. In many cases, contemporary or homegrown compositions found an audience only in close proximity to the composer.[19]

A few of the early Cape Breton bagpipe compositions by pipers Archie Beaton, Ranald Gillis and Malcolm Gillis were printed by Scottish music publishers in the early 20th century. The collection of traditional bagpipe music and information on the piping traditions in Nova Scotia was practically non-existent until fairly recently. Most local players who could read music concentrated their efforts on acquiring printed collections from Scotland, although a few early-20th-century handwritten manuscripts containing several previously unpublished tunes have recently been discovered in Nova Scotia. These resources, combined with homemade tape recordings from the 1960s and 1970s and personal interviews with the last of the old style pipers shed some light on the repertory, playing styles and roles of some of these community pipers.

Military Music and Dance Music

In Scotland, the army is credited with keeping the piping tradition alive. It has been said the Highlanders never marched anywhere without their pipers.[20] As mentioned earlier, grouping pipers and drummers together produced the first military pipe bands around the mid-1850s. Under these conditions the musical requirements for pipers began to change. Eventually dance rhythms gave way to march rhythms as the music of the dance was adapted to the music of the route march and the parade square. The emergence of the military pipe band necessitated the need for uniformity in playing and the development of a common repertoire. Some dance tunes, such as strathspeys and reels, the mainstay of many of the Highland social dances, were rearranged as marches and, in the case of William Ross's *Collection*, many of these melodies were also renamed.[21] During the 19th century an increasing number of prestigious competitions were held whereby pipers not only vied for top honours, but also for the chance of gainful employment as pipers to the aristocracy. Add to this changing role the detrimental effects of many well-established piping families emigrating to North America and changes were all but inevitable.

Writers in the early part of the 19th century echoed sentiments expressed by Samuel Johnson after his 1773 visit to the Western Isles. Johnson had found a decline in piping probably due to migration to the cities of Scotland and immigration to the colonies:

> The decline of piping standards by the early part of the 19th century is remarked by both James Logan in his *Scottish Gael*, 1831 and J. G. Dalyell in his *Musical Memoirs of Scotland*, 1849, present pipers, they believed, were inferior to their predecessors and getting worse.[22]

In Nova Scotia there was very little military influence on piping until the First World War and very little exposure to the changes taking place in Scottish piping. Rural areas were particularly unaffected. Pipers in the province served a more diverse and functional purpose than supplying marching music to soldiers or competing against one another for prizes or a chance at gainful employment on an estate. As community musicians they were responsible for providing music for a wide variety of social gatherings, such as dances, weddings and funerals.

One of the prime functions of community pipers in Nova Scotia was to supply music for dancing. The volume of the instrument made it an ideal choice for outdoor entertainment and almost every area of the province settled by Scottish Gaels appears to have included community dance pipers.[23] This was not unique to the Scottish Gaels because, as George Emmerson has commented, pipers had provided dance music throughout Europe for centuries:

> We have noted the supreme place of the bagpiper as the purveyor of dance music at all social functions of the ordinary people from medieval times. Most of these functions had to be conducted outdoors or in a large farm building, such as a barn and that when it was empty. The fiddle held sway indoors but it is not until the eighteenth century that one sees it offer serious competition to the bagpipe in popular social dance, and then particularly in the Central Highlands, Breadalbane and Strathspey.[24]

Types of Dances

When one thinks of Scottish dancing, two forms of it immediately spring to mind: Scottish country dancing, and the various solo exhibition dances, such as the sword dance, sean truibhas, Highland fling, etc.

Scottish country dancing was imported from France and England and developed in the ballrooms and assembly halls of late-18th-century lowland Scotland. Its performance later incorporated some regional dance styles. The Highland dances, although now performed following set rules and regulations, are believed to have originated among ancient rural dance forms.

One Scottish dancer in particular is given credit for changing the performance style of the ancient dance known as the *seann triubhas* (the old trousers) in the late 19th century.[25] Piper Willie MacLennan (1860-1898) was one of the first professional Highland dancers in Scotland to learn ballet technique and to employ it in the Scottish exhibition dance idiom. It was felt that Highland dancing at the time was marked more by "enthusiasm than grace," and his employment of ballet technique to enhance the impact of the Highland dances altered the whole approach to the art of exhibition dancing.[26] Other exhibition dances were similarly affected by European ballet styles. The current style of Highland dancing is both graceful and physically demanding and usually requires a lot of jumping. Subsequently, the rhythm and tempo of the music has been altered to accompany these changes, playing it much slower and moving the expression from simple time (rounded) to compound time (pointed). The "wildness" of Scottish dance music became slower and more subdued to reflect these changes.

For people in Cape Breton who remember the more ancient dance form of the *seann triubhas* the changes implemented have rendered the current form of the dance unrecognizable. As Margaret Gillis, the great-granddaughter of dancing master, Alexander Gillis, observed: "The *seann triubhas* was a different dance than the one that they do in Highland dancing today with piping. That wasn't the *seann triubhas* our early settlers had at all!"[27]

We are left to wonder what specific social dances the common people in the Highlands of Scotland performed in the 18th and 19th centuries. This period is too early for Scottish country dancing, and the sword dance and others cannot be termed social dances. There is no recollection of Scottish country dancing in Nova Scotia among the Gaels, which indicates that it was unknown at the time of immigration.[28]

The most obvious answer, but not necessarily the only one, is a form of dancing known as step-dancing. All indications suggest this was a popular form of entertainment in Europe two centuries ago. Remnants of this type of dance can be found in Ireland's *sean nós* dance tradition, Northumberland step-dancing, Appalachian "buck" dancing in the United States, French and Acadian dances in Quebec and the Maritimes, and Scottish step-dancing in areas of Canada's Atlantic provinces, most notably Cape Breton. For many of the new world Gaels, dancing was an important form of recreation and socializing. As George Emmerson discovered: "Browsing through the statistical accounts for the various Scottish parishes for this period (18th century), one finds time after time that their chief amusement is dancing"[29] and in Barra, "dancing to the music of the bagpipes was a favourite pastime."[30]

Step-dancing and Dancing Masters

Step-dancing involves the intricate movement of the dancer's feet in time to the music and is much less regimented than the current display dances performed at Highland games and competitions. Step dancers have the freedom of expression to insert particular steps or dance sequences to match the notes of the music to which they are dancing. This form of dance matches the style of dancing observed by Colonel Thornton in the Scottish Highlands in 1804, where he noted that "[the dancers] all shuffle in such a manner as to make the noise of their feet keep exact time."[31] In its more traditional form, the dancer remains almost motionless from the waist up, employing movement of the knees, ankles and feet to "beat out" the rhythm of the music. Step-dancing is also physically demanding and graceful, but in Cape Breton and parts of mainland Nova Scotia it is performed close to the floor when compared to modern Scottish dances. It requires the music to be played much faster than the display dances described above and in simple time, which is a much rounder rhythm than compound time.

Several dancing masters were among the early immigrants from Scotland. These dancing masters came from both the Hebrides and parts of the Scottish mainland, which gives an indication of how widespread the step dance tradition was in early 19th-century Scotland. A list of these professionals included:

> Mary MacDonald Beaton (1795-1880) [who] had been a distinguished dancer in Scotland and after immigrating to Cape Breton, set up a school near MacKinnon's Brook for the purpose of teaching that skill.[32]

> Allan "The dancer" MacMillan ... was born in Lochaber, Scotland. Around 1817 he came to America, and he came to Rear Little Judique in 1820. He was a celebrated dancer and, after coming to this country, kept a dancing class in both the settlements of Judique and Creignish.[33]

Other dancing masters included: John Kennedy, who immigrated from Canna in 1790; Angus "Ban" MacDougall, piper and dancer, an 1812 immigrant from Moidart to Cape Breton; Malcolm MacLean, who came from Mull in 1826;[34] and Alexander Gillis, who immigrated from Morar to Cape Breton, also in 1826.

The dancing masters would migrate from community to community, staying with friends or relatives. According to an account by the late James D. Gillis, the dancing master would set up a school in a community or area. The school would involve mostly young people and the training would extend over two or three days. In the beginning, graceful and simple moves would be introduced. This was followed over the next few days with more intricate dance steps.[35]

There has been much discussion during the past few years on the origins of "Cape Breton step-dancing."[36] The late Alex Currie was of the opinion that Scottish step-dancing originally came to Scotland from Ireland. Alex cited his father as his source for this theory, the well-known step dancer Peter Currie.[37] Purists might be aghast at such a suggestion, but Alex was of the opinion that the migration of this particular form of dance occurred several hundred years ago, when the Western Isles and Ireland shared a similar language and culture. Cultural exchanges during the 16th and 17th century would not have been uncommon. The MacMhuirichs, bards and chroniclers to MacDonald of Clanranald, were reputed to have had at least some of their training in Ireland, as were some of the pipers who founded piping schools based on the Irish model in Scotland. There are a few examples of the close ties between pipers in both Ireland and Scotland. One such story involves Donald MacDonald of Baleshare, North Uist, who sent his half-brother, Angus MacRury, to Ireland to learn the Irish method of curing bacon: "Angus brought his pipes along and while at Kilkenny was also in contact with Irish pipers where, it was noted, they had some common tunes but with different tune names."[38]

Certainly the old style (*sean-nós*) form of step-dancing sometimes seen in Ireland today bears a strong resemblance to Cape Breton dancing.[39] Absent, however, in Irish traditional dance is the type of music known as the strathspey, or strathspey reel. This indicates that if step-dancing did migrate to Scotland from Ireland, then some aspects of Scottish dance evolved outside the Irish influence.[40]

In medieval Europe, dance music was supplied by singers, or any one of the various forms of bagpipe at that time. As musical sophistication evolved, other instruments were created to provide music for dancing and listening. The introduction of the violin, with its musical range, dynamics and quieter sound when compared to the bagpipe, coincided with a growing trend to move entertainment indoors. Changes came slowly to the remote Highlands and Islands of Scotland. By the mid-18th century, dance musicians competent on both instruments began to appear and, as George Emmerson points out: "It is apparent too, from some of David Allan's pictures, that the piper sometimes alternated with the fiddler at weddings and the like. Sometimes the piper was also a fiddler, as was the case with Joseph and Patrick MacDonald." [41]

Occasionally the function of poet and musician was administered by a single individual. Duncan MacPhail, a piper, bard, fiddler, harper and composer from North Uist was a veteran of the Battle of Sherrifmuir during the Jacobite Rebellion of 1715. He was also credited with composing an elegy for James MacDonald to the melody of the *piobaireachd* "Sir James MacDonald of the Isles Salute." He died around 1795 at the age of 104. [42]

The descendants of many Highland immigrants in Nova Scotia continued this tradition of dual musicianship and many also fulfilled the function of local bard (Appendix B). In Scotland there would be some tunes common to both instruments but gradually the range and popularity of the violin enabled its players to develop a distinctly Scottish violin repertoire. This era, during the period 1740-1830, is sometimes referred to by Scottish violin music historians as "The Golden Age of Fiddling."[43] It is interesting to note that the second half of this "Golden Age" coincided with extensive immigration to Maritime Canada.[44]

Fig. 18. Three Piper/Fiddlers: "Black" Angus MacDonald, "Little" Allan MacFarlane, Angus Campbell Beaton, ca. 1930, Glendale, Cape Breton.

It is not known for certain when the violin penetrated the Western Isles, but by the late 1700s the bagpipe was still the main instrument used to provide music for outdoor dances which often followed very diverse and solemn ceremonies, such as religious celebrations:

> Outdoor communions were often devoid of pious solemnity, bur-lesqued by the presence of peddler's booths, confectioners' tables and whiskey tents. The celebrated Roderick MacLeod, a 19th century Evangelical Minister in Skye, described a scene which he witnessed during his boyhood at Dunvegan: ...as soon as the services, which were conducted in the open field, were ended, three pipers struck up music, and three dancing parties were formed on the green [where the communion was served].[45]

This is an important description in so much as it reveals the type of music played (i.e., dance music) in the late 18th century, as well as the close proximity to the famous MacCrimmon piping college at Boreraig. Some piping "authorities" in the 20th century maintained that *ceòl mór* (big music) was the only form of music performed by a majority of the 18th-century pipers, and that many of the family pipers considered *ceòl beag* (little music) as decidedly inferior.[46] Existing evidence does not support this view, and it would be tempting to imagine one or more of the MacCrimmons or their pupils playing for group dances such as the Scotch fours when not playing the classical music of the

Barry W. Shears

bagpipe. The concept of hereditary pipers playing dance music is further evidenced by the fact that one of the celebrated MacKays of Gairloch, John Roy, was sent by his father to Strathnaver to learn dance music.[47] Primary sources indicate that early immigrants and their descendants in the Maritimes were well acquainted with dancing as a form of social entertainment, as this description of Scottish Gaels landing at Prince Edward Island in the early 1800s illustrates:

> Another band of settlers, who, sailing from Moidart to Prince Edward Island, also enjoyed the good fortune to be accompanied by a piper. A descendant tells that when they landed they formed themselves into sets on the shore and danced a Scotch Reel to the music provided by Ronald MacDonald the piper; and Bishop Fraser, who was present at the celebration exclaimed with delight, "That man has the best little finger on the chanter I have ever known."[48]

Later descriptions of social dancing to bagpipe music appear in C. H. Farnham's article entitled "Cape Breton Folk," written in 1886 for *Harpers New Monthly*. In 1885, Farnham and a companion walked what later became the Cabot Trail in Cape Breton, and his observations offer a first-hand account of rural life on the island. Farnham mentions attending two gatherings, one a house party at Ingonish, the other a "Gathering of the Clans" held at East Lake Ainslie in 1885:

> Each of the platforms had about it a large crowd looking at the reels and jigs and piper. The dancing went on all day vigorously. The most impressive figure of all was the piper. The pipes go well with the national emblem: they are a very thistle in your ear; their weird barbaric strains are certainly inspiriting and martial, but you must be a Scotchman to love them. One of the pipers a very tall, very dark, very shaggy man, sat up with a rigid neck, stiff figure, puffed out cheeks, and looked like the presiding genius of some awful heathen rite. But he was one of the gentlest of men. I afterward spent a day with him noting some of the native airs of Cape Breton. [49]

Whether the author of this travelogue was referring to melodies composed in Cape Breton or simply to Scottish tunes played in Cape Breton we will never know. Since this encounter occurred at East Lake Ainslie, and judging by the description, the piper in question was in all probability, Farquhar "Mór" MacKinnon.

The MacKinnons of East Lake Ainslie were known as Clann Fhionghuinn a' Chiùil (MacKinnons of the Music) and the extended family included several pipers and fiddlers.[50] This family was descended from pioneer settlers who came to Cape Breton from the Island of Muck in 1820 and is further discussed below.

Farnham also mentions attending an all night party at Ingonish, "where reels and jigs helped pass the night."[51] It is unfortunate that Farnham didn't mention the names of the performers or what instruments, bagpipe or fiddle, supplied the music. One possibility might well be Rory MacDougall of Bay St. Lawrence.

Rory (Roderick) MacDougall (1848-1936) was a son of Donald MacDougall, who was born at Christmas Island, Cape Breton County, around 1802 and later moved to Bay St. Lawrence, on the northern tip of Cape Breton.[52] This family of MacDougalls had operated a grist mill for the MacNeils of Barra in the late 18th century. Although Rory was born at Bay St. Lawrence, he spent a great deal of time at Ingonish where his son, Dan Rory (1885-1957) later had a home. Both Rory and Dan Rory were well-known pipers who also played the violin and step danced. Not much is known about Rory's piping other than that he travelled all over Cape Breton playing for dances and frolics and was employed by a visiting horse trader occasionally to pipe up and down dusty roads to attract people's attention.[53] He also played the bagpipe with the local militia unit, the 94th Regiment, Victoria Battalion, in the 1890s.

Fig. 19. Dan Rory MacDougall playing for a dance, Ingonish, ca. 1955. Breton Books.

Barry W. Shears

More is known about Rory's son, Dan Rory, and stories still survive of his musicianship and stamina. On one occasion he is reputed to have walked from Ingonish to Cape North, a distance of more than thirty miles, to play for a wedding. According to local tradition, he played all night and most of the day, alternating between pipes and violin as physically demanding as this feat may have been, the fact that he could not read or write music and was still able to entertain for hours on both instruments indicates an extremely large repertoire of music. Music in this family of MacDougalls continued into the 20th century through Dan Rory's sons, Mike MacDougall (1928-1981), a gifted fiddler and composer, and Gabriel MacDougall (1925-1986), a player of both the bagpipe and violin.

The traditional dances brought by the first Highland settlers from Scotland consisted mostly of the eight-hand reel and the "Scotch" or single fours. The eight-hand reel was usually performed by four couples. The single fours were performed by two couples to strathspeys and reels and this format made it an ideal "wedding" dance with the bride and groom, best man and maid of honour participating. In many locations particular tunes were associated with these dances. In Christmas Island the wedding strathspey and wedding reel was danced to a strathspey called "Donald's Fair Daughter," and the reel was a variation of the tune "The Periwig."

Fig. 20. Wedding Strathspey from Christmas Island (based on the singing of Archie Alex MacKenzie).

Communal efforts in cutting wood and clearing land, known locally as "chopping frolics," were often followed by a supper and dance.[54] In areas such as Meat Cove, on the northern tip of Cape Breton, the piper would play for the Scotch fours and the fiddler would play for the square sets. Sometimes the fiddler and piper would team up and play together.[55] By the early 20th century, the Scotch four was gradually being replaced by more modern group dances, such as the Saratoga lancers and the quadrilles popularized by returning Gaels from the "Boston States." These imported dances, or their variations, were quickly adopted and now constitute the modern square sets or square dance in Cape Breton and parts of mainland Nova Scotia.

Fig. 21. Wedding Reel from Christmas Island (based on the singing of Archie Alex MacKenzie).

Fig. 22. Alex John MacIsaac and Hector Campbell, ca. 1930, Judique. Courtesy Charlie McIsaac.

In addition to these group dances there would be performances by solo dancers. This was an opportunity to demonstrate individual skills and introduce new steps. In some areas a lighted candle would be placed on the floor close to the dancer. When the performer was finished, he or she would snuff out the candle flame by clicking their heels together.[56] Other dancers demonstrated their skills by dancing with a small glass of water placed in the band of their hats, the finest dancers not spilling a drop.[57]

A piper was often called upon to provide dance music at wedding receptions, especially in areas with few fiddlers. In some instances there would be a friendly competition between the piper and fiddler.[58] Sometimes one musician played both instruments and would alternate between the bagpipe and violin or, as previously mentioned, pipers and fiddlers would play together. In areas with few pipers, fiddlers would sometimes play together during dances to compensate for the lack of volume of a single violin.

Since the spring and summer were the busiest seasons for farmers, most weddings in the 19th and early 20th centuries were conducted in the winter. The wedding reception or dance would extend from early evening to early morning the following day.[59] Usually there was no shortage of strong drink, be it government liquor or locally produced spirits. In some areas it was customary for the bride to present the first drink to the piper and the bagpipe before the dance began. Such was the case at a wedding in the Louisbourg area of Cape Breton described by Jim MacDonald, a piper, and son of one of the attendees:

> Piper John MacInnis of Kennington Cove near Louisburg was the official wedding reel piper in that district. Every time he would play the reel "More Rum for the Piper" he was given a water glass full of rum. When he thought he had enough he let the rest of the 90 over proof down the blowpipe. My late father used to tell me when the instrument got warm you'd swear there were doves flying out of the drone. In the wee hours of the morning when the pipes would stall he would walk home with two gallons of rum in an oversize bag—sheepskin with no cover on it.[60]

Similar traditions survived in early 20th-century Scotland, particularly in South Uist, as the following reference indicates, but by the 1920s step-dancing in Scotland appears to have all but disappeared:

> There was always a dance on the 15th of August [*Latha Feille Muire*], and a few in the springtime, and there was a dance at Christmastime. The music was provided by 'Giad'-Archie Campbell on the pipes, and he piped the whole night in the old school in Iochdar. We got a gallon of beer before we went and gave it to the piper. He was the oddest piper to watch, for he always piped for a dance sitting down, but he was the best of pipers to dance to. [61]

Funerary Customs

In Nova Scotia, dance playing was an important function for the piper in Gaelic society, but it was also incumbent upon these musicians to play for funerals. This was a time-honoured tradition which had parallels in the Western Isles of Scotland as Reverend Finlay McRae, North Uist, noted in his 1837 contribution to the *Statistical Accounts of Scotland*:

> At funeral processions, which had been, and still are conducted with remarkable regularity, the pipes, in strains of pathos and melody, followed the bier, playing slow plaintive dirges, composed for and used only on such occasions. On arriving near the church yard, the music ceased, and the procession formed a line on each side, between which the corpse was carried to its narrow abode. [62]

In Nova Scotia, as in Scotland, funerals would involve playing some tune or lament while accompanying the casket to the graveside. One common funeral melody in Nova Scotia was "The Flowers of the Forest." It was said that during Malcolm Gillis's funeral his close friend and fellow musician, Allan MacFarlane, played this tune on his bagpipe continuously during the four-mile walk to the cemetery.[63]

Funerary customs were almost universal among the Gaels of Nova Scotia. As C. H. Farnham observed:

> A wake, whether among the Presbyterians or the Catholics, gathers a great crowd in the house of the deceased; during two days the family is constantly at hard work, night and day, serving successive meals to those who arrive. It is considered a marked offence not to come to a wake, and, when there, not to eat and drink abundantly. Two or three funerals near together have actually ruined a family. The pious and aged in the room where the corpse lies generally occupy their time in reading and praying, while the young, in another room, solace their grief by eating, drinking and flirting. Many are more or less drunk when the procession moves on or collects about the grave, and generally it is then that the fight occurs, which seems a part of every good funeral.[64]

Bodies were washed and further prepared for burial by female relatives and laid out on "cold boards" until the coffin could be made from local timber. At the Gaelic settlement of French Road, the trees selected for making coffins were said to shine or have an eerie glow at night before they were cut down.[65] The coffin was usually carried on the shoulders of the pall bearers preceded by a piper. Several eyewitness accounts describe similar funeral processions such as the following by Jim MacDonald:

> In the old days a funeral took place in primitive style in Cape Breton. They had to travel footpaths except for the old French Road. No horses,

no sleighs, no hearses. Four men carried the bier on two poles on their shoulders to the nearest burying ground. A piper walked ahead of them playing a lamentable funeral dirge. They made their own coffins with white pine stained black with tint from burned alder wood.[66]

۞

Archibald MacKinnon

At East Lake Ainslie, another funeral-related story is recorded concerning Archibald MacKinnon, a member of the above mentioned "musical" MacKinnon family. Archibald MacKinnon (1784-1872), known locally as *Am Baitsealair Mor* or The Big Bachelor, was a piper and fiddler who had a premonition of his death. Eighteen years before his death he made a tombstone for himself, on which he engraved the MacKinnon crest and motto, a crescent star, and a record of his birth.[67] Several years before his eventual demise, he purchased five gallons of rum, which was intended for use at his funeral. Reverend Gunn, the local minister, heard of the will and the proposed availability of alcohol and, being a supporter of the temperance movement, tried to persuade the Big Bachelor to change his mind saying, "If you retain that clause in your Will, you will not get a man in East Lake Ainslie to bury you." Emphasizing the importance of "refreshments" at a funeral, Archie replied, "Oh Mr. Gunn, if they have five gallons of rum at my funeral there will be plenty of Big MacLeans from Broad Cove to bury me fifteen feet deep."[68]

Fig. 23. Archibald "The Big Bachelor" MacKinnon's headstone. Courtesy Eugene Quigley.

Despite the objections of the local minister, the Big Bachelor's funeral went as planned. When Archibald MacKinnon died, his remains were carried to their final resting place in the old Highland fashion: on the shoulders of the pallbearers preceded by a piper. Further instructions included stopping for "ample drams" of rum: first at the house where the wake was held, second at the gate of his niece's farm and finally at the graveside. This was reputed to have been the last funeral held at East Lake Ainslie at which liquor was served. [69]

Archibald MacKinnon taught several of his nephews and one niece to play the bagpipe before his death. Archibald MacKinnon's niece, Annie, was an accomplished performer on the violin and sometimes she and her brother "Big" Farquhar MacKinnon would "play the bagpipes each having one hand on the chanter."[70] Big Farquhar was a multi-talented individual. An impressive-looking Highlander, he stood six-feet-six in height. He played both bagpipes and violin, was an elder and precentor in the Presbyterian church, a farmer and a wood turner. Several of his nephews played the bagpipe and these included "Little" Farquhar and his brother Hugh Fred MacKinnon, Allan B. MacDonald and Hector MacQuarrie. Hugh Fred left Cape Breton and spent some time in the Klondike before settling in Edmonton, Alberta. While in the Canadian West, Hugh Fred won several prizes and medals "for the efficient handling of the chanter." Both Hector MacQuarrie and Allan B. MacDonald died when they were young men, and Little Farquhar became a popular dance player in early 20th-century Cape Breton.

Fig. 24. Hugh Fred MacKinnon, Edmonton, AB. Courtesy Eugene Quigley.

Little Farquhar was, like his grand uncle, a bachelor and his first love the music of bagpipe. When he was lying on his deathbed he longed for a tune on the pipes. He was too ill to blow a set of pipes and so he persuaded a close relative to inflate the bag for him while he fingered a few of his favourite tunes on the pipe chanter. After a few tunes the music ended and Little Farquhar passed on to his final reward—a fitting end to a well-respected community musician.

Fig. 25. "Little" Farquhar MacKinnon.

Funeral services today occasionally include a piper, but in some rural areas like Washabuck, Victoria County, the practice of playing the bagpipes at funerals was showing signs of waning as recently as the 1940s.[71] One explanation might be that out-migration had taken its toll and there were fewer pipers. Another reason might be changes in funerary customs which have occurred during the late 20th century. People are no longer waked in family homes and caskets are no longer homemade but mass-produced in factories.

Bagpipe Makers in Nova Scotia

As the number of pipers increased among the second- and third-generation Scottish Gaels in the 19th century, a small bagpipe-making cottage industry developed in Nova Scotia.[72] Bagpipes were expensive and difficult to acquire from Scotland. Unlike the bagpipe-making industry in Scotland, which began with a handful of musical instrument makers and later experienced unprecedented growth in the 19th and 20th centuries,[73] the small market for locally produced bagpipes in Nova Scotia peaked by about 1900 and, during the next few decades, disappeared.

Information on early bagpipe manufacturing in Scotland is sparse, especially in the late 17th and 18th centuries. Bagpipes were definitely played during this period, but who made the instruments remains a mystery. The increase in the numbers of Highland regiments raised during the Seven Years War and the American Revolution coupled with the numerous fencibles, or militia, battalions raised in the late 18th and early 19th century created a growing market for bagpipe manufacture, and several professional musical instrument makers established businesses in major centres such as Edinburgh, Perth, Glasgow, Aberdeen and London.[74] Three examples of early Scottish pipe makers are Hugh Robertson, who is listed in the 1775 Edinburgh directory as a bagpipe maker, Allan MacDougall, who set up a bagpipe-making business in Perth in 1792, and Adam Barclay (ca. 1740), of who not much else is known.[75] The number of known immigrant sets of bagpipes in Nova Scotia is about a dozen, and since they do not resemble any of the bagpipes attributed to the above pipe makers, one can conclude that early bagpipe-making in Scotland must have been quite localized at one time.

The romance of the Scottish Highlander and the inferred, kilted masculinity which blossomed under Queen Victoria's reign, enhanced the recruitment of a record number of Highland regiments (and pipers), a few of which were dispatched to various countries in the British Empire.[76] As Diana Henderson points out:

> The close links with bagpipe music, whose development in the 19th century was largely fostered through army pipers, the Gaelic bardic tradition of an heroic romantic culture, the works of Sir Walter Scott, the influence of the Highland Societies and the active support of a Monarch who came to associate herself with Scotland and in particular

with the Highland regiments, all affected Scottish attitudes to the army and recruiting.[77]

An increased demand for bagpipes for the pipers in these regiments resulted in new economic opportunities for these and several additional pipe-making firms. During the 19th century several large firms diversified their businesses by including the manufacture of other military musical instruments such as fifes and drums and various forms of Highland dress such as kilts, hose, sporrans (purses) and ornamental weaponry like dirks and the *sgian dubh* (stocking knives).[78] One bagpipe firm, R. G. Lawrie of Glasgow, also produced bowling green bowls or balls.[79] In the late 19th century, pipe-making firms such as David Glen, William Ross, Donald MacPhee and Peter Henderson extended their influence by publishing bagpipe tutors and music books, which put them at the forefront of musical literacy and standardization among pipers.

In Scotland, local woods such as fruitwood, holly, boxwood and larburnum were originally used in bagpipe manufacture.[80] During the 18th century, tropical hardwoods became more readily available and their superior tonal qualities and durability soon replaced the native hardwoods. Tropical woods such as ebony, cocus wood, lignum vitae and African blackwood all have a very close, straight grain and high oil content.[81] This makes these types of wood ideal for woodwind instruments and, eventually, they became the materials of choice for bagpipe, clarinet, oboe and flute makers.

These instruments were mounted with a variety of materials such as pewter, cattle horn, bone and stag horn. Mountings serve a practical as well as decorative purpose. The mounts are placed at strategic locations on the bagpipe to help prevent the wood from splitting. In Nova Scotia the most common hard woods for bagpipe making were apple wood and sometimes ash and pear wood.[82] Occasionally, if the maker lived close to a shipbuilding centre, some exotic woods like *lignum vitae* were available. Many instruments were turned on a lathe, usually powered by a foot treadle.[83] The task of making bagpipes in Nova Scotia fell to the wood turner, whose craft was already indispensable to pioneer society.[84] The manufacture of furniture, household items, spinning wheels and various farming implements were all part of that craft. In one area on the northern tip of Cape Breton, bagpipes were carved by hand and, in some cases, the conical shape of the pipe chanter was fashioned by using an old three-sided French bayonet as a reamer. Cattle horn, bone, brass and sometimes ivory from walruses and whales were used to adorn these home-made instruments. The overall design of the bagpipe has altered very little from the 18th century. The bells or terminals at the end of the drone, once almost pear-shaped, took on a smaller, slightly square profile. In Scotland the demands placed on the player and instrument in the army required a heavier bagpipe. The drones became thicker and, in some cases, longer.[85] This "army" pattern, with its large ornate mounts, has continued to present day.

Attributing an instrument to a particular pipe maker is very difficult. There are several problems associated with "pipe-maker" identification, not the least of which is a lack of suitable instruments with which to make a comparison. Pipe makers very rarely stamped their instruments, other than the pipe chanters, until the mid-19th century. The pipe chanter is the most delicate part of the instrument and quite often these have been worn and broken, or replaced as more desirable refinements in tonal qualities have been achieved. The overall appearance and design of the bagpipe is still the best way to identify who the maker was since, as Hugh Cheape points out, "the finish or shape and style of the drones, design of the mounts, is the trademark of a particular pipe maker."[86]

Judging by the number of immigrant bagpipes recently discovered in the Maritimes and the variety of styles of these instruments, it becomes clear that there were more instrument makers plying their craft in Scotland than the three early manufacturers mentioned above. It would appear, from the absence of documented evidence to the contrary, that several unknown pipe makers were supplying instruments to small, local markets and were only part-time manufacturers. It is also possible that individual pipers might have manufactured their own instruments, as was the case with 19th-century piper John "Ban" MacKenzie (1796-1864) and numerous other professional pipers in the 19th and 20th centuries which went on to establish successful pipe-making enterprises.[87] Certainly, the tradition of making a small number of instruments was carried on by several Nova Scotian Gaels during the 19th and early 20th century.[88]

Many of the early Highland immigrants to the Maritimes were pipers, and in addition to bringing Scottish-made bagpipes to Nova Scotia, they and their descendants constructed bagpipes using local materials.[89] Bagpipes were an integral part of the musical culture of the immigrant Gael and omnipresent among the Scottish Gaels who settled North America. Dr. Abraham Gesner, the noted scientist and inventor, commented in 1843 that "In a Highland settlement a set of bagpipes and a player should not be forgotten. I have known many a low-spirited emigrant to be aroused from his torpor by the sound of his national music."[90] The number of instruments available in these communities was disproportionate to the number of people who could actually play them, and in some areas of Nova Scotia one set of bagpipes would serve several family members. The early settlers and their descendants held the national instrument of Scotland in very high esteem. Many people could play a few tunes on homemade chanters, but very few could afford to purchase a new set from Scotland. As the numbers of pipers in the province increased, a growing market for inexpensive, locally produced instruments emerged.

The most notable features of the surviving examples of locally produced instruments are the number and size of the drones. Duncan Gillis, Grand Mira, made only two-droned sets at first, adding a bass drone when requested to do so. Two-droned sets of pipes were banned from competition by event organizers in Scotland after 1821 due to a perceived disadvantage on the part of several competitors,[91] and surviving examples of two-droned bagpipes are extremely rare. Many of the bagpipe-makers in Nova Scotia would undoubt-edly copy the sets originally brought from Scotland. This might explain why surviving examples of Nova Scotia bagpipes are noticeably smaller and more delicate in appearance than their modern Scottish counterparts.

Reeds for the instruments were made from a variety of materials. The MacIntyre pipers of French Road, Cape Breton County and later Glace Bay, made chanter reeds from old cane fishing rods.[92] Other pipers used small pieces of birchbark or maple tied to a copper or brass tube or staple. Sheepskin was normally used for the pipe bag since cowhide was too stiff. A single piece of hide would be folded over and stitched using a heavy needle (sometimes a porcupine quill) and waxed thread and affixed to the drone stocks.[93] To make the bag airtight, a variety of mixtures were used to dress or season the pipe bag. These included the whites of two eggs and a little sugar which produced an odorless rudi-mentary adhesive, or molasses or honey. Drone reeds were crafted from elder, known as *drumanach* in Gaelic.[94] Practice chanters, a small flute-like instru-ment used to initially learn the instrument and practise new tunes, were made from young maple trees. Once a small maple tree was selected and cut, it was left to dry for a few days and then the soft centre core or heart was burned out with a long wire rod heated in the fire. The positions of the finger holes were marked and then burned out in similar fashion.[95] Practice chanter reeds were usually made from a piece of oat straw flattened at one end.

Robert Ross

As far as is known, Robert Ross was the first person in Nova Scotia, and possibly North America, to make full sets of Highland bagpipes. Ross was born in Cuthill, Dornoch Parish, Scotland, in 1769 and emigrated to Pictou around 1816.[96] There is a family tradition that he was a veteran piper of the Battle of Waterloo, but this is unsubstantiated. Surviving documents indicate that he served a period of six months in the 75th Regiment and was discharged in 1809, six years before the Battle of Waterloo. The 75th Regiment was known as the 75th Stirlingshire Regiment which was raised as a Highland unit in 1787. It is perhaps no coincidence that 1809 is the same year in which the 75th Highlanders were re-designated as the 75th Foot and deprived of its Highland dress.[97] Changes to the regiment may have eliminated the position of company piper as well.

There is some evidence in Scotland to suggest Robert Ross was piper to George MacKay of Skibo (a son of Lord Reay), and that Robert's wife, Isabel MacKay, was a daughter of a MacKay piper.[98] The local tradition in Nova Scotia maintains that Isabel MacKay was the daughter of Lord MacKay, and that she eloped with Robert Ross against her father's wishes and emigrated to Pictou County. Census information in Scotland, however, indicates that several of the children were born in Scotland, so this claim can be challenged.

In the Nova Scotia census of 1838, Robert Ross lists his occupation as Piper, a designation which was shared with only two other pipers in the province: John MacDonald of Egerton, Pictou County, and Donald Stewart, Mira River, Cape Breton County. According to family tradition, Robert Ross applied for a land grant in Pictou County, but due to a delay in processing his request, several adult members of his family decided to move to West Bay, Richmond County, to take advantage of the recent land availability in Cape Breton. An examination of the surviving parts of a bagpipe attributed to him indicates that Ross used tropical woods for his bagpipes (three-droned) and mounted them with sea ivory. Ross eventually received his land grant and continued to live in Bayview, Pictou County, until his death in 1843. His will is registered as "Robert Ross, Piper," and lists among his many other possessions, "two pares [*sic*] of bagpipes." In his will he bequeaths to his oldest son Alexander, then living in Cape Breton, "all my tools for bagpipe making."[99] Two of Robert Ross's children, Alexander (1801-1861) and William, continued to work as wood turners in Cape Breton and in all likelihood continued to make and repair bagpipes.

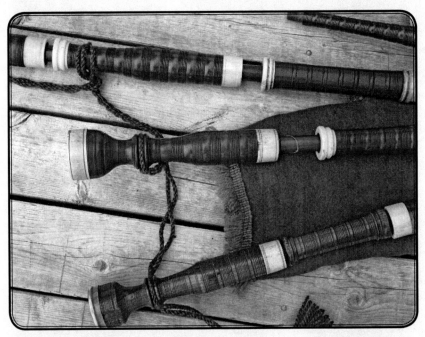

Fig. 26. A sample of Robert Ross's craftsmanship.

Barry W. Shears

Duncan Gillis

One of the most successful pipe makers in Nova Scotia was Duncan Gillis, Grand Mira, Cape Breton County. Usually referred to as Duncan "Tailor," he was born at Upper Margaree, Inverness County, around the middle of the 19th century but later moved to Grand Mira, Cape Breton County, to be closer to relatives. His occupation is listed as "Turner" in Lovell's *Nova Scotia Directory* of 1871, and in addition to making spinning wheels he made a profitable sideline of making and selling bagpipes around the province. Duncan Gillis made bagpipes from apple wood and mounted the instruments with bone, cattle horn and brass. An advertisement (Fig. 27) soliciting patronage, but with what appears to be a variation on Grand Mira, appears in an 1886 issue of the *Pictou News* where he claims to be "the only manufacturer of bagpipes in North America." Duncan Gillis

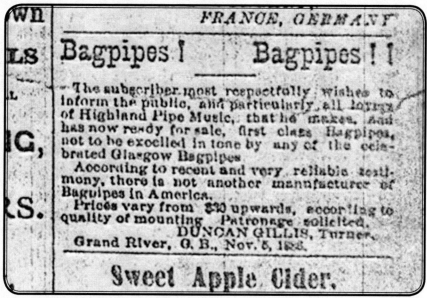

Fig. 27. Duncan Gillis advertisement, Pictou News, December 10, 1886. Nova Scotia Public Archives and Records Management (NSARM).

lived at Lewis Bay on the Mira River and not Grand River, which is in neighbouring Richmond County.

Gillis was so successful at making bagpipes that he was the subject of a Gaelic song, "*Òran do Dhonnchadh MacGill-iosa, am Mira, Fear a Tha Deanamh Phioban Ciuil*" (Song to Duncan Gillis of Mira, Maker of Bagpipes), composed by the Margaree Bard, Malcolm H. Gillis, in praise of his musical craftsmanship and upstanding character.

Fig. 28. Malcolm Gillis, The Margaree Bard.

Malcolm Gillis was a renowned bard and musician from South West Margaree. He could play the bagpipes, violin, piano, organ, Irish pipes and whistle, and several of his songs were published to wide acclaim in Scotland.[100] The poem alludes to a long-standing tradition of piping in Duncan Gillis's family and perhaps one of his ancestors also made bagpipes.

Thainig sgeul oirnn o chionn bliadhna,
Sgeul a riaraich mi neo-throm,
Sgeul bha taitneach leis gach Gàidheal
A chaidh àrach anns an fhonns':
Donnchadh Tàillear bho an Bhràighe,
Fear mo gràidh as aille com,
A bhith deanamh phiob am Mira:
Beannachd air a laimh nach lom!

     We received news a year ago
     News which pleased and cheered me
     News delightful to every Gael;
     Who was brought up in this area:
     Duncan Tailor of Upper Margaree
     My dear handsome man
     Is now making pipes in Mira-
     Blessings on his bountiful hand!

Beannachd air a làmh neo-chearbaich
A tha ainmeil air gach gniomh,

'S air an eanchainn anns 'n do chinnich
Móran grinnis 's am bi sgiamh!
'N a chuid obair cha bhi fàllinn,
Ach gu dealbhach, làidir, dion-
'S beag an t-ioghnadh 's gu 'n robh chàirdean
Eolach, talantach o chian.

> Blessings on his skilful hand
> Noted for every task,
> And on his intellect which produced
> Much artistic beauty:
> There will be no defect in his work
> It will be shapely, firm and secure,
> Small wonder as his people were
> Adept and talented long ago[101]

Duncan Gillis continued to make bagpipes until just after the First World War and in recent times samples of his musical instruments have turned up in such diverse places as Ontario and Glasgow, Scotland.[102] Another pipe maker from Grand Mira was "Old" Allan Gillis, who also made a few sets of bagpipes in the late 19th century. Allan "Turner," as he was known, was employed as a wood turner at a shipyard at Fourchu, Richmond County, and this job gave him access to tropical woods like lignum vitae, a very oily wood used in the manufacture of various items necessary on sailing ships such as pulleys, blocks and deadeyes.[103] A blood relationship between these two pipe-makers has yet to be established, but since they were from the same area, it is possible that Duncan apprenticed his trade with Old Allan Gillis.

In Inverness County, individual bagpipes were made by several pipers including Alex Dan MacIsaac, Dunvegan, Fred MacEachern, River Denys Mountain, and Alexander "Mor" MacDonnell, Kiltarlity.

Another area of Cape Breton where bagpipes were made was at Meat Cove, Victoria County, a tiny community originally settled by immigrants from the Isle of Skye. Here several pipers made their own bagpipes. For example, Johnnie Archie MacLellan did not possess a turning lathe and instead would carve by hand the various sections of the bagpipe from a solid piece of apple wood.[104] In the fall, the bones of a butchered steer would be collected, dried and carved for mounts using a knife and a "rat-tailed" file.[105] Also in the community were "piping" brothers Rory, "Red" John, Dave and Duncan MacKinnon. They were the sons of Alexander "Sandy" MacKinnon, also a piper. Sandy was married twice and in total his family consisted of nineteen children, most of whom could play an instrument or step dance, so there was no shortage of pipers.

Rory and John made bagpipes, sewed their own pipe bags, and made their own pipe chanter reeds using strips of birch bark. Later they used cane from chairs blown from the decks of passing ocean liners which sometimes washed up on the shore. The reed staple was fashioned from a .22 calibre shell casing.

left: Fig. 29. Alexander "Sandy Mor" MacDonnell, ca. 1910. Courtesy Janice Ferguson.

below left: Fig. 30. Rory MacKinnon, ca. 1950, Breton Books.

below right: Fig. 31. "Red" John MacKinnon, ca. 1920, Sea-Cape Music.

Barry W. Shears

Another turn of the century pipe maker was Peter MacNeil (1840-1910), commonly known as Peadar Dubh or "Black" Peter, of Christmas Island, Cape Breton County. He was born in the late 1800s and was a direct descendant of Rory MacNeil, family piper to the MacNeils of Barra. He was described as "a man of more than ordinary intelligence."[106] He was a talented craftsman, farmer and turner. He built several boats, houses and spinning wheels, as well as being skilled in the use of a lancet. Local sources indicate that he made three or four sets of pipes for use in the Iona-Washabuck area of Cape Breton.[106] The 19th century produced other bagpipe makers in various communities across Nova Scotia, two of whom immigrated to Boston in the late 19th century.

Ronald MacLean came from Stillwater, a small community close to the present town of Louisbourg. Ronald was a self-taught piper. He was a skilled carver of clocks and made at least one set of pipes. He immigrated to Boston in the early 1890s, where he was employed as a successful wood carver earning one hundred dollars a month.[108] While a resident of Boston, Ronald managed the occasional summer visit to his old home in Cape Breton.

A second bagpipe maker who left Nova Scotia for the United States was John MacDonald of Centredale, Pictou County. John's father and grandfather were both pipers and he may have learned the skill of pipe making from one or both of them. He immigrated to Boston in the late 1800s and made and repaired both bagpipes and violins in his shop on Tremont Street. [109]

Decline of a Cottage Industry

There were several factors which contributed to the decline and eventual disappearance of bagpipe manufacturing in Nova Scotia, and these included demand and durability. The demand for homemade instruments was never great and successful manufacturers only produced instruments as a secondary form of income. If cared for properly, a set of bagpipes could last generations. Industrialization and outward migration reduced the size of the rural population and constrained the markets for homemade instruments. The availability of factory-manufactured cloth, mass-produced furniture and modern farm implements reduced the need for a community-based craftsman such as a wood turner. The move to a wage-based economy supported by the province's coal mines, steel plant and small manufacturing no doubt increased the amount of disposable income available to pipers. Eventually, it became preferable and more prestigious to own a new set of pipes from Scotland, and the small market for locally produced bagpipes eventually disappeared. Despite competition from Scottish manufacturers, a handful of bagpipes continued to be made by wood-working hobbyists in the mid- to late-20th century.[110] Bagpipes made in Nova Scotia represent a functional device as well as a form of folk art. Fashioned from wood and decorated with fittings carved of horn, brass and bone, their creation was both aesthetic and utilitarian. Not only were they the product of a woodworker's craft, but in the right hands they provided hours of music for listening and dancing.

During the second half of the 19th century, piping in Nova Scotia and activities associated with piping, like impromptu dances, weddings and funerals, allowed the community piper to continue in his and her traditional role. The emergence of a small cottage industry in bagpipe manufacture indicates piping in Nova Scotia was in a healthy state. By the 1890s, the industry included several makers from various parts of the province (see Appendix C). The subsequent competition from both local makers and, later, Scottish firms curtailed the market share for bagpipes and as the need for wood turners diminished in industrial society, bagpipe-making on a semi-professional scale disappeared.

Conclusion

The rural piper continued to provide music for social dancing in the countryside in the 19th century and, in some areas of Cape Breton, for a good portion of the 20th century.[111] The increase in the number of pipers in Nova Scotia in the 19th century created a small market for locally made bagpipes, but these failed to be lasting ventures. For those pipers who had moved into Nova Scotia's towns and cities, the demand for their musical talents was substantially reduced by changes in entertainment preferences among many of the new generation of urbanites who, after being exposed to a dominant English culture and mass communication devices like the radio, came to equate Gaelic instrumental music with hick music.

The 20th century introduced to Nova Scotia's "ear-trained" community bagpiper a much different musical culture from the one which was brought with the early Highland immigrants. The problem was that during the 19th and early 20th centuries, pipers were being trained for roles in Gaelic society which were fast disappearing. The role of community piper (or blacksmith, or cooper, for that matter) was virtually eliminated during the 20th century. By mid-century there remained only a handful of these musicians who had experience in playing for social dancing. For those pipers who could not or would not change, their eventual fate was to be marginalized by modern methods of playing and their musical styles dismissed as incorrect by non-Gaels.

Chapter Four
Tradition in Transition, 1895-1930

A' Ghaidhlig agus ceòl na pìoba, 'S co-innnan leam fhin na dha dhuibh;
Chan eil sin' na aobhar ionghnaidh. O shiol nam pìobairean a tha mi.

Gaelic language and the music of the pipes, The two are the same for me;
That is no reason to wonder, Since I am descended from the seed of pipers.*

The period 1895-1930 can be described as one of profound change for most aspects of Gaelic culture in Nova Scotia. The first three decades of the 20th century witnessed a decline in the number of Gaelic speakers in the region and increased migration from rural areas to urban centres, both in Nova Scotia and other provinces of Canada and to the United States.[1] This period also heralded intense changes in Highland piping and the perceptions of Scottish culture among native Nova Scotians. In the case of Nova Scotian pipers the transition was from an ear-trained, community piper to a musically literate one, and from a bagpipe soloist to a pipe band musician. These changes were directly influenced by the increased use of Highland pipers in the military during the First World War and the arrival in Nova Scotia of several Lowland Scottish pipers following the province's industrial expansion. The growing urban centres became fertile ground for the development of civilian or citizen bands: both brass and bagpipe.

As noted, there is little evidence to indicate that the role of piper in Nova Scotian Gaelic society changed very much in the 19th century. Although very few individuals listed their occupation as piper to immigrant officials in Nova

---

*"In Praise of Gaelic" by Malcolm MacNeil, Ironville, Cape Breton County. Macleod, ed., *Bardachd a Albainn Nuaidh*, 59. English translation generously supplied by Jim Watson, Nova Scotia Highland Village.

Scotia, research shows that a number of immigrant Gaels were indeed pipers.[2] Ship passenger lists rarely mention piping as a profession and additional information must be gleaned from family lore, genealogical studies and census information compiled in Nova Scotia. Possible reasons for this would include the gradual decline of piping as a profession in Scotland and the reality that perhaps piping was not a wholly recognized profession among immigration officials. Piper, fiddler and bard were all specific functions within Gaelic society; the collapse of the old order proved trying for most people involved in these cultural pursuits. Indeed, it became apparent that they could not survive on these professional skills alone and so proceeded to adopt other occupations.

Angus Campbell of Salmon River, Cape Breton County, was one such professional who was intimately aware of the changes affecting poets and musicians after their emigration from Scotland. He left Scotland in the 1840s and took up farming in the rugged backlands between East Bay and the Mira River. Campbell was born in Benbecula, a small island separated by tidal fords from the islands of North and South Uist (now connected by a causeway). He was a piper, fiddler and bard and, although none of his fiddle or pipe music survived to the present day, several songs which he composed in Cape Breton remained in the repertoires of a handful of local Gaelic singers until the mid-20th century.[3] Described as "one of the sweetest singers that Gaelic poetry could ever claim, he was asked once if the gift of song was brought over from Scotland to America." He replied saying, "Certainly it exists here in America, but there is no one who appreciates a good poem in America. In Scotland the bard received a sovereign or even a guinea for an ordinary song, and then he could afford to forget even the ordinary cares of life while he was composing a much better one."[4] Unfortunately for Campbell there were no patrons of the Gaelic arts in Cape Breton, and this talented individual had to resort to farming and lumbering to earn a living.

The provincial census of 1838 lists several occupations and trades of many of the immigrant Highland settlers to Nova Scotia. Included in the census are the names of only three individuals who listed their occupation as piper: one in Cape Breton County and two in Pictou County.[5] This shows that piping was considered a profession by at least a few census takers and respondents. The 1838 census also paints a picture of the occupations of many more immigrant Gaels and their descendants. The information for Pictou County shows a preponderance of farmers, some miners and labourers, two turners, several blacksmiths and five fiddlers.[6] Comparison of this information with family and community history establishes that most pipers relied on other professions to provide most of their livelihood, and even well-known pipers were not recorded as such by most census takers.

Barry W. Shears

The list of pipers compiled in Appendix B shows that piping tended to be passed on within families, extended families and the community as a whole. The role of the piper in Nova Scotia Gaelic society shared many similarities with other cultural forms of expression such as Gaelic singing and storytelling. There is very little published material available on the development of repertoire and the transmission of songs and stories. There is even less on the parallel relationship between language, song and instrumental music, even though most tradition bearers claim that the Gaelic language and music were inseparable.[7]

Gaelic Song and Instrumental Music

The findings of John Shaw in two of his books on the subject of Gaelic songs and storytelling in Cape Breton, have direct relevance to various aspects of piping.[8] The conservative role of the community, the development of repertoire and the linear descent of tradition characterize not only the Gaelic song and storytelling traditions but also piping and fiddling. As English gradually replaced Gaelic, even in the rural areas, the function of instrumental music gradually changed. Shaw observed that:

> combined with other recent agents of cultural change, the language shift has effectively altered the social context for singing—interrupting the lines of transmission and changing the community's internal concepts of such fundamental aspects as function, performance, occasion and composition.[9]

Shaw's narrative describes the song tradition among the Gaels of Broad Cove, Inverness County, but it could apply equally to the piping traditions of rural Gaels—and not just in Cape Breton, but throughout the new world *Gaidhealtachd* (Gaelic-speaking area) as well. Similar descriptions of piping repertory development, retention and eventual decline within Gaelic-speaking communities have been mentioned in taped interviews with the late Alex Currie, piper, and the late Joe Neil MacNeil, storyteller.[10]

Alex Currie (1910-1997)

One of the strongest links to traditional piping in late 20th century Cape Breton was the late Alex Currie of Frenchvale, Cape Breton County. There were several families of Curries who came to Cape Breton from Scotland in the early 19th century. Alex's branch of the family was known locally as the "Bears" for an incident that happened to Alex's grand parents. Alex's grandfather, Donald Currie, was married to Elizabeth MacDonald of Cleveland, Cape Breton. One day she was washing clothes by a stream with her baby in a basket beside her when she was surprised by a bear.

Fearing for her safety and that of her infant, she raised the wooden bat which she was using to beat the clothes and struck the bear knocking it senseless. She then went and got her husband who came and shot the animal.

Alex Currie was born at Sydney Mines in 1910 and, starting at age ten, he acquired his piping knowledge almost entirely from within his own extended family. Alex's father, Peter, was a piper, as were his two grandmothers and two older brothers. From his father he learned to make homemade chanters from young maple trees and reeds from oat straw; from his mother and grandmother he learned his repertory of tunes entirely by ear. He was unacquainted with written music until he joined the army, enlisting with the Cape Breton Highlanders and later transferring to the PEI Highlanders during the Second World War. Alex learned to play the chanter sitting in a chair while his mother sang tunes in Gaelic and her own form of *canntaireachd*. Alex's mother represented a wealth of tradition. Her mother was a MacIntyre from Boisdale, Cape Breton, and her paternal grandfather's extended family included several well-known pipers in the area. This particular family of MacIntyres emigrated from South Uist to Boisdale, Cape Breton, around 1820.

Alex Currie's early training as a piper was indicative of many such musicians and singers in the province since it was within rural, homogenous societies that the early pipers developed many of their skills. The development of repertoire, which included memorizing literally hundreds of melodies without any written guide, was a long and laborious task. Alex's repertory of tunes consisted mostly of jigs, strathspeys and especially reels. As Alex learned most of his tunes from his mother's singing, he developed a rather unique fingering technique.

The methods of learning song and instrumental music were almost universal among the Gaelic communities in the Maritimes. As Shaw points out in his study of the Gaelic-speaking community of Broad Cove, Cape Breton:

> the daily routines in Gaelic-speaking rural communities of the early 20th century provided a nearly ideal environment for a child to become exposed to and drawn into the singing tradition. Here the lifelong learning process known to ethnomusicologists as enculturation or cultural learning began as a part of a wider process of the child's socialization. Generally, those destined to be active singers began at an early age, *"cho luath 's a thuigeadh iad facial is ceol"* (as soon as they could understand words and music), and often with active support from women.[11]

Compare this observation to Alex Currie's memories of learning to play the chanter under the watchful eye and ear of his mother, a descendant of the MacIntyre pipers of Boisdale, Cape Breton. The comparisons become obvious:

> Here's the way I learned. My mother would jig [a word used in Cape Breton to indicate singing] the tune as it was written in the olden days, and she was a better jigger than my father. She jigged in words—in Gaelic. She pronounced the words in Gaelic, and the note would be the same as it would be written in the book! The old people who came over from Scotland—her father and her grandfather—they took that over here with them. She couldn't play the pipes, though. But if I didn't hit a note right, she'd say "That's not right! You gotta put a little more stir to it—a little livelier." In that way I had the tunes *more* accurate than the ones that are written in the book! But she had no books; it was all in her head! She'd jig tunes night and day; she had all kinds of them.

> But they play with a different style today; there's really no Scotch to it, you know. But when I play a tune, it's as it was played two hundred years ago! But when I was a young fellow starting, I could sit down three or four hours in the evenings with the lamplight and nothing else to do but play the chanter—and I was quick to catch on. My mother would help me every time I wanted to play. Ah! Those were the good old days! After supper she'd be jigging while she was knitting or quilting or making mats. My mother and father were proud as could be when I learned how to play.[12]

Fig. 32. Dance piper Alex Currie, 1996, Frenchvale, Cape Breton.

For Alex Currie, the learning of a particular tune usually included Gaelic words and sometimes background information on the melodies. In an age of homespun entertainment, pipers learned not only tunes but also the history surrounding various melodies. Pipers such as Rory "Shim" MacIsaac of Ben Eoin, Cape Breton County, (who was reputed to have tunes "as old as Noah"), could supply approximate dates of composition for some melodies, another similarity with the retention of a song or story repertoire among Gaelic speakers. Piping, fiddling and singing remained strong in the more isolated areas of the province, but with increased outward migration and demographic changes, especially after 1920, these skills remained with only a handful of traditionally trained musicians and bards.

But just how popular were the bagpipes as a dance instrument in Cape Breton in the first three decades of the 20th century? According to several sources, violin players were a rare commodity in several areas of Cape Breton and many of the older residents preferred dancing to the bagpipes. In a reference to dance piping by William Gillis (quoted below) it would appear that some areas of Inverness County had only a few violin players in the 19th century. The continued popularity of the piper as a purveyor of dance music was also pointed out by Alex Currie during an interview with Ron Caplan of *Cape Breton's Magazine* and substantiated by other sources. As Alex Currie pointed out:

> Pipes were more common than the violin. You go to a party and the old people wanted the old music, you know. It was dancing, and step-dancing. My sister and my brothers, my mother and my father, were good dancers, too.[13]

In Inverness County, one of the strongholds of modern Cape Breton fiddling, a similar observation at Glencoe Mills concerning the entertainment preferences of the older Gaels in the community and the new generation, was made in 1929 by George Pearson, a reporter with the *Toronto Star*:

> Early though it was in the afternoon the big barn already shook with the ardor of the main body of the dancers. The harrows and rakes and other implements piled upstairs out of the way for this occasion, shook and rattled noisily. Sleighs jingled merrily in fitful starts at each "thump" of the dancing feet below.

> The big room down there was dark and the floor was jammed with young dancers. Two fiddlers sawed valiantly away in lively tunes as the dancers circled and swung with Scotch determination to lusty shouts of "Swing 'er round," "All the Way," "Grand right and left." Four sets were going at a time with moving figures barely discernible through clouds of rising dust which no one heeded.

> Scorning such fancy new-fangled things as these square dances and the effeminate Sassenach music of the fiddles, in a smaller building, the older people danced with great vigor and more joy than the younger ones. Scotch fours, reels and solo dances to the tune of the pipes;

and at times the smaller children joined them. One of the Campbell girls, Dolena [?], a dainty little ten-year old girl, danced with precision, grace and dignity an old Scotch solo which brought from her elders Wild highland cries of proud acclaim.

Amid these older people each dance was a ceremony unto itself, and one set only occupied the floor while all others watched with faces only less grave than those of the dancers. They stepped the intricate measures of dances as old as their race, and no shouts of direction marred the beat of their feet no[r] the poetry of their movement.[14]

A strong affection for pipe music could be found in other areas of the Island. For some dances held at the parish hall in Grand Mira, dance music was supplied for the older residents of the community by local pipers Joe Hughie MacIntyre and Dan MacIsaac. While they played on the main floor a fiddler in the basement provided the music for the younger generation.[15] The sentiments expressed by one local piper that "when he was a boy almost every second house in Grand Mira had a set of bagpipes" was probably no exaggeration.[16] By the end of the 1930s, the development of a parallel piping culture was well on its way in Cape Breton, although the competitive musically literate piper was still largely confined to the urban centres of both mainland Nova Scotia and Cape Breton Island.

Another question that arose during the course of this research was how pipers in Nova Scotia compared with their Scottish counterparts. Perceptions differ from person to person depending on their musical and cultural background and there is no consensus. No doubt during the immigration period pipers in Nova Scotia played the same way as pipers in Scotland, since they had merely changed their location. Some native Nova Scotia pipers left the province looking for work, and during their travels influenced music in the areas in which they settled. Others were influenced by current trends in bagpipe playing and musical literacy by interaction with later Scottish immigrant pipers to North America.

One such individual who carried the music with him from Nova Scotia was "Red" Dougald MacIsaac, a fiddler, piper and step dancer from Antigonish County. MacIsaac immigrated to Bay St. George, on the west coast of Newfoundland, in the latter part of the 19th century, and he taught these Gaelic musical disciplines to several local musicians and step dancers.[17] The case of Dougald Gillis of Pleasant Valley, Antigonish County, was just the opposite. Gillis had left Nova Scotia for Montana in the early part of the 20th century. While in Montana he was a member of local pipe band which included several immigrant Scottish pipers. One Scottish piper who lived in that area at the time was D. C. Mather, a former gold medal winner and composer.[18] Upon his return to Nova Scotia, Gillis passed on some of what he had learned in Butte, Montana, to two of his relatives, Hugh and Allan Cameron of Springfield, Antigonish County. This interaction introduced modern concepts of pipe music and Highland dance to one area of mainland Nova Scotia in the early 20th century.[19]

The Beatons of Pleasant Valley, Pictou County

One of many outstanding pipers from Pictou County was David Walter Beaton (1855-1922), or, as he was known after his father's death, Walter Beaton. Beaton was somewhat of a child bagpiping prodigy born at Pleasant Valley, Pictou County. His older brother, Norman, also played the bagpipes and violin, which suggests a family tradition of musical training. David's first foray into playing the bagpipes in public was at the age of five during Pictou's "Scottish Gathering" held around 1861. He was a mere boy at the time and so small his father had to assist in holding the pipes for him while he played.[20] In 1866, at the ripe old age of nine, he placed third in the local competition against a field of fourteen competitors.[21] No list of competitors survives, but it appears the competition was open to pipers of all ages and that first and second prizes were won by adult competitors John MacKenzie and Hugh Fraser respectively, who were much older than Beaton. In 1866, the *Eastern Chronicle* included a special mention of "the exceedingly good pipe music played by several little boys under twelve years of age,"[22] which indicates that he was possibly not the only juvenile competitor. In keeping with family tradition David Walter also played the violin, although by all accounts he concentrated on piping.

During the 1880s David Walter Beaton left Nova Scotia and joined his brother Norman in San Francisco, California. Norman had emigrated from Nova Scotia in the mid-1880s and secured a job as manager of the Scottish Hall in San Francisco.[23] He was a dance teacher and well-known competitor in the San Francisco area and according to the history of the club he enlivened many a gathering with his piping. Norman died in 1891 and for the first time in the organization's history the Scottish Hall was used for a funeral. It also hosted a grand concert to provide financial aid for his widow.[24] The following is an excerpt of his funeral announcement:

> Norman Beaton died on July 13, 1891, and on July 15 his funeral took place at the Hall, with the Club and other organizations to which he belonged being represented. Orthodox Presbyterian and Oddfellows funeral services were said, and the procession, led by pipers, to the graveside was impressive. Beaton was a magnificent piper in life and his piping associates, who had competed with him at the Games piped him away on this occasion. The description of the funeral ceremony is quite touching.[25]

David Walter eventually returned to Nova Scotia after his brother's death and, according to local tradition, competed at a major piping competition at the Columbia World's Fair held at Chicago in 1893. The World's Fair set aside a week for a major North American Highland gathering and representatives were sent from the various Highland and Caledonian societies across North America to compete in a variety of events. David Walter Beaton is reputed to have won the piping competition, an event which was billed as a world championship and one which included representatives from most of the Caledonia societies across North America.[26]

The Beatons of Mabou, Inverness County

Another home-grown "champion piper" was Archie A. Beaton (ca.1840-ca.1923). Beaton was born at the Mabou Coal Mines area of Cape Breton. The source of his piping knowledge is unknown, but one incident concerning his playing abilities has been retained in local folklore.

In August 1895, a piping competition was held in Prince Edward Island under the auspices of the Charlottetown Caledonia Club. Pipers came from Scotland to attend the function and to observe the state of piping in this part of North America.[27] Among the pipe music adjudicators was David Manson, a recent immigrant from Scotland. He had moved to Nova Scotia shortly before the competition and had become official piper to the North British Society in Halifax. David Manson was former Pipe Major of the 72nd Highlanders, as well as a champion Highland dancer. He was reputed to have been one of the top five pipers in Scotland in his day.[28]

Several pipers from Nova Scotia, Prince Edward Island and New Brunswick were in attendance, and after all had played Archie Beaton approached the judges to see if he too might compete. With their approval, he played a selection of tunes and when finished he was pronounced the winner. The pipers from Scotland are reported to have stood and up and told him, "You are not only a piper, you are a professor of pipe music. To our knowledge we have heard no one in Scotland who would dare compete with you."[29] From that time on he was referred to as "Professor" Archie Beaton. A tune composed by Archie A. Beaton entitled "The Charlottetown Caledonian Club" was originally published in David Glen's *Edinburgh Collection*, appearing later in *The Gathering of the Clans Collection, Volume One*. Beaton's competitive success at the discretion of at least one Scottish adjudicator on the judge's panel raises several questions. The results of the competition may indicate that perhaps there was very little difference between the styles of music played in Nova Scotia and in Scotland in the last few decades of the 19th century especially for those pipers born in the 1850s. There is also a distinct possibility that Beaton's interpretation of pipe music might have represented a style of performance which had all but disappeared in Scotland. Unfortunately, no other evidence exists to explain why he was given the title "professor." As far as is known, only one other piper was conferred with this title. John MacArthur, a member of the Skye piping family who for years ran a piping college, was often referred to as "Professor" John MacArthur.

During the early 20th century Nova Scotia boasted several top-drawer pipers scattered in various communities around the Province. In Inverness County dance music was provided by several leading pipers and piping families.

The MacKinnons of Deepdale, Inverness County

John MacKinnon (1869-1936) was known as Am Piobaire Loisge or "the Burnt Piper" owing to an injury to his hands in an industrial accident. He started off as an "ear- player," but while he lived in Pictou in 1897 he learned to read music from David Walter Beaton, who had recently returned from California and was then living at Westville, Pictou County.

The "Burnt Piper" had the tips of his fingers blown off and his hands burned in a coal mining accident and it looked like his piping days were over. Some of the older residents, well versed in homemade remedies and cures, suggested he use eel oil as a natural rehabilitative substance. Taking their advice he chopped up a freshly killed eel into small sections and placed the pieces in a Mason jar filled with water. The directions required that the jar be sealed and left on a sunlit windowsill for a few weeks. The resulting secretions of oil were then collected and rubbed into his hands and knuckles. After several months the desired effects were realized and the Burnt Piper was again able to play.[30] He eventually regained his prowess with the instrument and was considered a superb player. John had a younger brother, Joe MacKinnon (1878-1963), who was a very musical player. Joe was an "ear-player," having learned to play on a homemade chanter with a piece of oat straw for a reed. Piping continued in the family for another generation and two of Joe MacKinnon's sons, John Paul and Alex Dan, also played the bagpipe.

A brief sketch entitled "Pipers 1790-1890," written by Willie Gillis, one-time Pipe Major of the Cape Breton Highlanders and grandson of the Burnt Piper, alludes to pipers in Inverness in general and Joe MacKinnon in particular. It illustrates just how commonplace piping was in Inverness County at one time. It also explains why some pipers played in a seated position, a style of playing which has recently been copied by pipers imitating the older step dance rhythms of piping. It should be noted that not all dance pipers played sitting down and there were just as many who played for step dancers in a standing position:

It will be remembered that from 1790 to 1890 there was but a few violin players in this area, while on the other hand there was [sic] many, many pipers. We could name most of them but for this note in history we will name but a few: Jim MacDonnell, Neil

MacDonnell, Alex MacMaster, Sandy MacDonnell, and of course the 28 pipers on Gorry's Mountain.[31] Of course the best of these, and in demand, was Joe MacKinnon....

Now the question comes up, why did these pipers play sitting on [a] chair? As we have already said violin players were not too plenty. So pipers were in demand to play for step-dances and the five figure square set. So it was much easier to sit on a chair [to play].[32]

The 20th century would introduce major changes to playing styles in Scotland, changes which had no effect on the way Nova Scotia pipers played dance music. The evolving differences in the performance of dance music such as phrasing, tempo and rhythm between Scottish and Cape Breton pipers is alluded to in a story which dates to about the end of the First World War, a generation after Archie Beaton's victory in Charlottetown. The tale, recounted by Hector MacMaster, a step dancer and piper originally from Judique, Inverness County, to Archie MacDonald, Grand River, compares the playing ability of two very famous pipers, John MacColl of Scotland and John MacKinnon, Am Piobaire Loisg (the Burnt Piper), of Inverness, Cape Breton.

Many Nova Scotian musicians are aware of the fame and reputation of John MacColl through one of his students, the itinerant 20th-century Scottish piper Sandy Boyd. John MacColl (1860-1943) was a successful athlete, competitive piper and talented composer.[33] Several of his compositions such as "Miss Jeannie Caruthers," "Mrs. J. MacColl" and "Arthur Bignold," are still played today by pipers, fiddlers and accordion players.

The late Hector MacMaster of Judique, later of Boston, was scouting various bagpipe manufacturing firms in Glasgow in order to purchase a new set of bagpipes to bring home after the First World War. MacMaster entered the shop of R. G. Lawrie while then manager John MacColl was making some final adjustments to a set of bagpipes. When MacColl discovered that MacMaster was interested in purchasing a new set, he kindly offered to play a few tunes so the perspective customer could hear the quality of the instrument. According to local tradition, MacColl blew up the bagpipe and proceeded to play a selection of marches, strathspeys and reels. When he was finished, Hector MacMaster remarked on the quality of the bagpipe sound and complimented MacColl on his march playing, but rated his performance of Strathspeys and Reels well below those played in Cape Breton by the Burnt Piper, John MacKinnon.[34]

Fig. 33. John MacKinnon,
Am Piobaire Loisg (the
Burnt Piper). Courtesy
Roddy MacLennan.

Some people will contend that this story, which so obviously places a Cape Bretoner's interpretation of dance music above that performed by one of Scotland's most successful pipers, is based on regional bias. One must remember, however, that MacColl was a frequent competitive piper and Highland dancer who won fame performing for a panel of judges while the Burnt Piper could play step dance music all day and all night for the eight-hand reel, Scotch fours and quadrilles to crowds of enthusiastic dancers.[35] From this anecdote one can conclude that Scottish piping was well on its way to becoming "Art Music," while functional dance music performed on the bagpipes continued to have a strong following in Cape Breton and parts of mainland Nova Scotia.[36]

Not all accounts of the quality of piping in Nova Scotia are as complimentary as MacMaster's assessment. Other interpretations of piping in Cape Breton come from two Scottish pipers who had an opportunity to listen first-hand to local pipers in the 1920s.

Pipe Major John Carson

John "Jock" Carson was originally from Greenock, Scotland,[37] and he immigrated to New York at the turn of the last century. He later lived in Boston and when the First World War broke out he came to Nova Scotia to enlist in the army. He joined the 25th Battalion, Canadian Expeditionary Force (CEF), and was appointed Pipe Major of the Battalion pipe band. After the war, Carson married a girl from West Bay, Richmond County, and for a short period of time he lived at West Bay.[38] During a gathering of pipers one evening a local piper approached Carson to ask his opinion of a particular tune setting and related technical difficulty. Carson shrugged his shoulders and replied rather contemptuously, "I learned that tune in the Boys' Brigade when I was a young lad!"[39] It was obvious from this comment that Carson thought little of the playing of at least one local piper. Unfortunately, no other references survive of Carson's overall assessment of Cape Breton piping or how it compared to his own style of playing. He did serve in the 25th Battalion pipe band with two other Cape Breton pipers, Mike MacDougall, Lewis Bay West, and Dan Morrison, Blues Mills; Morrison served as pipe sergeant. Jock Carson didn't stay in Cape Breton long and a few months later he was back in Boston leading another pipe band and playing at numerous engagements throughout the city.

Fig. 34. Pipe Major Jock Carson, ca. 1930, Boston. NSARM.

Pipe Major David Ferrier

The second assessment of pipers in the Maritimes comes from Pipe Major David Ferrier.

David Ferrier was a Scottish piper who immigrated to Boston in the early 1900s. In Scotland he was a pupil of "Old" John Cameron and had been in the Cameron Highlanders.

Fig. 35. Pipe Major David Ferrier, ca. 1930, Boston.

He was a successful competitor in the Boston area winning top prizes against other Scottish immigrant pipers such as Bob Ireland.[40] He judged at least one piping competition in Sydney in the 1920s. Ferrier's opinion of step dance piping comes from the recollections of his pupil Archie MacDonald.

Archie was born at West Bay, Richmond County and moved to Boston in the 1920s, where he was employed with the police department. He returned to Cape Breton in the 1960s, retiring to Grand River, Richmond County, and was a wealth of information on the piping traditions of both Cape Breton and the Boston area.

During the early decades of the 20th century it was not uncommon for pipers from Cape Breton to visit and perform at outdoor events in the Boston area. During a Highland gathering in Boston in the 1920s, a Cape Breton piper was playing a few tunes for step-dancers by a tent on the field. Ferrier, who was standing close by, remarked to Archie MacDonald that the player lacked the proper finger technique. Ferrier did confess to Archie, however, that he thought there was something in the step dance piper's playing that he [Ferrier] could not reproduce.[41] Unfortunately, the name of the piper in question has not been recorded. During an interview in 1989, Archie reflected on the event some sixty years earlier. Archie felt it was the "Gaelic" in the piper's music which separated him from the modern Scottish style. Archie also believed that the turn of the century was the heyday for dance pipers in Cape Breton. The relationship between musical performance and language can still be found today; in Cape Breton, musicians are often said to "have the Gaelic" in their music which, among both pipers and fiddlers, is considered very high praise. This Gaelic "flavour" or *blas* is not an intangible quality but usually means a lift or lilt in the performance of instrumental music.

The same factors which contributed to the decline of Gaelic language in Nova Scotia also contributed to the decline of piping. These factors included a gradual move by the rural population to urban centres, increased outward migration, a changing cultural and social milieu, and the after-effects of the First and Second World Wars.

Representatives of several piping families, such as the Jamiesons, MacInnises, MacPhees, MacNeils and MacIntyres, relocated to the mining areas in and around Glace Bay, with several members eventually continuing on to the United States. Regardless of the location, once the move was made from rural to urban dweller the result was always the same: the Gaelic language and other cultural art forms levelled off, declined and eventually disappeared. For example, despite the significant numbers of pipers who moved to Glace Bay in the late 19th and early 20th centuries, piping eventually died out in these families. Industrial Cape Breton is peppered with the descendants of famous bards, pipers and fiddlers, but very few have any knowledge of their ancestors and fewer still appear to have much interest in researching their rich cultural past.

The coal mines and steelworks were one of the biggest attractions for rural Nova Scotians during the latter half of the 19th century, drawing not only rural Gaels but also European immigrants. After the formation of the Dominion Coal Company in the early 20th century, professional miners were brought in from England, Lowland Scotland, Italy and several eastern European countries. This pattern of immigration gradually diluted the Gaelic majority. The introduction of radio, and later television, also helped wrest the control of culture from the Gaels. Over time, the concepts of entertainment (including music, song and dance) were influenced by forces far removed from the Gaelic cultural community.

Outward Migration

Outward migration from Nova Scotia also had a profound effect on culture. In the closing decades of the 19th century, large numbers of Nova Scotian Gaels were seeking their fortunes in the United States.[42] The drain of inhabitants from rural areas did not go unnoticed by early 20th-century social observers such as William D. Cameron and Michel D. Currie.

Cameron, who was known by the pen name Drummer on Foot, was an Antigonish school teacher who wrote a weekly article on genealogy for the local newspaper, the *Casket*. In a 1913 article, he drew attention to the after-effects of depopulation. Cameron lamented the fact that parts of rural Antigonish County, such as the community of Springfield, had lost up to 75 per cent of their population by that time, with "a large majority of them being in the United States."[43] The land was being rapidly reclaimed by the forest and many farms had been abandoned completely. Similar sentiments were expressed almost a decade later by Michael D. Currie, a schoolteacher from Cape Breton.

Michael D. Currie was also a well-known local genealogist and a few stories survive of his life in his beloved Cape Breton. One account describes a near fatal accident which happened to him during a particularly harsh winter.

Michael D. was returning home across the frozen Mira River one night after visiting a friend's house when he fell through the ice. Currie's calls for help went unnoticed and he feared the worse. Realizing he hadn't much time before hypothermia set in, Currie removed his mittens and placed them on the ice in order to retrieve his Rosary and what few coins he had in his pocket. The money was for his family and the Rosary for his funeral. It was a bitterly cold night with howling winds and as Currie struggled to get these items from his trousers he noticed something odd about his mittens. The wind had frozen both mittens to the ice and they were frozen solid enough that Currie was able to grab them with his hands and pull himself out of what would have certainly been a watery grave.

An article written in 1922 by Michael D. Currie highlighted the far-reaching effects of depopulation in one area of Cape Breton County. The article was republished in 1932-33 in *Teachdaire Nan Gaidheal*, and referred to the descendants of the three hundred South Uist immigrants who came to Cape Breton in 1832 on the *Northumberland*:

> The emigrants who came here from Scotland in 1832, as I already observed, settled in rear lots or "Back Lands", as these localities were called, at East Bay, North and South, and also at French Road and elsewhere in Mira. I know several of their descendants—MacDonalds, MacPhees, Morrisons, Fergusons, MacCormicks, Curries, Campbells, MacKinnons, MacMullins, MacLeods and Thomases. But their progeny are more numerous in the United States, Western Canada, the City of Sydney and the mines of Cape Breton, than they are in the farming districts where their grand fathers and great grand fathers settled when they came to this country, and the old farms are deserted.
>
> In the rear settlements of East Bay, North and South, the population is scarcely as large as it was in 1840. On the road from Huntington's Mountain, at Salmon River to King's Road East Bay, a distance of ten miles, there is not one inhabited house. At Gillis Lake, where there was a large population in the middle thirties of the last century, there are only three or four families.[44]

The observations of Cameron and Currie described a problem which was widespread among Gaelic communities across Nova Scotia, especially in the late 19th and early 20th centuries. Gradual movement away from a rural cultural base would manifest itself in a declining population and a language and culture in crisis.

The First World War and the Citizens Band Movement in Nova Scotia

The First World War also had a negative impact on both the Gaelic language and traditional piping. Thousands of Nova Scotians volunteered for service overseas and, as one informant put it, the Gaels who went overseas became more "worldly" and viewed their language and culture in a very different light upon their return.[45] The high casualty rates during this conflict were keenly felt and it was sometimes said that there was not one house between New Campbellton and New Harris (on Bras d'Or Lake) which did not lose a family member during the war. Several Nova Scotian pipers (Appendix B) who had enlisted to fight overseas during the First World War were added to the list of more than a thousand pipers from Great Britain and the Empire (later the British Commonwealth) who were either killed or wounded during the four-year struggle.[46]

Pipers who volunteered for service in the army received instruction in modern piping techniques from several British army pipers during their period of enlistment. Those pipers who managed to survive the First World War passed on these new skills to a new, albeit smaller, generation of pipers in Nova Scotia.[47] The efforts of these homegrown pipers to modernize piping in Nova Scotia were aided by the arrival of more than a dozen immigrants from Scotland (Appendix E).

Shortly before the First World War, industrialization in Nova Scotia began attracting a very different sort of immigrant piper from Scotland. Unlike their predecessors, these immigrant pipers were non-Gaelic-speaking Scots, most of whom were musically literate, and almost all of whom had some previous form of military or civilian pipe band experience. These Scottish musicians were scattered throughout industrial counties such as Cape Breton, Inverness, Pictou and the cities of Halifax and Dartmouth. The end product of this influx was the emergence of Nova Scotia's first civilian pipe bands.

The development of these first pipe bands paralleled the emergence of numerous citizens' brass bands in Nova Scotia. The development of these volunteer organizations, both brass and bagpipe, was influenced by the numerous regimental bands of British army. The early civilian pipe bands, like the first citizens' bands, benefited from the training of these musically literate and often professionally trained musicians. The full impact of these musicians on the civilian band movement in Nova Scotia has yet to be fully studied. Professional musicians in the British army brass bands tended to teach locally during their tour of duty in Nova Scotia, but this was not restricted to brass bands.[48] As William O'Shea points out in his book *The Louisburg Brass Bands*:

> In Nova Scotia there is a tradition, not yet fully studied, of public band entertainments provided by the various garrisons stationed here during the 18th and 19th centuries. The military bands helped to develop a local appreciation for band music and provided a source of professional instructors to the community. By the 1870s, the band master sergeants in the British army were graduates of the Royal School of Music, established in 1857, and were replacing civilian bandmasters. Still to be studied, as well, is the influence of British bandsmen who came to Nova Scotia to work in the collieries.[49]

The regiments of the British army were stationed mainly in Halifax, but some had individual companies rotated throughout various parts of the province, at various times in the province's history. [50]

The first civilian pipe band was formed in Nova Scotia in either 1896 or 1898, and it was soon followed by the organization of several other pipe bands around the province.[51] This first pipe band was known as the MacIntyre Pipe Band and it originally consisted of four MacIntyre brothers and several cousins.[52]

The MacIntyre Pipers of French Road, Cape Breton County

Members of the MacIntyre family who comprised this band were descended from South Uist immigrants who settled at French Road, Cape Breton, around 1828. This family of MacIntyres were direct descendants of Duncan MacIntyre, MacDonald of Clanranald's piper in 1759.[53] One question which arises when researching this particular family is why John MacDonald of Clanranald chose the previously mentioned, Robert MacIntyre of Rannoch as his personal piper in the late 1780s and not one from among the established MacIntyre pipers of South Uist presently being discussed? There are several possibilities. Duncan may have been dead by that time or, perhaps, with an increased interest by Clanranald and his cousin MacDonald of Boisdale in Presbyterianism in the late 1760s, a break with family tradition and hereditable positions was necessary. It is also a distinct possibility that the Rannoch and South Uist MacIntyres were more closely related than many piping historians have assumed; blood is thicker than water.[54] Regardless of the circumstances, the name MacIntyre no longer appears associated with the position of family piper for the Clanranald family after John MacDonald's death in 1794.

The first member of this South Uist piping family to come to Cape Breton was Donald MacIntyre. There is no record as to when MacIntyre died or his age at the time of his death so his relationship to Duncan, whether son or grandson, is more difficult to ascertain. Vital statistics and land grant information for much of the early 19th century in Cape Breton are meager and, in some areas, nonexistent. A good case can be made that the MacIntyres who settled at French Road, Cape Breton, were the celebrated "Pipers of Smerclate (Smearclait)," a prominent South Uist piping family who, according to Scottish folklore, immigrated to the new world in the early 19th century and whose prowess on the bagpipe was said to rival the famous MacCrimmons of Skye.[55] In Scotland, the Pipers of Smerclate were said to have been descended from the family pipers to MacDonald of Clanranald, a similar claim established for the immigrant Donald MacIntyre and his descendants in Cape Breton.[56] Successive generations of the family have continued to maintain a tradition of pipe music within their family from the mid-18th century to the present day, and the family was also well-known as performers and teachers of pipe music throughout Cape Breton.

According to local tradition, Donald MacIntyre had seven sons, most born in Cape Breton, and several of whom were pipers. A number of family members relocated to the coal mining districts of eastern Cape Breton in the latter part of the 19th century seeking steady employment and

Fig. 36. "Big" Jim MacIntyre, ca. 1880. From a water-stained charcoal etching.

opportunity. One son, James MacIntyre (Seumas Mòr mac Dhomhnuil 'ic an Tailear) was known locally as "Big" Jim MacIntyre.

"Big" Jim MacIntyre was born at French Road in 1833, a few years after Donald's arrival in Cape Breton. He was a celebrated piper and step dancer and he later relocated to an area of the town of Glace Bay known as Caledonia to work in the coal mines. Four of his eleven children, Archie, Dan, Joe and Mickey were pipers and dancers and were founding members of the MacIntyre Pipe Band.[57]

The band was subsequently augmented by two other pipers, John and Charlie Jamieson. Charlie Jamieson later married a daughter of "Big" Jim MacIntyre, which led to a local saying that in order to get into the pipe band you had to marry one of the MacIntyre women.

Fig. 37. Charlie Jamieson and Katherine MacIntyre. Courtesy Kevin Kelleher.

The Jamieson family was from Piper's Glen, Inverness County and all the children in the family, as well as the father, Neil (1838-1931), could play the bagpipe.[58] Neil's father, Lachlan had immigrated from the Isle of Canna in the early 19th century. Neil and his family joined thousands of Gaels moving from rural communities to industrial centres. Neil took some of his family to an area of the city of Sydney known as Whitney Pier where he continued to work as a shoemaker. He died there in 1931 at the age of 93. Two of Neil's sons settled at Glace Bay and several other family members settled in the United States.

Fig. 38. Neil Jamieson, Sydney, 1887. Courtesy John MacDougall.

Fig. 39. John Jamieson, 1940, son of Neil, Glace Bay.

When the family left Piper's Glen, their departure was commemorated in a Gaelic song composed by Neil's friend, neighbour and fellow piper, Angus "Ban" MacFarlane:

Dh'falbh thu bhainn a Glean a' Phiobair,
Ch'uir sin mighean air mo nadur,
S'ann ort fhein air do chuid cloinne
Chaidh a shloinneadh, the iad ag raitinn.

> You have gone away from us from Pipers Glen,
> and that sheds gloom on my spirits,
> It was after you and your children that
> the glen was named, they say.

Seinnidh Iain grinn a phiob dhuit
Seinnidh Sine agus Tearlach,
Eachann, Floiri agus Seumas
Mary Jane's May's Charlotte

> Handsome John can play the pipes for you
> Jean can play and Charlie
> Hector, Flora and James,
> Mary Jane and May and Charlotte

Ho gur misde, he gur misde
Ho gur misde learn mar than 'chuis;
'S misde learn gu'n d'rinn thu gluasad
Null gu tir a ghail a thamhachd

> Oh I'm the worse, Oh I'm the worse
> Oh I'm the worse as things have turned;
> I'm the worse since you have moved away
> to stay in the country of coal[59]

The MacIntyre pipe band was assisted in its early training by an immigrant Scot named Alexander "Sandy" Bowes. Bowes was originally from Hamilton, Scotland, but later emigrated to Cape Breton around 1898, where he was employed with the Sydney and Louisburg Railway. The band was kept busy playing for a variety of events such as picnics, parades and fairs and there is some evidence that the MacIntyre pipe band was later associated with the 94th Regiment, Victoria Battalion, a local militia unit. Several members of the MacIntyre family joined the army during the First World War and during the tumultuous miners' strike of 1925, members of the pipe band staged concerts featuring piping, fiddling and step-dancing to raise money for the striking miners.[60] The

MacIntyre band lasted until about 1940, when the band folded due to recruitment by the army during the Second World War and the loss of most of the original members due to age.

Fig. 40. The MacIntyre Band, Glace Bay, 1902. (Left to right) "One-eyed" Dan MacIntyre, Charlie Jamieson, Joe MacIntyre, Mickey MacIntyre, John Jamieson, Peter MacIntyre, "Long" Joe MacIntyre and Archie MacIntyre.

During this period of time two small pipe bands were formed in Pictou County: one under the leadership of David Walter Beaton and the other with Andrew Holmes and his son Fraser. These bands lacked any standard uniform and its members either purchased kilts in their own tartans or wore used military jackets and kilts.

Fig. 41. Pipers on parade, Pictou, NS, 1912.

Fig. 42. Pictou County Pipe Band, ca. 1906. (Left to right) Seated Clarence Sinclair, Jones, Billie Barr, Fraser Holmes. Standing: Edward MacKenzie, Murdock Macleod, ? MacLean, Andrew Holmes.

When the First World War broke out, Sandy Bowes enlisted with the army and instructed several pipers before they went overseas. After the war, Bowes moved to Louisbourg where he founded a local pipe band in the 1920s. In addition to Pipe Major Sandy Bowes, other recent Scottish immigrants were settling in Nova Scotia and soon began to teach piping. One of the most influential of these early 20th-century Scottish immigrant pipers was George Dey.

George Dey

George Dey (1878-1967) was born at Bonniebridge, Scotland, and began piping at age ten. George Dey was a piping student of former Inverness Gold Medalist John MacDougall Gillies and as a young man started off his working life in a Glasgow foundry. Dey maintained that although it was extremely hard work, his years in the foundry gave him "hard hands," something he considered essential for good piping. Prior to leaving Scotland, Dey apprenticed in Peter Henderson's shop in Glasgow and made a set of pipes for himself which he mounted in aluminum. His job at Henderson's shop consisted of assembling, repairing and tuning bagpipes before they were sold.[61] He was reputed to have a good ear for setting up a band and, according to one of his former piping students, he could set all the chanters in a pipe band in ten minutes.[62] MacDougall Gillies thought so highly of him that when Dey left for Canada he [Gillies] wrote a letter of recommendation and gave George Dey a plaid brooch he had won in a previous piping competition; the pipe band presented him with an engraved, silver-mounted practice chanter. When Dey came to Canada he brought with him several books and manuscripts of pipe music, including handwritten pieces of *ceòl mór* by Gillies and a bound collection of tunes written by various pipe majors serving in India in the 19th century. Dey served for ten years with the Volunteer Battalion of the Highland Light Infantry before coming to Halifax in 1906. He was attracted to Halifax by another Scottish immigrant piper, Robert Thomson, formerly of Galasheilds, Scotland. Thomson was a successful building contractor who, along with his three sons, had a small pipe band in Halifax. Thomson advertised in Scotland for a professional piper to come to Canada and help with the band and improve piping in the city.

Fig. 43. John MacDougall Gillies, Glasgow, Scotland. Courtesy Ian Gillies.

In 1906 George Dey came to Halifax, but did not stay. He moved on and after a brief sojourn in the United States, he moved west to Vancouver where he was pipe major of the Vancouver Pipers Society Pipe Band. He moved around to several Canadian cities before he returned to Halifax in 1912, eventually marrying one of Thomson's daughters. Dey served in the Canadian army during the First World War and was official piper for the North British Society for fifty years. Over his lifetime George Dey instructed several individuals and pipe bands in the city including a school pipe band at Queen Elizabeth High School. In the 1950s Dey appeared with the QEH pipe band on an episode of the *Jackie Gleason Show* in New York. He was an active piper until 1962 when he suffered a debilitating stroke.

Dey was a successful competitive piper both in Scotland and Canada. Before coming to Canada, he had won numerous piping prizes in Scotland, placing third in 1902, and second in 1903, for the gold medal at the Argyllshire Gathering in Oban, one of the most prestigious awards in competitive piping. In addition to being a successful solo competitor, Dey, also adjudicated competitions throughout Nova Scotia and taught numerous pipers and Highland dancers, both young and old, in the Halifax-Dartmouth area. George Dey probably had some Highland dance experience before he left Scotland and during his time in Canada and the United States he learned Highland dancing from Angus MacMillan Fraser, a Canadian-born piper and dancer who toured with Scottish entertainer Harry Lauder between 1913 and 1920.

~~

According to his obituary, Angus MacMillan Fraser was born at Lost River, Quebec, in 1873 but census records show the family had lived in Ontario for a time, possibly in Glengarry County and there is a tradition that Fraser was the inspiration for a reel composed by D. C. Mather entitled "The Man from Glengarry." The *New York Herald Tribune*, March 9, 1938, reported that New York City Scots sent Fraser off with "the biggest funeral parade ever to be seen in the city of New York and continued for six full city blocks." The parade included five pipe bands and piper John Sabiston [?] played "Lament for the Children" as Fraser's coffin was lowered into the ground. According to the newspaper Angus MacMillan Fraser was instrumental in the establishment of piping and dancing in the eastern United States, especially in the New York area.

~~

George Dey's capacity as competitor, piping judge and teacher helped to successfully transplant modern Scottish musical standards in the capitol region and raised the bar for competitive piping in Nova Scotia based on the modern Scottish model. On mainland Nova Scotia, George Dey, with his military and musical backgrounds, proved to be a major influence on piping, especially in the Halifax area.

Fig. 44. Angus MacMillan Fraser, The Man From Glengarry.

Fig. 45. George Dey with his niece, Annie Thomson (left) and daughter Margaret, ca. 1924, after they won the Senior and Junior Canadian Highland Dancing Championship. Courtesy Randy Smith.

Pipe Major Kenneth MacKenzie Baillie

During most of the 19th century, military piping had little effect on traditional piping in Nova Scotia. By the 20th century the army played a major role in the transition of traditional Gaelic-flavoured pipe music in Nova Scotia to the modern Scottish idiom.[63] A full examination of this subject would require a separate study. However, the army's influence on piping in rural Gaelic-speaking communities in Nova Scotia in the early 20th century is exemplified by native-born Nova Scotian, Kenneth MacKenzie Baillie.

Pipe Major Kenneth MacKenzie Baillie was born in Nova Scotia but learned to play the bagpipes while living in Britain. Baillie was born in 1859 at Pictou, a month after the accidental death of his father. He was raised in the Gaelic-speaking home of his uncle at Balmoral, Colchester County, where he learned to play the violin. It is unknown who taught him to play, but the area surrounding the Highland community of Earltown, Colchester County, boasted several fine fiddlers such as Robbie MacIntosh.

~~

MacIntosh was born in the Parish of Rogart, Scotland, in the early 19th century, settled with his parents at Earltown in 1822, and soon became one of the most popular entertainers in the district. He learned to play the violin from his father, and in 1860 Robbie was invited to Halifax to perform for the visiting Prince of Wales (later King Edward VII) and received a handshake from the Prince and a fancy hat from the Prince's personal wardrobe for his efforts.[64] MacIntosh was also an exceptional dancer who would often finish his performances by step-dancing and playing the fiddle at the same time,[65] a skill revived by a few fiddlers in the late 20th century.

~~

The 1870s were a period of economic decline in Nova Scotia and under these conditions Baillie and his brother went to Boston, ostensibly to work in a relative's tailoring business. He worked for a short time at the stockyards in Boston, but later he shipped aboard a cattle boat for England. In 1879, at the age of nineteen, he enlisted in the Royal Marine Artillery, a corps which "lived with the navy but fought on land."[66] This was the age of "gunboat diplomacy" and Queen Victoria's "little" wars, and Baillie served in several campaigns during his military service. Baillie had an outstanding military career which included being part of the marine complement of the HMS *Temeraire* in Egypt and the Sudan, from 1880 to 1884, and he took part in the bombardment of Alexandria and the relief of Khartoum.[67] During the expedition to the Sudan, Baillie's Royal Marine

Artillery was paired with the Black Watch and dispatched to relieve the British garrison at Sin Kat.[68] By the time Baillie and the others arrived they found nothing remained of the garrison but "a pile of their bones bleaching in the sun." On their return to Tamei, Sudan, Baillie's column was attacked by the Sudanese and in an effort to repel the enemy, the units hastily formed a British Square. On the right hand corner of the Square was the artillery, while in the centre were camels, supplies and the sick and wounded.[69] Despite the superior firepower of the British, the Sudanese, armed mostly with spears, attacked the British Square and managed to break through the area of the square manned by the Black Watch—a feat which later inspired the poem "Fuzzy Wuzzy," by Rudyard Kipling. Reduced to hand-to-hand fighting during the exchange, Baillie received a spear wound through the leg, but the Sudanese dervishes were driven back and the square reformed. This was reputedly the first time a British Square had ever been broken.[70]

Baillie also served on board HMS *Inflexible*, the first ship in the British navy outfitted with electric lights, and HMS *Eurylas* on the African west coast. During the Niger River expedition the British captured King Jaja,[71] a slave who had bought his freedom and, due to his almost monopolistic control over the lucrative palm oil trade, became one of the most powerful men in the eastern Niger Delta and a thorn in the side of mercantile interests in Britain.

During a Samoan hurricane in 1889, all ships of a Royal flotilla were lost except Baillie's HMS *Calliope*, known later as "The Hurricane Jumper." The *Calliope* was one of the last two corvettes powered by steam and sail in the British navy. In 1889 it was dispatched to Samoa as part of the Royal Navy Australian Squadron to protect British interests in the Pacific. A hurricane wrecked twelve of the thirteen ships anchored in the harbour including three warships from both Germany and the United States.[72] The storm was so intense that its aftermath and destruction was described by well-known author Robert Louis Stevenson as: [There was] "no sail afloat and the beach piled high with the wrecks of ships and the debris of mountain forests."[73] When the ship returned to port, Baillie piped Queen Victoria aboard and, according to family lore, he was immediately appointed Pipe Major by her Majesty.[74] Naval historians will dispute this story, but it should be noted that, at the time, the title of Pipe Major was an appointment, and not a specific rank, and so the story does have merit.

Baillie began to learn the bagpipes as a pastime while serving with the Royal Marine Artillery. He was later promoted and managed to be posted as a recruiting sergeant in Glasgow in the 1880s in order to perfect his piping abilities. According to family lore he competed successfully in London, England, in the 1890s against some of the top pipers then resident in the city, but this has not been substantiated. To further his study of music, especially *ceòl mór*, he transferred to Inverness where he came under the influence of a former Inverness Gold Medalist, Pipe Major Sandy MacLennan. Baillie studied piping with MacLennan for several years, and married Sandy's only daughter, Catherine.[75]

Fig. 46. MacKenzie Baillie, ca. 1900, with some of his piping medals.

The MacLennans, Town Pipers of Inverness

The MacLennan family of Inverness was renowned as pipers. Sandy was descended from the 16th-century MacLennan town pipers of Inverness. Sandy's grandfather, Duncan, had been a piper at Waterloo in 1815, and Sandy's great grandfather, Murdoch, had been a piper at Culloden in 1746. Sandy MacLennan's father, Donald "Mor" MacLennan, had received some instruction in piping from the celebrated MacKays of Gairloch, before the MacKay family emigrated to Pictou in 1805 and was highly sought after as a piping tutor. Donald Mor taught some very prominent pipers in the early 19th century, such as John "Ban" MacKenzie and Donald Cameron, in addition to his two of his sons, Sandy and John. Sandy won the prize pipe (a bagpipe awarded for the best performance in competition) at Inverness in 1857 and the gold medal in 1860.

Sandy's younger brother, John MacLennan, was piper to the Earl of Fife and was also an Inverness Gold Medalist, having won the medal in 1854 and the prize pipe in 1848. Sandy MacLennan enlisted first with the 78th Highlanders and was pipe major from 1843 to 1850, before transferring to the Inverness-shire Militia.[76] Sandy's daughter Catherine was also an accomplished musician. She could play both the bagpipe and piano and, according to one account, she was a better piper than MacKenzie Baillie,[77] who she later married. When she came to Nova Scotia she brought with her several pieces of furniture, a piano and all her late father's awards and Highland regalia. These included an English sword recovered by one of her ancestors, possibly Murdock, from Culloden's battlefield, the prize pipe and the Inverness gold medal, an award presented by the Highland Society of London[78] and still coveted by pipers today.

In 1901, the Baillie family retired to a farm at Loganville, Pictou County, and from this base, they influenced the musical development of a large section of mainland Nova Scotia. Baillie joined the 78th regiment, Pictou Highlanders,[79] and piping became his life's work. Both he and his wife Catherine taught numerous pupils in west Pictou and Colchester counties, and their fluency in Gaelic allowed them access to communities not readily accessible to other teachers. After his return to Nova Scotia, Baillie, who received a small pension from the army, toured most of the major cities in North America as a Scottish violinist. Pipe Major Baillie was also involved in recruiting in Canada and the United States during the First World War and instructed several pipers who had enlisted for service overseas.

Fig. 47. Pipe Major Kenneth MacKenzie Baillie, 1916.

Among his piping students were Fraser Holmes of New Glasgow and Rod Nicholson from Cape Breton. These men were very influential in training new pipers in both mainland Nova Scotia[80] and Cape Breton during the mid-20th century.[81]

Fig. 48. Catherine (MacLennan) Baillie, ca. 1920.

Catherine Baillie instructed several young pipers from Pictou and Colchester Counties prior to her death in 1927. Her husband was away for much of the year either training with the militia, judging piping competitions throughout the Maritimes or touring as a Scottish concert violinist.[82] To look after the many chores required on a farm, Catherine would often take in young boys from neighbouring communities willing to perform farm work in exchange for piping lessons.[83] Several of her piping students, such as the Henderson brothers of Camden and Alexander Sutherland, Earltown, learned in this fashion and in turn went on to instruct students of their own in Truro and Dartmouth.

It is difficult to gauge the influence of the Baillie family on piping in Pictou and Colchester counties. Certainly many of their piping students, including their son Sandy Baillie, went on to teach literate, army-influenced piping to a whole new generation of musicians on mainland Nova Scotia at a time when Gaelic was in full decline in most areas. What has yet to be considered is Pipe Major Baillie's influence on the fiddle traditions of Cape Breton. Baillie was a trained musician capable not only of reading written music, but also of playing the Highland bagpipes, violin and bellows-blown Irish bagpipes. The pipers who attended the two-week

Fig. 49. Alex Sutherland, ca. 1924.

summer camp with the militia each year were not only from mainland
Nova Scotia, but also from Cape Breton, and a few of these pipers were
also known as fiddlers. These included Angus "the Ridge" MacDonald of
Lower South River, Kenny Matheson, River Denys, Rory MacDougall,
Ingonish, James D. Gillis, Inverness, and several MacIntyres from Glace
Bay. Musicians have always exchanged tunes with each other, and Baillie's
influence might explain the existence of late 19th-century published
Scottish pipe tunes in the repertoires of ear-learned fiddlers in 20th-
century Cape Breton.[84]

Although both George Dey and the Baillie family heavily influenced the
promotion of turn-of-the-century Scottish piping in Nova Scotia, they
were essentially from two separate schools of thought with regard to
performance technique and style. Dey represented a style which has
been dubbed the "Cameron School" in Scotland, and heavily promoted
by John MacDougall Gillies of Glasgow. Pipe Major Baillie and his wife,
Catherine, meanwhile, reflected the "MacLennan School," which had its
origins in the north of Scotland. The performance of *ceòl mór* in Scotland
has been always been controversial and this lack of consensus on playing
styles continued among early 20th-century pipers in Nova Scotia. It would
appear that there was no organized attempt at converting or training new
pipers in a homogeneous Scottish style in Nova Scotia. Twentieth-century
immigrant Scottish pipers to Nova Scotia simply passed on methods of
reading and performing music, then current in Scotland, to their pupils.
The problem for many Nova Scotian pipers was that the method of

learning and playing the bagpipe, and its function within Scottish society, had changed substantially in Scotland since their forbears emigrated to the new world. Increasingly, the public's perception of Scottish culture in Nova Scotia was equated with such events as competitive Highland dancing and pipe bands.

Conclusion

As the realities of population shift and urbanization began to settle in, ties with traditional Gaelic culture began to weaken among the Gaels of Nova Scotia. Outward migration had thinned the ranks of many Gaelic cultural strongholds and this decline continued after the First World War. Many rural Gaels born during the early 1920s were raised bilingually, having a good command of both English and Gaelic, while their younger siblings born in the second half of the decade and in the 1930s, lacked confidence in the language and tended towards increased use of English.[85] There are several plausible reasons for this. First, the education system in Nova Scotia had failed miserably to educate Gaels in their native language.[86] A shortage of trained teachers who could converse in Gaelic and translate lessons from one language to another limited the effectiveness of the classroom, and in a few instances the education system produced some students functionally illiterate in both languages. Secondly, the early 20th century witnessed the deaths of many immigrant and first-generation Gaels and this, coupled with the advance of English, diminished the need for bilingualism. The language decline in Nova Scotia was accompanied by a corresponding decrease in all but sentimental attachment to old ways and customs.

During the 1920s there seemed to be an overwhelming interest in playing the bagpipes in the more modern Scottish style, reflecting the renaissance in Highland piping then occurring in Scotland.[87] This conscious decision was influenced by the returning pipers from the First World War and a new generation of immigrant pipers from Scotland, such as Sandy Bowes, the Baillie family and George Dey. Increasingly, newly trained pipers turned their backs on traditional piping in favour of a literate, competitive and military style of playing, a trend that continued for most of the 20th century as the need for step dance pipers declined.

In an increasingly Anglocentric society, piping, fiddling and singing, along with other aspects of Gaelic culture, such as storytelling and step-dancing, were considered backward and decidedly inferior. This trend was not without its detractors, however, and according to local folklore, several of the older MacIntyre pipers in Glace Bay were adamant that their children avoid musical literacy for fear it would change the performance style and thereby affect the role of the piper in Gaelic society. Such pleas proved in vain and, in deference to modern Scottish standards, many of the old traditions were gradually pushed aside.[88]

Chapter Five

Piping in the Army

Now we wear the feather, the Highlander's feather
We wear it with pride and joy,
Take fake advertiser, old Billy the Kaiser
Shall hear from each Bluenose boy,
When trouble is brewing our bit we'll be doing,
To hammer down Britain's foes,
With the bagpipes a-humming,
The Highlanders coming,
From the land where the maple leaf grows!*

Highland regiments were raised in Scotland as early as the 1700s, and while pipers were not recognized in an official capacity they were certainly present—sometimes hidden under the term drummer or fifer. According to some sources the government in Britain realized a need to harness the warlike nature of the Gaels, but in reality it was a way to engage a former enemy, thereby lowering the risks of another rebellion. The notions of clan loyalties and regional patriotism were resurrected and several distinctive Highland regiments were raised. During the 18th and 19th centuries many of these units were stationed in mainland Nova Scotia and Cape Breton Island.

Nova Scotia's position on the eastern seaboard of North America was of immense strategic importance for both France and England. France had built the

---

*This is the chorus from a First World War song entitled "The 85th Feather," author unknown. Each battalion of the Nova Scotia Highland Brigade wore a feather in their Balmorals—the 85th, 193rd and 219th Nova Scotia Highlanders wore blue feathers while the 185th, Cape Breton Highlanders, wore green feathers.

fortified town of Louisbourg in 1719 to protect its interest in the cod fishery. England countered by establishing fortifications at Halifax in 1749 which, due to a large ice-free harbour, eventually became the largest British naval base on the east coast of North America—the temporary home to dozens of British regiments stationed there at various times throughout its history. Several of the regiments stationed in the province were raised in Scotland and were to have a significant impact on Highland settlement in Nova Scotia.

❂

The Fraser Highlanders

Lord Lovat's son, Simon Fraser, first raised the Fraser Highlanders (the old 78th and 71st) in 1757. Although dispossessed of land because of his family's participation in the rebellion of 1745, Simon Fraser was able to raise more than eight hundred of his clansman for the regiment in only a few weeks. Among the recruits were "thirty pipers and drummers."[1] They embarked for Halifax, Nova Scotia, in 1757. The Fraser Highlanders participated in the capture of Louisbourg in 1758 and the fall of Quebec in 1759. Among the ranks of the Fraser Highlanders during these important campaigns for supremacy in North America, were several veterans who would eventually settle in Nova Scotia or at least influence future settlement.

Several of the ships carrying the 13,000 troops, including the Fraser Highlanders, sailed from Halifax to Louisbourg, but were prevented from landing and taking up position when inclement weather delayed the battle. The flotilla spent six days in rough seas at Gabarus Bay waiting for the weather to clear, and during this period many soldiers suffered from seasickness. During the eventual assault on the beach, one boat containing several members of the Fraser Highlanders was riddled by musket fire so badly that some of the Highlanders had to stuff their plaids into the holes to prevent the boat from sinking. This badly damaged landing craft was eventually recovered and sent to Britain for display, to the utter amazement of all who saw it.[2]

One soldier serving with the Fraser Highlanders during this campaign was Neil MacPhee of South Uist. He survived both the Louisbourg and Quebec offensives and, returning to Scotland, no doubt entertained many of his friends with tales of the war. Several of his descendants eventually left Scotland and settled at French Road, an area which borders on Gabarus Bay, close to Louisbourg.

Simon Fraser's original corps was augmented with an additional six hundred men from various areas and commissioned officers. Several of these were killed during the intense fighting which ensued the following year on the Plains of Abraham in 1759. At one point during the battle it appeared as if the French defenders might repulse the Highlanders. One of the commanding officers, who had ordered the pipes to be silent during the fighting, was advised of the importance of pipers to the morale of the Highlanders and was prevailed upon to rescind his order. The pipers struck up their instruments and rallied their comrades on to eventual victory. The officers who fell that day on the Plains of Abraham included Captain Simon Fraser of Inverallochy and Lieutenants Hector MacDonald of Boisdale, Alexander MacDonald of Barisdale and Roderick MacNeil of Barra.

Roderick MacNeil, a son of the laird of Barra and the fifth Roderick in succession, was also known as "Roderick the Turbulent." He was accompanied to North America by his attendant and piper, Malcolm MacNeil, known as Calum Piobaire, or Malcolm the piper. An interesting story was preserved among the descendants of Calum Piobaire MacNeil in Cape Breton concerning the unfortunate circumstances surrounding the death of Roderick on the Plains of Abraham in Quebec, and it demonstrates what a close clannish bond the two men enjoyed.

During the battle, Roderick MacNeil had his jaw broken by a French musket ball. A devoted Malcolm chewed his food for him, enabling Roderick to live for another three weeks before eventually succumbing. Lieutenant MacNeil was buried at Quebec and Calum Piobaire returned to Barra and continued to serve the old laird.

Lieutenant MacNeil's father, sometimes referred to as "Old" Roderick MacNeil, died in 1763 and was succeeded as laird by his grandson, also named Roderick (the sixth Roderick in succession). As attendant, Malcolm accompanied the young clan chief to North America to fight in the American Revolutionary War. During this time a similar tragedy was averted when the young chief received a life-threatening wound to his wrist. Fearing that another MacNeil chief would be buried in the wilds of North America Malcolm sucked the poison from his wound likely saving his life. After dressing Roderick's wound Malcolm remarked "that if he didn't have the blood of the Chiefs of Barra in him before he had plenty of it now."[3]

It is not absolutely certain if Malcolm MacNeil came to Cape Breton in 1802. Some of his children eventually settled at Piper's Cove, Cape Breton County, and it is currently unknown how many family members were pipers.

Malcolm's brother, Hector, settled at Piper's Cove and his grandson, Black Peter (Peadar Dhuibh) made bagpipes there. Black Peter's son, Tom, was also a piper and as a young man went to the coal mining village of Bridgeport, situated between the towns of Glace Bay and Dominion. When he arrived at Bridgeport he spoke only Gaelic. At the time this did not represent a significant problem since most of the residents of the coal mining towns had some knowledge of the language. According one of his sons, he continued to play the practice chanter every day until his death in the 1960s at an advanced age. Unfortunately, since no recordings were made of this tradition bearer, his tunes and style of playing were buried with him.

Calum Piobaire's younger brother Donald immigrated to Cape Breton in 1817. His petition to the governor of Cape Breton for a land grant lists his occupation as piper and his age as sixty. He had come from the Island of Barra (Barray) with several children and eventually settled at a point of land on Bras d'Or Lake known as Rudha Dileas. Donald's son, Murdock Beag (little) also settled in Cape Breton around the same time. Although many members of this particular MacNeil family were known as "The Pipers" for several generations, only a few continued the family piping tradition.

Fig. 50. Malcolm J. MacNeil, 1946, One of the last MacNeil pipers of Piper's Cove.

~~

Another Barraman involved in the capture of Louisbourg was Donald "Og" MacNeil. According to local folklore, he was on board a ship in pursuit of a French vessel which had entered the Bras d'Or Lake to escape capture after the Battle of Louisbourg. Donald Og took particular notice of the surrounding area and remarked to his comrades how much it reminded him of his native Barra. The chase for the French vessel continued across the Atlantic and ended in failure when the vessel made safe harbour in France. Since it was too late in the year to return to North America Donald's ship sailed on to Britain. Donald Og spent the winter in Barra where he regaled his friends and relations with stories of the area in and around the Bras d'Or Lake he had seen.[4] The following year, Donald returned to North America where he was killed by a French sniper while "he was hoisting a flag to the mast for Wolfe at Quebec."[5]

Within a few decades of his visit, large numbers of MacNeils, including two of Donald Og's sons, started arriving in Cape Breton from Barra and began settling on the shores of the Bras d'Or Lake at places such as Iona, Christmas Island, Piper's Cove, Castle Bay and Washabuck. The inhabitants of Barra were renowned as sailors in Scotland, and they continued their seafaring activities in Cape Breton, choosing land for settlement which was close to water. It is little wonder that the grand inland body of water in Cape Breton known today as the Bras d' Or Lake was once known as *"Loch Mór Nam Barrach"* (The Big Loch of the Barramen).

~~

Another veteran of the Fraser Highlanders, Alexander MacKay, chose not to return to Scotland after the Seven Years war had ended. Instead, MacKay accepted a grant of land at East River, Pictou County, in 1784. During the Seven Years War, Alexander MacKay received a French musket ball to his leg and carried that souvenir of the campaign with him to the end of his 97 years.[6]

84th Regiment, Royal Highland Emigrants

The 84th Regiment was raised in 1775 by Allan MacLean[7] under royal decree to counter the growing hostilities towards Great Britain in the Thirteen Colonies. The 84th regiment had the distinction of being "the first Highland regiment raised in the Americas."[8] Its recruits hailed from the numerous Highland settlements found in North America at the time. The original intent was to enlist experienced soldiers in the form of veterans of the Fraser Highlanders, Montgomery's Highlanders and the 42nd who decided to stay in North America after the peace of 1763.

The 84th consisted of two battalions of ten companies each. The First Battalion was the Royal Highland Emigrants raised by MacLean, largely from Highland settlers in Quebec, Ontario and the Mohawk Valley. The Second Battalion, raised by Major John Small, was formerly known as the Young Royal Highlanders. Its volunteers were from Nova Scotia and what are now Prince Edward Island and New Brunswick.

Only a few of the names of the battalion pipers have been recorded, but their presence has been confirmed by the recent discovery of a Grenadier Orderly book belonging to Murdock MacLaine and a piper's Banner. According to MacLaine's notes:

> Drum Major and Drummer Robert Ross of the Grenadier Company (appointed to assist him as fife major to instruct the boys intended for fifers) as well as the regimental pipers will attend practice and playing near the men employed at camp duties or fatigue. The drummers to practice at some distance during the interval the men are unemployed.

Murdock MacLaine appears to have had his own company piper, in the person of his cousin, Neil MacLaine, for on May 18, 1776, MacLaine also made a reference to "Piper Neil MacLain of the 5th Company disallowed £4.13s.4p pipe set."[9] Neil must have obtained a set of pipes for which his Captain had refused to pay. It was noted in May, 1777, however, that an additional premium of "£3 additional pay, [to] Neil Mclaine, pyper" was made to MacLain.[10] This extra pay may have been to cover the purchase or repairs to a bagpipe or an additional payment to a company piper and may allude to early government support for pipers in the British army. Neil MacLean returned to Scotland where he served as piper to Murdock MacLean.[11] Neil MacLean died in 1820, and he appears to have lived out his final years with family on MacNab's Island near the mouth of Halifax Harbour.

Pipers who served with the 84th, Royal Highland Emigrants, included Alexander MacGregor, Alexander Ferguson and Neil MacLain (McLean) and possibly Evan MacPhee. MacGregor settled at Rawdon, Nova Scotia, and MacPhee at Nine Mile River. Evan MacPhee had a son, John (1790-1870), and a grandson, Alexander (1827-1912), both of whom were pipers.

Another indication that the Royal Highland Emigrants had pipers within its ranks was the recent discovery of a pipe banner now housed at the York and Lancaster Regimental Museum, England, which predates the disbanding of the 84th in 1784, following the end of the American Revolution. It is a heavily embroidered pipe banner from the Second Battalion, 84th Regiment. The banner is quite large, measuring .6 m by 1.2 m (2 ft by 4 ft). It is faded blue in colour and lined with pink silk. On the left-hand side there is the badge and emblems of the Royal Highland Emigrants and on the right side eight lines of writing in Gaelic, translated as:

PRAYER OR WISH OF THE GAEL OVER HIS ENEMY

Decisive victory in time of battle, shoulder to shoulder, with their weapons and highland garb around them, that they keep up as was their custom, the fortitude and bearing of gentleman and retain like a precious thing, the renown their forbears had handed down to them. Let them have their sword, their shield, pistol, long gun and dirk and, instead of music of harp or fiddle, let them have the war music of the pipes to march to.

Fig. 51. Pipe banner of the 84th Royal Highland Emigrants. Courtesy of Kerry Delorey.

In 1784 the 84th was disbanded and many of its members settled on large government land grants on mainland Nova Scotia, at Rawdon and Douglas townships, with additional grants at Pictou County.

The Black Watch

At least three veteran pipers of the Black Watch and of the Napoleonic Wars settled in Nova Scotia. These included Donald MacLeod, Neil MacVicar (mentioned above) and Robert Ferguson. Also serving in the regiment at this time was a member of the famous MacCrimmon piping family in Skye who was both a veteran of the American Revolution and the Peninsular War.

Patrick, son of Iain *"Dubh"* MacCrimmon, is mentioned as "a piper at Dunvegan Castle and subsequently a piper in the 42nd Highlanders (Black Watch): served at an early age in the American War of Independence, and in the Peninsular War under Sir John Moore at the battle of Corunna."[12]

One of the most senior regiments in the British Army, the 42nd Regiment, or the Black Watch, originated with six independent companies raised in 1725 to police the Highlands of Scotland after the failed Jacobite Rebellion of 1715. It wore a dark tartan and because of this was called in Gaelic Am Freiceadan Dubh or the Black Watch. The regiment itself was stationed in Nova Scotia at several times during its long history.

In October 1783, the regiment was sent to Halifax where, on January 1, 1785, it was presented with new colours by Major General John Campbell, the commander of the forces in Nova Scotia. In 1786, six companies of the Black Watch were sent to Cape Breton Island and two companies to the island of St. John, now Prince Edward Island. After almost six years the Black Watch left Nova Scotia and returned to Britain in 1789.

The regiment was sent to Spain during the Peninsular War and was also part of the Highland Brigade at Quatre Bras and Waterloo. Many Scottish Gaels who had enlisted during the Napoleonic War ended up as cannon fodder, and for many years in Nova Scotia tales were told and retold by veterans of the horrors of that particular campaign.

One of the many immigrants to Cape Breton who had first-hand experience on the battlefield of Waterloo in 1815 was "Wild" John MacDonald. Although not a piper, his story is probably typical of many Gaels who took the "King's Shilling" and enlisted in the army during this period. John MacDonald was from North Uist, and he and his brother Allan "Ban" joined a company of the Black Watch which was recruited in North Uist around 1798-1799. He served as a front line soldier in the regiment for more than fifteen years, seeing action with Sir Ralph Abercrombie in Egypt and Sir John Moore in Spain. The day after the Battle of Waterloo he and several other Highlanders were selected to go around the field with the surgeons and gather up the wounded and bury the dead. Over the next six days those wounded individuals the surgeons could not save were put to death. "Wild" John and his brother eventually returned to North Uist and within a few years they joined many of their friends and relatives boarding immigrant ships bound for Cape Breton.

Sir John Moore

Sir John Moore, the brilliant commander of the British forces in Spain during the Peninsular War also had connections with Nova Scotia. His father's sister, Letetia Moore, married James Densmore and in 1772 they settled in Hants County, Nova Scotia, where many of their descendants still reside.[13] John Moore was stationed as a young ensign in the 51st Regiment in Nova Scotia during the American Revolution and also served in the 82nd Regiment.

John Moore, the son of a Scottish physician, was born in Glasgow, Scotland, in 1761. Moore dabbled in politics, but eventually went on to a stellar career in the army. He served as a Member of Parliament for Linlithgow in 1784 and was stationed in Corsica in 1793-1794 where he raised the ire of Horatio Nelson and others for becoming too friendly with the local population. Moore was described as "the first soldier in the army" for his efforts to modernize and remodel the British army and improve morale.[14] He became a Brigadier at age thirty-four, and a Lieutenant-General at forty-three.[15] Moore had witnessed war first-hand while serving in North America, Corsica, the West Indies, Ireland, Holland and Egypt. As a professional soldier Moore studied tactics and training methods and reintroduced discipline and pride to many of the soldiers he commanded. He personally oversaw the development of several light infantry units which were to prove so successful during the army's retreat to Corunna and later at the Battle of Waterloo.[16]

In 1808 Sir John Moore was sent to Portugal and Spain where he eventually took command of the British forces on the Iberian Peninsula. Abandoned by the Spanish allies, Moore was forced to retreat to the coast in order to save the British forces. The 400 km (250-mile) march to the port of Le Coruna (Corunna) was marred by bad weather, fatigue, low morale and mountainous terrain. Despite these obstacles the retreat was successful and most of Britain's 40,000 troops then in Spain were evacuated and safely transported back to England by ship. Moore did not get a chance to enjoy the honour bestowed on him by a grateful nation for saving almost the entire British army at the time. He was mortally wounded and buried at the citadel at Le Coruna on the night of January 16-17, 1809.[17]

During the early part of the 20th century the education system in Nova Scotia focused mainly on the triumphs and successes of the British Empire. Nova Scotia history was British history and so it was not surprising that during this period school children throughout Nova Scotia (and indeed the Empire) learned to recite the poem "The Burial of Sir John Moore," a memorial to the commander who died after saving most of the British Forces during the Peninsular Campaign; this particular strategic manoeuver helped set the stage for the final defeat of Napoleon at Waterloo, six years later.

Donald "Waterloo" MacLeod

Donald MacLeod (1791-1875) was a sixteen-year-old piper who enlisted in the Black Watch in 1807 and, being a Skyeman, he no doubt knew MacCrimmon and may even have had lessons in piping from him. He was with the regiment in Spain and participated in the harassing skirmishes developed by Moore as a means to slow down an enemy advance during the retreat to Corunna. Here, he was slightly wounded and was able to escape capture by the French. Donald was rescued by a rearguard officer, who recognized him as a piper and "realizing a piper's worth in keeping up morale, took him on his horse."[18] He was in very close proximity to Sir John Moore when a cannonball took away part of Moore's shoulder. Moore was removed from the field of battle on a blanket carried by six Highlanders and eventually died from loss of blood. MacLeod received the Waterloo Medal and the Peninsular Medal with four bars, Corunna, Bernice, Salamanca and Toulouse. A local tradition claims that the Highland soldier shown in the famous painting of the Burial of John Moore is in fact Donald MacLeod.[19] After the Napoleonic Wars, MacLeod settled at Landsdowne, Pictou County, where he was known locally as Donald "Waterloo." He cleared land later known as Battery Hill, and even as an elderly man he would walk back and forth atop the hill playing his bagpipe. A popular musician, Donald Waterloo was called upon to pipe at various functions and events. In 1867 Donald piped to welcome the first train into Pictou County and over his lifetime taught several of his descendants to play the bagpipe. The bagpipe he played at Waterloo is now in the possession of a Cameron family from Pictou County.

Robert Ferguson

Robert Ferguson of North Uist was referred to as "Master Piper of the Black Watch,"[20] but it is unknown what this term may have meant. The term Pipe Major seems to be a mid-19th century appointment in the British Army, although there is a reference to John MacKay as pipe master in the British Legion of 1779.[21] Both Robert Ferguson and Neil MacVicar settled in the Catalone area of Cape Breton in the 1820s. Robert Ferguson's grandson, "Big" John Holland, was a piper but many of the family's piping related memorabilia was destroyed in a house fire several decades ago. Another grandson of Robert Ferguson, Angus Ferguson, was Captain of the ill-fated ship *Dorcas*, which sank off Eastern Passage, outside Dartmouth, Nova Scotia, in 1893, resulting in the loss of twenty-four lives.[22] This event was commemorated in "*Cumha an Dorcas*" (Lament for the *Dorcas*), a lament composed by the late Mrs. Alex Ferguson of Broughton, a local bardess who composed several songs and hymns in Gaelic.[23] Several of her relatives perished on the ill-fated voyage.

Another veteran of the Napoleonic Wars, regiment unspecified, was John Gillis (born ca. 1781).[24] In 1816 he petitioned for land in Cape Breton and at least one of his sons, Simon, a grandson, two great-grandsons, and a great-great-grandniece became pipers.

Return to Halifax

The Black Watch was dispatched to Halifax again in 1851 with companies dispersed to Cape Breton, Prince Edward Island and Annapolis. Anxious to meet former members of the regiment, they brought Donald Waterloo MacLeod to Halifax for two weeks and feted him while he recounted some of his experiences during the Napoleonic Wars.[25] During their stay in Halifax two other members of the regiment also decided to settle in Nova Scotia. John "Jock" Patterson (1822-1892) was a veteran piper of the Crimea. He settled in Dartmouth and continued his military career as a member of the Dartmouth Scottish, later the 63rd Rifles. During the Northwest Rebellion in 1885, and at the ripe old age of sixty-three, he accompanied twenty-nine men and officers to Fort Saskatchewan and served in that conflict for three months.[26]

Fig. 52. "Jock" Patterson with family and Colonel Sinclair, ca. 1875.

Jock Patterson was eventually employed as a piper and servant to Robert Bligh Sinclair, Adjutant General of Militia for Nova Scotia. Sinclair was a Colonel in the 42nd Regiment, Black Watch, who had married a local woman while stationed in Halifax and rather than leave his wife and family behind when his regiment was ordered back to Britain, he sold his commission and moved to Dartmouth, Nova Scotia. This is quite possibly the same John Patterson who won first prize at a piping competition at Pictou in 1867 and is definitely the same man who listed his occupation as piper in the 1881 Canadian census for Nova Scotia. Jock Patterson was the official piper to the North British Society for more than fifty years; after his death the Society erected a large headstone in his memory.

78th Highlanders

The 78th Highlanders, also known as the Ross-Shire Buffs, were raised in 1793 by Francis H. MacKenzie, later Lord Seaforth. Nearly all of the men recruited for the battalion were from the MacKenzie estates in Ross-Shire and Lewis. The 78th Highlanders were stationed in Nova Scotia from 1869 to 1871. It had a complement of six pipers, including Robert Meldrum, a future gold medalist and later pipe major of the 93rd Sutherland Highlanders, and Pipe Major Ronald MacKenzie, who won the Northern Meeting gold medal when a lad of seventeen. Pipe Major Ronald MacKenzie taught at least one piper while stationed in Halifax. John MacLachlan, son of John Senior, described as a successful businessman and gentleman of some means. Alexander MacKenzie, editor of *Celtic Magazine*, also spent some time at the MacLachlan home during his tour of Canada in 1878 and made the following observations:

> Having met Ronald at the last Annual Assembly of the Gaelic Society of Inverness, I told him I was going to Halifax. "Well if you are" said he, "you must call and see my old pupil, John MacLachlan, son of MacLachlan the tobacco manufacturer there, and one of the best Highlanders I ever met from home. Before I left Halifax, the pupil could almost play as well as the master, and if he continued to practice and progress as he did when I was there, I expect he will be equal to, if not better than myself."
>
> I called as requested, and had an evening of the pipes, played in perfect style. I never heard a cleaner finger on the chanter, and for time, spirit and accurate playing, I honestly believe that the teacher's prediction has been verified, and that the pupil really is as good a player as his master. I strongly recommend him to go to Scotland and compete at the Northern Meeting, where I feel sure he would carry away some of the principal prizes and possibly the medal. He is however only a gentleman amateur, and he is loth [*sic*] to compete in public; but as he has ample means, I trust his master will ere long have the satisfaction of seeing him in the Highland capitol competing for and possibly carrying off the Gold Medal. He has no competitor within sight on the American continent, and I am satisfied that he has few, if any superiors at home.[27]

It is not known what eventually happened to MacLachlan the piper, or if he ever passed on his piping skills to any local players. He may have died young or moved away. He must have had previous instruction in playing the bagpipe before MacKenzie arrived since it would be extremely doubtful if he could have achieved such a high level of proficiency on the instrument in just a few years. As for the claim he had "no competitor on the American continent," it must be mentioned that MacKenzie had only encountered a few pipers during his trip to New York, Halifax and Pictou in 1878. There were far more pipers in Nova Scotia than those mentioned in *Celtic Magazine* as appearing at the various Highland gatherings. Many pipers simply did not compete in Nova Scotia during this period in history.

Nova Scotia Militia

Nova Scotia has had a long and honourable affiliation with the military. Beginning with the earliest accounts of regiments stationed in Sydney and Halifax, to the current existence of a Highland Militia unit, the province has maintained a unique Scottish identity. Canada was founded on July 1, 1867. The first Dominion of Canada Militia Act became law in 1868. In the absence of a regular army, many of the smaller centres and rural areas were encouraged by the government to establish one or more companies of riflemen for defence. In areas of Highland settlement, the rifle companies usually included a piper. The Antigonish Rifles marched to the music of John MacQuarrie, a recent immigrant from the Isle of Eigg. John competed successfully in Nova Scotia, winning a prize sporran at a competition held at MacNab's Island, Halifax County, in the 1860s. Other rifle companies were recruited in Cape Breton. One unit trained at an area known today as Militia Point and had as its piper a young immigrant from Scotland. Donald MacInnis was a boy of twelve when he and his family emigrated from Moidart, Scotland, to River Denys Mountain in the 1840s. He learned his piping in Cape Breton (apparently from a MacColl piper who later returned to Scotland), and in addition to supplying music for the militia he also proved to be a popular local musician. In 1875 he performed during the opening of the new church in Glendale.[28]

Further development of the fledgling militia in Nova Scotia produced among other units the 94th Victoria Battalion of Infantry (Argyll Highlanders), headquartered in the village of Baddeck, Victoria County, and the 78th Pictou Highlanders, Dartmouth Scottish and the Halifax Rifles on the Nova Scotia mainland.

~~

Charles Campbell (1819-1906), a wealthy Baddeck merchant, helped organize the 94th Battalion in Cape Breton. Campbell was born on the Isle of Skye and his father had been an officer in the Argylls. Campbell was not only a successful merchant, but he also owned coal mines and had several shipping interests. He served four terms in the provincial government as Member of the Legislative Assembly and twice represented Victoria County as a Member of Parliament in Ottawa. In the early 1870s, the 94th was referred to in militia reports as the Cape Breton Provisional Battalion. During an 1874 inspection of the 94th by the minister of Militia it was observed that the Battalion was well trained and turned out, "but as many of the men only speak Gaelic and do not understand English, it is necessary to interpret all orders and explanations to them, and the progress, therefore, is not so rapid."[29]

Fig. 53. Piper Gillis, The Victoria Provisional Battalion, "Argyll Highlanders," later the 94th Battalion, ca. 1887. Courtesy of the Gillis Family.

Fig. 54. Unnamed piper from the 94th, ca. 1912. Courtesy of John Clarke.

Barry W. Shears

The musical requirements of the 94th Battalion were supplied by various citizens' bands such as the Baddeck Brass Band, and later the Glace Bay Brass Band. The piping component of the 94th relied heavily on members of the MacIntyre Pipe Band, also of Glace Bay.

The 94th Victoria Battalion was mobilized during the First World War for home defence and was attached to the 6th Battalion Canadian Garrison Regiment. It also served as a training battalion for the Nova Scotia Highland Brigade. It had the distinction of being the only unit in the British Empire with more than 75 per cent of its officers and men being Gaelic speakers.[30] Other pipers in the ranks were brothers Dan S. and Steve MacInnis from Morley Road and two officer pipers Captain Angus J. MacNeil (1867-1917) and John MacKinnon.

Fig. 55. (L - R) John L. MacKinnon and Angus J. MacNeil, officer pipers of the 94th. Captain MacNeil is playing a set of bagpipes made in Cape Breton by Duncan Gillis.

First World War

Out of a total of 260 numbered battalions raised in Canada during the First World War the following were Highland units, meaning their numbers were made up primarily of people of Highland descent. Many of these infantry battalions were later disbanded or absorbed by other Canadian units on the Western Front:

13th Battalion, Royal Highlanders of Canada
15th Battalion, 48th Highlanders of Canada
17th Battalion, Nova Scotia or Seaforth Highlanders

42nd Battalion, Royal Highlanders of Canada
72nd Battalion, Seaforth Highlanders
73rd Battalion, Royal Highlanders of Canada
85th Battalion, Nova Scotia Highlanders
92nd Battalion, 48th Highlanders
96th Battalion, Canadian Highlanders
105th Battalion, Prince Edward Island Highlanders
113th Battalion, Lethbridge Highlanders
119th Battalion, Algoma Overseas Battalion (Highlanders)
134th Battalion, 48th Highlanders
154th Battalion, Overseas Battalion (Highlanders)
173rd Battalion, Canadian Highlanders
174th Battalion, Cameron Highlanders of Canada
179th Battalion, Cameron Highlanders of Canada
185th Battalion, Cape Breton Highlanders
193rd Battalion, Nova Scotia Highlanders
194th Battalion, Edmonton Highlanders
219th Battalion, Nova Scotia Highlanders
231st Battalion, Seaforth Highlanders of Canada
236th Battalion, MacLean Highlanders
241st Battalion, Canadian Scottish Borderers
246th Battalion, Nova Scotia Highlanders
253rd Battalion, Queens University Highland Battalion

Most of the above battalions had pipe bands. This was in addition to non-designated highland units such as the 1st and 4th Canadian Mounted Rifles, whose pipe band performed on horseback, the 107th Pioneers, 35th Forestry Battalion, Princess Patricia's Canadian Light Infantry (PPCLI) and the 25th Battalion.[31]

25th Battalion

Nova Scotia had already contributed to several Canadian units with the outbreak of the First World War. One of the first infantry units raised in Nova Scotia was the 25th Battalion CEF (Canadian Expeditionary Force). Of the 5,092 officers and men who passed through its ranks only eight were taken prisoner.[32] Organized at Halifax in 1914, it had recruiting centres at Amherst, Sydney, Truro and Yarmouth. Although not raised as a Highland battalion, because of the number of native Nova Scotians among its ranks, it held a strong attachment to the Highland tradition and this included a pipe band.[33] The 25th Battalion pipe band was comprised of several pipers from Cape Breton and a few ex-patriot Scots, some of whom had volunteered via Boston, Massachusetts.[34]

Barry W. Shears

During the First World War pipers performed a variety of tasks. They were used to march soldiers to and from the front lines and would often pipe their comrades "over the top." In some units pipers would compete for this honour, a tradition which originated among the Scottish Highland Regiments:

> The 25th marched to the pipes as they moved from Boulogne to their baptism of fire at Kemmel; on the march from their ordeal at the Somme up to the Vimy sector: at Vimy itself their pipes played them over the top in a display of valour outstanding even at that day of Glory; and in the proudest moments of all—the triumphal entry into Bonn and the victory march in London—the shrill defiance of the pipes seemed to symbolize the very soul of the Empire.[35]

Fig. 56. 25th Battalion Pipe Band.

Pipers W. Brand and Walter Telfer piped their companies into action at the battle of Vimy Ridge and both were awarded the Military Medal. Telfer was badly wounded, but continued to play until he fell. Due to the severity of his wounds, one leg was eventually amputated. Pipe Major Jock Carson of the 25th Battalion, Nova Scotia, reputedly had his bagpipe shot from his shoulder during the battle of Courcelette. In recognition of his bravery the officers and men of the battalion purchased a new set of bagpipes which was presented to Carson on their behalf by the Prince of Wales in 1917.[36]

The toll on pipers during this conflict was devastating. More than one thousand pipers from Britain and the Commonwealth countries were estimated killed in action, with many more being wounded.[37] Realizing the danger this practice placed on pipers, it was decided to transfer the musicians from combat to support roles. In addition to entertaining the troops, pipers and drummers were employed as messengers, stretcher-bearers and ammunition carriers; to relieve boredom when not performing these tasks some pipers were sent on training courses to "improve" their piping abilities.[38]

The Nova Scotia Highland Brigade

Increasing demands on men and resources precipitated the raising of the 85th Battalion, Nova Scotia Highlanders. This was followed shortly by the establishment of the Nova Scotia Highland Brigade with the addition of the 185th, 193rd, 219th Battalions and later the 246th. The uniform chosen for the Highland Brigade was the Government or Black Watch tartan, red-and-white-diced hose and a white horsehair sporran with four short black tassels arranged in a diamond pattern, one tassel representing each of the four original battalions of the Brigade. Recruitment levels were met and exceeded in a few weeks and a Gaelic regimental motto was chosen. *Siol Na Fear Fearail* (Breed of the Manly Men) was selected by then Premier George H. Murray.[39]

Fig. 57. Piper John MacKinnon, Framboise, Richmond County.

The war effort in Nova Scotia was a communal one, and several societies were organized to raise money for supplies and equipment to comfort the enlisted men during training and at the front. These included the Blue Feather Society, Green Feather Society and The Catholic Ladies Patriotic Front. These organizations supported the troops by supplying various articles of clothing and acquiring musical instruments for both the Highland Brigade's pipe and brass bands. Cape Breton was represented in the new brigade by the 185th Cape Breton Highlanders. Recruitment was swift and soon the battalion was at full strength. The 185th Battalion's Cape Breton headquarters were located at the tiny town of Broughton.

Today not much remains of the once thoroughly modern early-20th-century town of Broughton. The abandoned buildings have long since been cannibalized for their scrap lumber, windows and doors and all that remained by the end of the 20th century were a few crumbling foundations nestled among the spruce trees. The story of Broughton can be considered a minor tragedy and a major waste of time and money.[40] The town had been designed by well-known architect William Harris at the behest of British investor Colonel Horace Mayhew. The town was planned, constructed and inhabited before clear title to the surrounding property had been established or a reliable method of transporting coal to market had been secured. In its heyday Broughton boasted the first revolving door in North America and two hotels, one of which, the Broughton Arms, was considered the most modern hotel east of Montreal at the time.[41]

Its perfectly designed streets and ample accommodation after the mine closure in 1915 made it an ideal spot to billet the 185th Battalion while it waited to embark for England. It had a branch railway, power plant, water system, two hotels and forty-three cottages. This friendly "occupation" was marred when a fire started by a welder's torch destroyed the town's largest hotel, The Broughton Arms. This proved to be a setback to the battalion, but a highlight of the unit's stay in Broughton was the presentation of several musical instruments to the pipe band:

> A feature of the Battalions occupation of Broughton was the presentation of the pipes and drums to the various companies. A large representation of the citizens of Glace Bay made the first visit and in an address of thrilling interest couched in the eloquence of the Gaelic language, a representative of the party presented the valuable gift of 4 pipes and 3 drums. Next came some of the citizens of Sydney, and in the name of the Royal Yacht Club, made a similar presentation to D Company. Victoria Day a great many visitors witnessed the presentation by Col. Thomas Cantley of New Glasgow to A Company a set of pipes and drums, while Mrs. W. S. Thompson of North Sydney, on behalf of the Green Feather Societies of North Sydney and Sydney Mines,

presented C Company with a set, thus forming when massed, a pipe band of 16 pipes and 12 drums.[42]

After a brief stay in Broughton, the 185th Battalion, Cape Breton Highlanders moved on to Aldershot, Nova Scotia, and eventually England. During their stay in England the pipe band competed in the 15th Canadian Infantry Brigade regimental band contest in 1917 at Witley Park and won first prize. The piping judge for the competition was Pipe Major G. D. Taylor.

~ ~

Fig. 58. 185th Bn. Pipe Band, Cape Breton Highlanders, Winners 15th Canadian Infantry Brigade Regimental Band Contest, Whitley Park, Surrey, July 19th, 1917," photographer G. West and Son; NSARM D.M. Wiswell Collection, 1988-412

George Douglas Taylor was piper and Highland dance teacher in London. He was Pipe Major of the Royal Scots from 1902-1904, and in 1914 he was appointed pipe major of the 7th Battalion Kings Own Scottish Borderers (KOSBs).[43] He was severely wounded at the Battle of Loos and was invalided home where he managed to move around with the use of a cane.

~ ~

The only part of the Nova Scotia Highland Brigade to see action in the First World War was the 85th Battalion, Nova Scotia Highlanders; the other battalions were disbanded and its members used as reinforcements for the 85th and other Canadian units. Cape Breton pipers Steve MacGillivray and Norman Ross served with Montreal's Black Watch and Toronto's 48th Highlanders respectively. By the end of the war the pipe band of the 85th Battalion consisted of sixteen pipers. Six were native Cape Bretoners; four, including the Pipe Major, A. Dares, were from Ontario, and the rest was made up of immigrant Scots.[44]

Barry W. Shears

Fig. 59. 85th Battalion with mascot, photographer unknown, n.d.; NSARM, D.M. Wiswell Collection, 1988-412.

~~

The first casualty of the 85th Battalion was piper Alex Gillis (sometimes spelled Gillies), (1877-1921). Alex and his brother Allan, also a piper, had immigrated to Port Hood, Cape Breton, from Eilean Shona, Moidart, Scotland, in 1905. Despite being in a non-combative role, he was gassed during a German shelling at Vimy Ridge in 1915. Alex was a splendid performer on the bagpipe and was appointed Lance Corporal in the pipe band.

After the war Nova Scotia faced another economic downturn and many native sons and daughters left the region for work in other jurisdictions such the Boston States, Ontario and western Canada. Alex left Cape Breton for Vancouver, where he died in 1921 largely due to the injuries he received at Vimy Ridge. He was buried with a full military funeral at Port Hood, Inverness County. Many of his former comrades rented a train at their own expense for the thirty-mile journey from Inverness Town to Port Hood. The following description of Alex's funeral procession shows the high regard many residents of Inverness County had for Alex Gillis:

> All Port Hood was there and a large attendance from the country round besides a special train was run in from Inverness with returned soldiers and friends. When the time to march had arrived the bugle sounded and two stalwart highlanders with piobrochs sounding, started to the van, next came the returned

soldiers, a goodly number, so many that they could not be easily counted: then came the hearse bearing the coffin draped in the flag he had served so well, immediately after came Allan, and after him, the multitude.[45]

The 85th Battalion, like so many units, sustained heavy casualties at Paschendaele in 1917. One hundred and forty-two men and officers were killed; 350 were wounded, including those in the pipe band. The brass band was brought up to play them off the field. Major Ralston supervised the roll call and only 65 of 557 men of the battalion answered their names. The pipe band had gone in as stretcher-bearers and fallen to the last man. This led to the famous exchange between Colonel Borden and the Sergeant Major:

> "Where are the others?" inquired the Colonel.
>
> "Sir, there are no others!" came the reply.[46]

Misfortune followed another piper from the 85th. Archie A. MacLellan was from Margaree and learned to play the pipes from the numerous local pipers in the area. He originally enlisted with the 185th Battalion, Cape Breton Highlanders, but on their breakup he was transferred. In the last days of the war he was transferred again to the Royal Canadian Regiment and on November 11, 1918, he was shot and killed by a German sniper who was apparently unaware of the Armistice. Archie was the last piper killed serving in the First World War although he was not believed to be performing the duties of a piper at the time.[47]

Fig. 60. Archie A. MacLellan. Courtesy Janice Ferguson.

~~

Three other pipers from Cape Breton killed during the First World War included Steve MacGillivray, D. J. Nicholson and John R. MacIsaac. Steve MacGillivray was from a family of pipers. This particular branch of the family was from Glen Morrison, Cape Breton County. He was killed while serving with 13th Canadian Infantry Battalion (Quebec Regiment). Donald J. Nicholson (1894-1917) was from Gillanders Mountain, Inverness County. He was wounded while piping the troops of the 85th Battalion into action at the battle of Lens and died of wounds June 29, 1917. His brother, Roddy Nicholson, was also a piper serving in the 185th Battalion. John R. MacIsaac was the son of Rory "Shim" MacIsaac, a piper and fiddler from Ben Eoin, Cape Breton County.

Fig. 61. John R. MacIsaac.

John R. was killed while serving as a gunner in the 5th Battalion, Canadian Field Artillery, rather than as a piper. When news of John R.'s death reached East Bay, Rory was so affected by the death of his youngest son that he never played the bagpipes again.

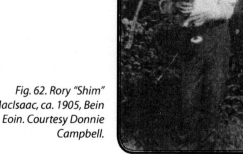

Fig. 62. Rory "Shim" MacIsaac, ca. 1905, Bein Eoin. Courtesy Donnie Campbell.

The losses to the MacIsaac family, and quite likely the Nicholson family, may have been the inspiration for the song "The Ghost of Bras d'Or," by local poet, Merriam Crewe Walsh. The song, which received a certain amount of radio play from 1958 onward, is considered a Canadian folk standard.[48] An adaptation of the poem was recorded by local singer, Charlie MacKinnon, using a variation of the third part of the bagpipe tune "Donald MacLean's Farewell to Oban" as the melody. The poem begins:

> Piper Donald John MacPherson volunteered for overseas
> With the plaid of the MacPherson gaily swinging round his knees.
> On Farewell leave from Halifax he marched along the shore;
> And his parents went to meet him by the waters of Bras d'Or.[49]

Near the end of the war the spirit and musical talent of the Highlanders were displayed at a Highland Gathering held at Tincques, near Arras on July 6, 1918. Present were representatives from all the Highland Battalions in the Canadian Corps as well as virtually all the battalions in the 15th (Scottish), 51st (Highland) and 52nd (Lowland) Divisions.[50] The events for the day included solo and band competitions, Highland dancing and various athletic events although no records of the winners appear to have survived. It was reported that the games apparently ended with a massed pipe band display of 264 pipers and 148 drummers.

Between the Wars

After the First World War most units were demobilized, others were returned to reserve status and communities were left to erect monuments to their war dead. Several war memorials across the province in communities like Judique, Inverness County, Amherst, Cumberland County and Chester, Lunenburg County, depict a kilted soldier from the Nova Scotia Highland Brigade. One of the most unique war memorials in Canada and a fitting tribute to the many pipers who served their country can be found in the Town of New Glasgow, Nova Scotia.

The monument, known as "The Piper in Bronze," was unveiled during a ceremony at Carmichael Park on September 25, 1929. Designed by Scottish sculptor Massey Rhind and cast in a Scottish foundry, the figure depicts a man in standard British Empire piper's uniform, playing an "eternal" lament on his bagpipe. The ceremony included speeches from local politicians, a kilted guard of honour from the Pictou Highlanders and performances from the local brass band. Pipe Major William "Tug" Wilson, a former Boer War veteran with the Cameronians, played the lament in remembrance of fallen comrades.

The town of New Glasgow also boasted a school pipe band which was founded in 1937. The New Glasgow High School pipe band was an army cadet unit which trained many "boy" soldiers who would later see active service during the Second World War.

Fig. 63. War Memorial, Amherst, NS.

Fig. 64. The Piper in Bronze, New Glasgow, NS.

The Second World War

When war was declared in 1939, Nova Scotians again answered the call and once again pipers were recruited to go overseas. The military need for pipers transcended standard protocol and even non-Highland regiments utilized these musicians for a variety of functions. Although not designated a Highland unit, the West Nova Scotia Regiment maintained a pipe band in the early years of the Second World War. The commanding officer, Colonel Jeffrey, had been a boy drummer during the Boer War. He realized the importance of a pipe band and saw to it the band was attached to the Battalion Headquarters at Aldershot, Nova Scotia. They were kept busy playing for route marches, church parades and public concerts for the surrounding communities.

The Pictou Highlanders and the North Nova Scotia Highlanders on mainland Nova Scotia continued the traditions of several of the early militia units such as the old 78th Pictou Regiment, the 93rd Cumberland Regiment (later the Cumberland Highlanders), and the Colchester and Hants Regiment (formerly the 76th Colchester and Hants Rifles and the 81st Hants Regiment). The Pictou Highlanders and the North Nova Scotia Highlanders both maintained pipe bands.

Fig. 65. West Nova Scotia Regiment Pipe Band, ca. 1941, Aldershot, NS.

Fig. 66. Pictou Highlanders Pipe Band, 1942, Halifax.

Barry W. Shears

One piper who served with the North Nova Scotia Highlanders was Duncan MacIntyre, a member of the French Road MacIntyre family and a direct descendant of Clanranald's piper, Duncan MacIntyre. With the outbreak of the Second World War he joined the Cape Breton Highlanders but later transferred to the North Nova Scotia Highlanders.

While overseas he attended several month long classes with Pipe Major Willie Ross at the Army School of Piping, Edinburgh Castle. In addition to being a piper Duncan MacIntyre was an excellent violinist and Pipe Major Willie Ross, chief instructor at the Army School of Piping, apparently showed some interest in Cape Breton fiddling. Duncan was asked on a few occasions to play the violin for Pipe Major Ross and during one such session he was accompanied on the piano by Willie's daughter, Cecily.[51] Duncan successfully blended both styles and could play either dance music or competitive music. He competed successfully in Scotland during his time overseas and upon his return Duncan continued to remain an active member of the North Nova Scotia Highlanders Pipe Band. He moved to Amherst, Nova Scotia, where he instructed piping to many youths in the area. Duncan's son Ben is also a piper.[52]

Fig. 67. Duncan MacIntyre, North Nova Scotia Highlanders, ca. 1943. Courtesy Hazel MacIntyre.

The Cape Breton Highlanders

The Cape Breton Highlanders perpetuate the traditions of the 185th, Cape Breton Highlanders and the 94th Regiment, Victoria Battalion. By the Second World War the unit had several Gaelic speakers within its ranks. The pipe band attracted much attention during the war especially outside Cape Breton. A Saint John, New Brunswick, newspaper article written about the Cape Breton Highlanders while they were stationed there describes the varied talents of the members of the pipe band:

> Eight Highland Pipers Can Speak Gaelic as Well as English; Two compose Marches, Strathspeys and Reels. The Pipe Major, 'Black' Jack MacDonald, has written bagpipe marches for Colonel Chisholm, Miss Elizabeth MacKinnon, and Colonel Small. Private Gordon MacQuarrie has written music for the pipes and a book on Scottish music, and Piper George Sutherland who, by employing a technique called circular breathing, is said to be able to perform the difficult feat of playing the practice chanter for a solid day without taking the instrument from his lips.[53]

~~

"Black" Jack MacDonald was from Soldiers Cove, Richmond County, a locality named for two veterans, Hugh and Ronald MacDonald, who served under Wellington during the Napoleonic Wars. Black Jack was a veteran of the First World War and, due to his age, he was subsequently sent home from England during the Second World War and replaced by William Gillis. "Red" Gordon MacQuarrie was from Dunakin, Inverness County. He was a piper and fiddler who compiled *The Cape Breton Collection of Scottish Melodies for the Violin* published in 1940. This collection highlighted the compositions of not only MacQuarrie, but several other pipers and fiddlers from Inverness County. George Sutherland was a neighbour and piping student of MacDonald.

William Gillis was quite a character and widely known and appreciated for his wit. One day he was on a training course on tactical warfare conducted by a junior officer in the Brigade. Standing in front of blackboard the officer drew a diagram depicting a small lake with an enemy machine gun nest on one side and a detachment of Highlanders on the other. The problem was obvious: How to eliminate the enemy position?

"Do you have any suggestions Pipe Major Gillis?" The officer inquired.

"Well," replied Gillis, "I'd get a small boat and row across the lake under the cover of darkness. Once on the other side and in range

I'd lob a few grenades at the enemy and finish them off with small arms fire."

"Very good!" said the officer emphatically. "But one question, Pipe Major. Where would you get the boat?"

"The same place you got the lake, Sir!" came the reply.

Two pipers from Cape Breton were killed during the Second World War. The first casualty of the Cape Breton Highlanders was piper Gordon MacDonald of New Waterford. He was killed while manning an observation post in Italy.[54]

The second was Angus Nicholson. Angus was descended from immigrants from Kilmuir on the Isle of Skye, and his extended family included several pipers and fiddlers in both Victoria and Inverness Counties. Angus Nicholson (1911-1943), a fluent Gaelic speaker, was originally taught piping by his father, a piper and fiddler, Sam Nicholson (born ca. 1864). As a young man Angus moved to Kirkland Lake, Ontario, to work. When the Second World War broke out he joined the 48th Highlanders of Canada and while on leave in Scotland he found time to visit his grand uncle, Neil Nicholson, Skye. In 1943 Angus was tragically killed in a train accident in England and is buried there. His brother Archie, who later settled in Ontario, was also a piper.[55]

Fig. 68. Cape Breton Highlanders Pipe Band. (Left to right) rear: ?, George Sutherland, ?, Gordon MacDonald. Row: "Black" Jack MacDonald, J.J. MacMillan, William Gillis, "Red" Gordon MacQuarrie, John MacMillan.

Postwar Years

After the Second World War the Canadian military was further reorganized with active regiments being disbanded, reduced to militia status or combined into new units. The Halifax Rifles (old 63rd) were reduced to reserve status and maintained a pipe band until 1968. The Pipe Major was Jim Cant, 25th Battalion veteran of the First World War. His age forced him to relinquish the appointment to his son Allan, although he continued to play in the band and teach piping in the Halifax area.

Fig. 69. The Pipe Band of the Halifax Rifles parading down Gottingen Street, Halifax, ca. 1953. Allan Cant, Pipe Major.

Fig. 70. Second Battalion, Nova Scotia Highlanders Pipe Band, 1971, Sydney. The author is seated 2nd from left.

Barry W. Shears

The Pictou Highlanders, the North Nova Scotia Highlanders and the Cape Breton Highlanders were amalgamated to form the 1st and 2nd Battalions, Nova Scotia Highlanders in 1954. They now have a combined battalion pipe band.

Conclusion

The army has been a major vehicle of change for bagpipe music both in Scotland and Canada. From the earliest days of clan pipers to the development of a full pipe and drum band, the army successfully grafted the solo piping tradition of the Highland clans to an army one, first as company pipers and later, combining pipers and drummers together to produce the first pipe bands. The result of so many local musicians serving in the armed forces during the major conflicts of the 20th century helped influence the development of a more homogeneous form of piping. These changes also fuelled the civilian pipe band movement not only in Scotland, but wherever pipe bands were formed. This homogenized style of piping included such things as standardized fingering technique and repertory and even something as rudimentary as under which arm the pipe bag was held while playing.

Alex Currie, one of the last of the "old-style" pipers in Cape Breton had learned to play the bagpipe entirely by ear and was taught to hold the bagpipe under his right shoulder with his right hand on top of the chanter. He joined the Cape Breton Highlanders during the Second World War, but later transferred to the Prince Edward Island Highlanders. During the war he was told to play with the pipes on the left shoulder because that is how everyone else played and from an aesthetic point of view, a right-shouldered piper would ruin the appearance of the band, especially during counter-marches. The other army pipers even tried to get Alex to reverse his hand position on the chanter to make things more uniform, but to no avail. After playing the chanter that way for twenty years it was too late to relearn.[56] Alex did succeed in learning to hold the pipes on his left shoulder but his unique fingering style remained virtually unchanged until his death in 1997. It is interesting to note that three of the earliest portraits of pipers, the Laird of Grant's piper, Allan MacDonald and John MacGillivray, indicate that the bag was held under the right shoulder, right hand uppermost on the chanter.

From a practical standpoint not all changes implemented by the army were bad. Pipers had time to practice and improve their playing ability, although sometimes non-military tunes were performed. In many instances the pipers who received training in the army and who made a conscious decision to adopt the modern Scottish style became, by modern standards, much better players. This is supported by the success in overseas competitions by musicians such Pipe Major Baillie and Duncan MacIntyre. These individuals, as well as numerous others in turn passed on what they learned to new generations of pipers, not only in Nova Scotia but throughout Canada. It is no coincidence that during the mid-20th century the development and expansion of civilian pipe bands in Nova Scotia relied heavily on former army pipers and drummers. Without their knowledge, experience and commitment the number of pipe bands in the province would have been much smaller.

During the past several years it has become commonplace to criticize the involvement of the army with Highland piping and in many instances such diatribes can be considered unfair. While it is true the army helped standardize the way bagpipes are played and were at the forefront of the development of the pipe band, its involvement was very much a double-edged sword. It provided employment to a host of professional pipers in Scotland and, to a much lesser extent, Canada. Many of the most influential pipers of the 20th century had some attachment to the military and many were full-time soldiers. These included John MacDougall Gillies, John MacDonald, William Lawrie, G. S. MacLennan, Willie Ross, Donald MacLeod and John MacLellan.

The army, by its very nature, requires uniformity and this extended to pipers and pipe music. This effectively suppressed individuality and ultimately eliminated regional variances in playing styles such as technique and expression. At the same time, however, if it weren't for the army and the opportunities it provided for pipers, there would a lot fewer people playing the instrument today.

One of the main attractions to piping for many people, young and old, is the kilted spectacle of the pipe band, whether playing in a street parade or on a competition field. The pipe band, which is based on the traditions of the British army, is still the single most effective means of recruiting individuals to learn to play the Highland bagpipe and discover its significant corpus of related history and folklore.

Chapter Six

1930-1997 - The End of an Era

Wi' a hundred pipers, an a', an a', Wi' a hundred pipers, an a', an a',

Well up an' gie' them a blaw, a blaw, Wi a hundred pipers, an a', and a' *

T he 20th century was pivotal in the transformation of the Nova Scotian piper from folk musician to pipe band enthusiast and tourist icon. As the need for community pipers subsided so too did significant roles for the piper in Nova Scotia society. By the 1960s, pipers were rarely called upon to play for dances, and opportunities to perform continued to decline. As outlined, many pipers were trained during a time when the Highland bagpipe served specific functions within Gaelic society in Nova Scotia and as Gaelic culture retreated on mainland Nova Scotia, traditional piping eventually died out. Traditional dances such as the Scotch fours and eight-hand reels had been displaced in the early 20th century by foreign group dances from the United States, such as the Saratoga lancers and quadrilles. These modern dances were introduced to rural Nova Scotia by returning Maritimers from the Boston States. Pipers adapted their repertoires to provide music for these dances, but with the advent of electric amplification the fiddle, with its dynamics and musical range, usurped the bagpipe as the favoured instrument for dance music among much of the Gaelic population. The sheer volume of the instrument

*Traditional Scottish songs. http://www.rampantscotland.com/songs/blsongs_100.htm. This was a Scottish song associated with Bonnie Prince Charlie and the Jacobite Rebellion of 1745.

was one reason the bagpipe had displaced the harp in Highland Gaelic society during the 17th century. Ironically, it was a stringed instrument, the violin, which pushed aside the bagpipe as a social instrument in mid-20th-century Nova Scotia.

By the 1950s there remained a few ear-trained pipers in rural areas like Grand Mira, Bay St. Lawrence, Tarbot and Mabou, but with a growing movement towards pipe band performance, and its emphasis on "correct" or 20th-century piping techniques, the older musicians were increasingly marginalized. These regional variances in fingering technique and tune repertory were viewed by some in the 20th century as a poorly developed tradition, which bordered on musical immaturity, rather than a healthy form of folk music. But those musicians represented styles of playing largely unaffected by external forces, unlike the situation in Scotland, and reflected their respective areas of Highland settlement. In essence they played a 19th-century style and were, no doubt, the last exponents of these styles left in the world. However, Gaelic and traditional piping influenced by the language did not fit into modern concepts of Scottish culture. Because there were no apparent efforts to collect information from the old pipers regarding function and linear descent of tradition, it appeared that no one was interested in preserving the old tunes and stories associated with Nova Scotia's rich piping traditions. A musical contradiction developed. The decline in traditional piping was accompanied by a marked increase in the number of students learning to play the modern Scottish style of bagpipe music in urban areas of Nova Scotia. Similarly, Gaelic language and culture declined in importance as Nova Scotia Gaels increasingly adopted modern definitions of Scottish culture. The dream of Premier Angus L. Macdonald that one hundred pipers would march across the Canso Causeway during its official opening in 1955 would be additional evidence that the "Romance of the Scottish Highlands" was alive and well in Nova Scotia.[1] This despite the fact that Gaelic was in decline in northeastern Nova Scotia and that it had already been virtually eliminated in places like Pictou and Colchester counties, and with it many features of Gaelic culture such as traditional piping.

The Establishment of the Scottish Tourist Industry in Nova Scotia

The influence of the various Highland Societies in Nova Scotia, the establishment of Highland games at various communities across the region and further contact with Scottish pipers, especially during and after the Second World War, all conspired to displace the indigenous bagpipe tradition. Highland games were initially established to help foster traditional Gaelic arts but by the mid-20th century, and with very little Gaelic content, they also became vehicles of change, promoting pipe band competitions and the various forms of Scottish "display" dances. In addition, outward migration continued unabated for much of the 20th century and this would continue to affect the overall number of pipers in the province. The further development of civilian pipe bands in urban areas increasingly alienated what little remained of the Gaelic-flavoured piping. The success of "tartanism" as a tourist strategy in

Nova Scotia during the 1940s and 50s, as described by Ian MacKay,[2] mirrored on a much smaller scale the development of the tourist trade in Scotland in the 19th century.

In Angus L. Macdonald's defence the tourist strategy pursued by the provincial government after the Second World War was an attempt to cushion the fluctuations of a resource-based economy. Macdonald's options were limited. The Dominion Atlantic Railway had already exploited the tourism potential of the Acadian Expulsion with the erection of a statue representing the Henry Wadsworth Longfellow's fictional character, Evangeline, at Grand Pré in 1920, and with the war just ended the German settlements around Lunenburg would have been a "hard sell" from a tourism perspective. Macdonald instead concentrated on the second largest ethnic group in the province and one of which he was a member—the Scottish Gael. Contrary to Ian MacKay's assessment that Scottish tradition was largely invented in the province by Macdonald and his government, it should be noted that some members of urban society from Halifax to Sydney occasionally wore tartan kilts during the 19th and 20th centuries. In addition, most Highland games in Nova Scotia offered prizes for "best Highland costume" and during the First World War the 85th Battalion, Nova Scotia Highlanders, wore kilts; public displays of tartan in some areas of the province were not an uncommon sight. Still the success of Scotland's tourist industry must have given local promoters and politicians more than a slight glimmer of hope in transforming the local Gaelic culture into a more attractive and visible tourism tool.

❦

In May, 1940, *National Geographic Magazine*[3] published an article entitled "Salty Nova Scotia," which included several photographs of kilted pipers and Highland dancers posing on wharfs and concert stages:

> In friendly New Scotland Gaelic songs still answer the skirling bagpipes. [And there] you will find kilted men in gay Glengarry bonnets proudly bearing tasseled bagpipes upon which they skirl their ancestral airs.[4]

The article, while giving the impression that both Gaelic singing and "traditional" piping were in a healthy state, presented to its readership a part of the world relatively untouched by progress. Over the next few decades Nova Scotians of Scottish Gaelic descent increasingly identified with these images.

In 1971 a group of individuals met to select committees to oversee the planning of the 1973 celebrations of the landing of the ship *Hector*. Although the actual landing of the Highland settlers at Pictou was in late September 1773, it was decided to select dates for the celebrations for either July or August "because of the better weather, and the important tourist trade, to say nothing of the vacation periods."[5] In 1973 the provincial government had delivered on a promised grant of fifty thousand dollars to assist in operating expenses,[6] a commemorative stamp had been issued by Ottawa and an invitation had been sent to Queen Elizabeth II to participate in the celebrations.[7] To increase the authenticity of these celebrations it was decided to invite several clan chiefs to attend the festival, and to achieve that end "the Hector Committee offered to assist financially with the visit."[8] The celebrations would also include a one-hundred-man guard of honour and a full pipe band supplied by the local militia regiment, dressed in period costumes. The history of Highland immigration to Nova Scotia, its causes and effects, was overlooked in order to conform to Victorian stereotypes of Scottish culture and to market Nova Scotia as a bastion of this culture in North America.[9] The presence of royalty, clan chiefs and pipe bands during the *Hector* celebrations simply reinforced these stereotypes. The language and culture of that first significant group of immigrant Gaels to Nova Scotia had been transformed into a sea of tartan and parades of pipe bands.

In 19th-century Scotland, change was inspired by the writings of Sir Walter Scott and James Logan; in Nova Scotia, it was the Highland societies, the Department of Tourism and the Gaelic College[10] that were the major factors of change. These manifestations of modern Scottish culture were particularly evident during the increase in the number of Highland games held throughout the province, the promotion of Nova Scotia's Scottish history in tourist brochures and advertisements and the increasing influence of the Gaelic College during the second half of the 20th century.

Large-scale exposure to modern piping technique and musical literacy among Nova Scotia pipers occurred during the First World War. During this conflict Nova Scotia raised several units for service overseas and a number of these battalions included pipe bands whose members received at least some training.[11] Many of the pipers who enlisted during the war benefited from instruction in piping overseas.[12] During the Second World War the Cape Breton Highlanders, North Nova Scotia Highlanders, Pictou Highlanders, and, for a short period of time, the West Nova Scotia Regiment, retained pipe bands. Several members of these bands also received instruction in Scotland at the Army School of Piping,[13] and according to local tradition, the senior piping instructor at Edinburgh Castle, remarked that the playing of the Cape Breton pipers had improved "one hundred times" since the First World War.[14] However, it was still the immigrant Scottish piper who proved to be the greatest force for change in Nova Scotia.

Sandy Boyd

One of the most influential Scottish pipers of the post-Second World War period was Sandy Boyd, a piper from Largs, Scotland[15] who was not only musically literate but could also play *ceòl mór*. Sandy came from a piping family. Two of his uncles played, as did two of his brothers. He started learning to play the bagpipes with the Boys Brigade and was an extremely talented piper in the 20th-century Scottish style. After he came to Canada in 1942, he joined the Pictou Highlanders in Halifax and was later appointed Pipe Major.[16] After the war and a failed marriage Sandy adopted the life of an itinerant musician. He moved around the countryside, staying with host families and performing in rural areas, towns and villages, not just in Nova Scotia, but in Saint John, New Brunswick, and parts of Ontario such as Huntsville and Maxville.[17] As an itinerant piper Sandy Boyd also had a major impact on Cape Breton fiddling in the postwar period. Sandy amassed a large collection of music books from Scotland and was in close contact with many pipers in the "old country." Since he played regularly in homes, concerts and Legion halls across the Province he introduced literally dozens of bagpipe tunes to fiddlers such as Angus Chisholm, Cameron Chisholm and Winston Fitzgerald. Marches by John MacColl and William Lawrie, reels by Peter MacLeod, and Donald MacLeod's "Crossing the Minch," a tune recorded and popularized by Winston Fitzgerald under the alternative title, "MacNab's Hornpipe," can all be traced to the influence of Sandy Boyd.

Sandy Boyd seldom worked at anything other than piping. He instructed individuals and pipe bands wherever he went. Sometimes he moved in for extended periods of time with host families and, in exchange for room and board, he would often instruct family members and local children in how to play the bagpipes.[18] During the 1960s and 70s, Boyd's students were well represented at the various piping competitions around Nova Scotia both as individual players, pipe band instructors and piping adjudicators.

As more and more Nova Scotians began learning to play the bagpipe, one of the first aspects of the music to suffer was the repertory of new pipers. The traditional requirements for pipers, which included those recognized community functions within Gaelic society such as playing for dances, weddings, baptisms, funerals and gatherings, was replaced by a greater reliance on pipe band performance and a uniform Scottish musical tradition. Instead of memorizing hundreds of dance tunes, as their fathers and grandfathers were required to do, the new generation of pipers were content with learning a handful of band tunes, usually marches and competition-style strathspeys and reels, types of pipe music which had limited appeal to non-pipers.[19] Pipe bands are only as

Fig. 71. Pipe Major George Dey and The Clanranald Pipe Band, ca. 1940, Halifax, NS. Courtesy Randy Smith.

good as their weakest players and so arrangements of tunes had to be adjusted to reflect the various levels of playing within a band.

During the 20th century, additional influences continued to erode traditional piping in Nova Scotia. The sporadic arrival and influence of non Gaelic-speaking, Lowland Scottish pipers (Appendix E) was reinforced with further interaction between Scottish and Canadian pipers during the Second World War. Outward migration due to poor economic conditions in the province thinned out the numbers of traditionally trained pipers and left all but the most remote areas of the Nova Scotia *Gaidhealtachd* susceptible to change.[20]

On mainland Nova Scotia the pipe band movement continued to expand. In Halifax, the Clanranald Pipe Band was organized under the directorship of Pipe Major George Dey during the tenure of Premier Angus L. Macdonald, whose Liberal government at the time helped maintain the band.[21] After a cross-Canada tour by the Canadian Women's Army Corps (CWAC) pipe band in 1944 and a tour a few years later by the Vancouver Ladies Pipe Band, several interested parents in Nova Scotia decided to form all-girl pipe bands. This resulted in the formation of four all-female pipe bands in Pictou County.[22]

Most of these organizations recruited former army musicians as their piping and drumming instructors. Mike MacDougall, a veteran piper of the First World War, was the first piping instructor of a band in Glace Bay; in his honour the band was named the MacDougall Girls Pipe Band and wore the MacDougall tartan. Sandy MacBeth and Ross Stone, former pipers with the

North Nova Scotia Highlanders during the Second World War, were chosen as the piping instructors for the Balmoral Girls Pipe Band of Stellarton and the Truro Girls Pipe Band respectively. Fraser Holmes, another First World War veteran piper, instructed the Ceilidh Girls Pipe Band of New Glasgow. The development of these all-female bands, dressed in tartan kilts and plaids (tartan sashes which drape over the shoulder, affixed by a brooch), silk jackets, blouses and lace cuffs, were the epitome of Scottish romanticism and made the promotion of Nova Scotia's Scottish heritage all the easier. The tartan-clad pipe band, although barely one hundred years old, came to represent a substantial segment of the musical culture of the Gael in Nova Scotia.[23]

The changes which resulted in this transformation among pipers, and possibly the entire concept of Gaelic culture in Nova Scotia, had their origins in the various Scottish and Highland societies which were formed in the early decades of the 19th century, the influence of the military on piping and, in the second half of the 20th century, the Gaelic College at St. Ann's, Cape Breton.[24]

Highland Societies and Highland Games

From the mid-18th century onward, several societies devoted to the traditions and culture of Scotland emerged in Nova Scotia, New Brunswick and Prince Edward Island.[25] In Nova Scotia these included the North British Society of Halifax (1768), the Highland Society of Nova Scotia (1838), the Caledonian Society of Cape Breton (1848) and, later, the Antigonish Highland Society (1861). These organizations tended to mimic the parent Highland Society of London, both in structural composition and goals and in their support for local Highland Games.

The men who filled the offices of many of these societies were drawn from the upper crust of society and included successful businessmen, government officials and local politicians. Other than supporting the occasional Highland Games, St. Andrew's banquets and, much later, Robbie Burns dinners, there appears to be very little interest among these societies in preserving anything but the outward trappings of Scottish culture in the Maritimes.[26] It is unknown how much Gaelic, if any, was included in the regular meetings of these societies. The aims of the branches of the Highland Society of London established in North America were one of Anglo-centricity, education, loyalty and an implied deference to the parent body:

> The Branches of the Highland Society of London which are established in America, have been endeavoring to promote a loyal system of education among Scotch youth. Such societies are eminently calculated to advance educational objects and to train up the tender minds of youth in feelings of veneration for the wise and time-honoured institutions of England.[27]

Venerating the "wise and time-honoured institutions of England" may seem an odd goal for a society founded to preserve the language, music and culture of the Gael, but it must be remembered that the society was based in London and its membership included members of the aristocracy and a future King. The incongruous nature of this organization in its relationship to actual Gaelic culture in Scotland did not deter the Highland societies of Nova Scotia from adopting the Highland Society of London's goals and aims.

The first traditional Highland Games in North America were reputed to have been held in Prince Edward Island in 1838, under the auspices of the Caledonian Club of Prince Edward Island. This was followed by similar gatherings sponsored by the Caledonian Society of Cape Breton at Sydney in 1848, the Highland Society of Antigonish in 1863[28] and the New Glasgow Caledonia Club in 1866.[29] Also in Cape Breton, the Glace Bay Caledonia Club held its second gathering in 1870 where members gathered to

> celebrate their anniversary and giving to Scots and others the opportunity of witnessing feats of strength as displayed in our athletic games. Sports of the day opened with an old fashioned "Scotch Reel", after which regular games for prizes were awarded.[30]

At this particular gathering John MacDonald of Big Glace Bay was chosen "Best Piper," although local newspaper coverage did not describe which types of bagpipe music were performed.

These Highland Games shared a common program of competitions in track and field, solo piping and step-dancing and, by the mid-19th century, Gaelic reading, Gaelic song and best Highland costume.[31] The number of Highland games held in Nova Scotia increased during the mid-20th century. In addition to the Antigonish Highland Games, the village of Pugwash initiated the Gathering of the Clans, held in conjunction with their Dominion Day celebrations; New Glasgow's Festival of the Tartans; and the week-long celebrations at the Gaelic Mod at St. Ann's. Several smaller, short-lived Highland games were held at Glace Bay (1967), Inverness (1972) and at various times Sydney and Halifax. These Highland gatherings emphasized competition in solo and band piping, drumming, Highland dancing and some athletic events. By the 1970s there ceased to be any Gaelic events.

The Gaelic College

Despite pockets of literate piping throughout Nova Scotia it was not until the mid-1950s that a concerted effort was made to fully develop piping in Nova Scotia, via Cape Breton, on the modern Scottish form. This would be instituted by the Gaelic College in Victoria County, one of the most Gaelicized areas in Cape Breton.

A major step to promote the Gaelic culture as a living, breathing entity was achieved in 1939 with the founding of the Gaelic College, at St. Ann's, Cape Breton. Its original plan was to develop extension courses in the Gaelic, music and poetry, but within less than two decades it was barely recognizable as a Gaelic and cultural centre and was more of a driving force for the importation of literate Scottish piping and modern "Scottish-ness" such as tartan and Highland dancing.[32] This effort was spearheaded by an immigrant Scot, Rev. A. W. R. MacKenzie (1891-1967). AWR, as he became known, was born at Portree, Isle of Skye. He immigrated first to the United States and later to Canada. After service with Canada's Black Watch during the First World War he eventually became a Presbyterian minister and in 1935 accepted a pastoral charge at Baddeck, Cape Breton.[33]

MacKenzie's dream was to rekindle a pride in the areas of Scottish heritage and transform Cape Breton into a miniature "Scotland in North America." MacKenzie was keenly aware of the precarious position of Gaelic culture in eastern Nova Scotia and was at times critical of the way the Gael of Nova Scotia was

> [a]llowing his rich heritage of Gaelic to decline: bagpipe music could be heard in a few isolated glens; Highland dancing had died completely; Clan sentiment and Clanship lore were being forgotten; the whole island could boast only a single Pipe Band outside military circles.[34]

MacKenzie was only partially correct in these assertions. Piping in rural areas was in decline and, during the years between the First and Second World Wars, fared little better in the urban districts. Scottish Highland dancing was a relatively new dance form in Nova Scotia, mostly associated with the early 20th-century immigrant Lowland Scots, such as George Dey and others, and generally confined to the larger cities and towns. It had not, however, "died completely" because the present form had never existed among the Gaelic population. Courses in indigenous Cape Breton step-dancing and fiddling would have to wait forty years after the Gaelic College's founding before they were finally (in 1979) considered to be acceptable, teachable subjects.

A. W. R. MacKenzie sought to establish a centre for promoting Gaelic language, music and dance. While the concept was accepted by many, the subsequent introduction of a modern 20th-century romantic view of Scotland eventually alienated those who were part of the indigenous Gaelic culture:

> Almost from its beginnings, the Gaelic College fully embraced the modern cultural stylings and stereotypes of Scotland. It largely ignored Nova Scotia's own native Gaelic traditions or gave them a decidedly secondary status and set about introducing one "Scottish" expert after another to help educate local people in the error of their ways.[35]

In 1949, Major Calum Iain Norman MacLeod was brought over from Scotland to teach at the Gaelic College and was subsequently appointed Gaelic advisor to the Nova Scotia Department of Education. Although a fluent Gaelic-speaker, scholar and piper, he appears to have had little interest in local Gaelic instrumental music:

In spite of his qualification as a Gaelic scholar, there is little evidence that Macleod ever realized that he was in an environment with a richer, more traditional form of instrumental music and dance than he had known in Scotland. He appears to have taken little interest in the Nova Scotian Gaelic traditions but instead threw himself into the task of introducing the modern Scottish varieties—piping in the modern style, Highland dance in the *very latest style*, and even Scottish country dance, which had no basis in Gaelic culture whatsoever.[36]

For a cultural centre such as the Gaelic College, situated as it was in a declining rural region, the cost of flying and feting overseas instructors every summer was an expense the College could ill afford.[37] A. W. R. MacKenzie set about raising money from a variety of sources from all over North America. During the 1950s he instituted a "Celtic Tour" taking kilted pipers, drummers and Highland dancers on pilgrimages to major North American cities in effort to secure future funding.[38] During one of these trips the College pipe band was invited to perform on the lawn of the White House in Washington, DC.

MacKenzie eventually alienated local members of the Gaelic community and, as the College became focused on romantic distortions of Highland culture, it was nicknamed "The Tartan Circus" by its detractors. MacKenzie defended this shift in direction for the Gaelic College by recognizing that Gaelic was actually in decline in Cape Breton and as such had to be replaced with something. He wrote in 1964:

Fig. 72. The Gaelic College Pipe Band returning from a fund raiser in Chicago, ca. 1953. On the left dressed in suits are A.W.R. MacKenzie and piping instructor Danny MacIntyre. Courtesy Hazel MacIntyre.

Barry W. Shears

Lest the reader of this article may conclude that altogether too much space has been devoted to Highland Clan Promotion at the Gaelic Mod, it may be profitable to consider again the various elements of value within the bounds of Gaelic (Highland Scottish) Culture. True it is that language is the basic ingredient in any culture as Gaelic truly is in the Celtic culture but, language may decay and die as a medium of expression among any people and may be replaced by another language as is the transition now rapidly taking place in Cape Breton as well as in Scotland. However, human individuals may outlive their native language, as a racial group, as also, clanship can outlive the language that cradled it as in Scotland today. Therefore, Gaelic Mod Directors regard Clanship equally important with the Gaelic Language as a vehicle perpetuating the true spirit of Highland Scotland to generations yet unborn.[39]

The Gaelic College had certainly been successful in raising the awareness of the island's Gaelic language and culture during the first ten years of its existence. The problem was that most Gaels living in Cape Breton had become increasingly ambivalent toward their language. Without the continued support of the local Gaelic community the Gaelic College became more of a tourist centre, relying on donations, volunteer workers and proceeds from its successful gift shop to keep the College afloat.[40] By the 1970s, the financially burdened Gaelic College became a ward of the provincial government.[41]

It is interesting to note that the Gaelic College was not taken over by the Department of Education, as one would expect for an educational institution, but instead by the government department responsible for Tourism. While government support was necessary to keep MacKenzie's dream alive, this action hastened the metamorphosis from Gaelic cultural centre to tourist attraction. Using the idea of tartans and other props, the government of the time continued to tie the provincial tourism strategy to a modified Victorian concept of Scottish culture.[42]

During its first decade and a half, local piping instructors were hired by AWR, but by the mid-1950s, professional pipers from Scotland were employed during the summer to teach the newer Scottish style at the expense of the regional forms of pipe music. Traditional dance was also affected. James L. MacKenzie, a champion Highland dancer from Scotland, was engaged to teach Highland dancing, to the detriment of Cape Breton's Highland immigrant dance styles. Writing in the *Piping Times* in January, 1995, Seumas MacNeill reminisced about his and James L. MacKenzie's early days at the Gaelic College and, in typical colonial attitude, criticized the native dances of the Scottish Gael in Nova Scotia:

> The great James L. MacKenzie spent an evening learning some of the steps, which of course he picked up very quickly. When it was

suggested to him that this was a form of dancing which had come from Scotland but had died out in the home country, he laughed at the idea. To him it was obvious that this was a form of Irish dancing but in a country where Ireland and Scotland are fused together in people's minds it was probably wishful thinking to attribute the dance to the wrong source.[43]

While such barbs against local tradition and its simplicity were not isolated occurrences it did not hinder MacNeill's acceptance as an authority on "traditional" piping by local promoters during his brief visits to Cape Breton. In retrospect, it is astounding that personalities such as C. I. N. MacLeod, Seumas MacNeill and James L. MacKenzie could influence an entire generation against the merits of their own culture. This influence highlights the precarious position of traditional piping within the context of a changing social milieu and re-evaluation of what constituted Scottish culture.

The Gaelic College did employ local pipers as instructors in the early days including J. J. MacKinnon, piper, fiddler and Gaelic playwright, of Sydney,[44] Bill Sutherland, a Presbyterian minister at Marion Bridge[45] and Roddy Nicholson,[46] a veteran piper of the First World War. MacKinnon lasted a few years and Sutherland, who was originally from Ontario, joined the army as a chaplain, went overseas during the Second World War and did not return to Cape Breton.

When the Gaelic College embarked on its series of summer school sessions in the early 1950s, Rod Nicholson became the chief instructor. Nicholson had been a piping student of Pipe Major MacKenzie Baillie and while overseas had several classes with some of the premier Scottish army pipers at the time. In 1951, the Gaelic College decided to offer a summer school at St. Ann's, the first of its kind in the world, and a winter session for pipers and drummers in Sydney. Extension courses in piping were held at the Venetian Gardens in Sydney and in preparation for the celebration surrounding the opening of the Canso Causeway in 1955, almost one hundred piping students were learning to play the bagpipe. The Gaelic College enlisted the services of Pipe Major Danny MacIntyre, and later his brother Peter, to teach the winter sessions and assist MacNeill during his summer visits. Danny MacIntyre was a devoted instructor who had learned piping first from his father, Joe Hughie MacIntyre, a traditional-style dance piper from French Road, Cape Breton County. He later embraced the modern piping traditions espoused by military-trained pipers such as Rod Nicholson of Sydney. Danny spent much of his leisure time teaching modern piping for little or no remuneration and even less recognition. He taught bagpiping at the Gaelic College for sixteen years. While Danny and, to a lesser extent, Peter MacIntyre instructed students for a good part of the calendar year during the 1950s, it was Seumas MacNeill, who after spending a few weeks each summer at St. Ann's, starting in 1954, was given most of the credit for the progress and success enjoyed by many of the pipers.

Seumas MacNeill

The Gaelic College employed the services of Seumas MacNeil, Principal of the then recently founded College of Piping in Glasgow, Scotland, in an effort to attract world recognition for the quality of its summer school staff. The plan succeeded and over the next few summers students from all over Nova Scotia and indeed North America were spending a few weeks of their summer holidays studying Scottish bagpipe music, drumming, Scottish Highland dancing and Gaelic, and the mandatory wearing of the kilt. By the mid-1960s one-third of the students attending the College summer school were from Cape Breton, one-third from the rest of Canada and one-third from the United States:

> The finest instructors in piping, dancing and Gaelic were brought over from Scotland; the standard of teaching seemed unequalled, not only in North America, but in Scotland itself. In the United States, enrolment in the summer classes conferred a social cachet upon young students, and wealthy families planned vacations to suit a Scots college in distant Nova Scotia.[47]

Unfortunately, MacNeill possessed no knowledge of Nova Scotia Gaelic musical traditions and very little understanding of Gaelic culture in his

Fig. 73. (L - R) Sandy Boyd and Seumas MacNeill, 1954, Gaelic College. Courtesy Hazel MacIntyre.

own country.[48] His job, as he perceived it, was to re-educate the local populace on the proper way to play the bagpipe and, as the co-author of "a new and improved" bagpipe tutor (which would eventually sell over three hundred and fifty thousand copies), he set about to denigrate any existing local musical traditions.[49] He dismissed local pipers as being decidedly inferior to the Scottish model and, with the help of A. W. R. MacKenzie and the local media, managed to reinforce the modern style of piping, especially in Cape Breton.[50]

MacNeill was not alone in his dismissal of local traditions; successive piping and dancing instructors at the Gaelic College from Scotland and, later, Ontario (where traditional forms of piping had been eliminated much earlier) continued to disparage local traditions by branding them as second rate. What seemed to be at stake were the promotion of "traditional" pipe music and the ownership of tradition. Scottish pipers claimed to be the true exponents of "traditional" pipe music (much of which was no older than the early 20th century) and totally dismissed the notion that there existed in Cape Breton an older, more authentic form of bagpipe playing. MacNeill came to Cape Breton, not to learn but to teach and to promote his own musical interpretations and notions of correctness. He was not interested in researching differing piping styles, tunes or piping folklore. This is unfortunate since some of the local pipers he met during his summer visits to Cape Breton were only two or three generations removed from the early-19th-century Highland piping styles of the West coast of Scotland. MacNeill dismissed the musical interpretations of Nova Scotian Gaels as practically worthless and was confident that Canadian pipers only became worth listening to after they were systematically retaught by Scottish pipers, particularly himself.[51]

In one sense, MacNeill epitomized the neglect Nova Scotians had shown toward their own musical culture. For much of the 20th century, the goal of the piping establishment in Nova Scotia was to dismiss any local tradition and "to copy, as closely as possible, the prescribed style laid out by cultural traditions in the Scottish Lowlands."[52] The Gaelic piping traditions of Nova Scotia were eventually overshadowed by the more powerful members of the piping establishment in Scotland. There was a lot at stake. Several members of the piping community in Scotland were associated with thriving businesses in bagpipe-related paraphernalia such as the production of instruments, tutor books and music collections, and the manufacture of tartan kilts, jackets and other accoutrements associated with Scottish culture. In addition, the concept of a bagpipe summer school, which had its origins at the Gaelic College, was being adopted by other areas of North America, such as the Thousand Islands School of Scottish Performing Arts in Ontario, Seumas MacNeill Summer School of Piping in California and similar summer schools in Saskatchewan and Idaho. The piping instructors at these various summer schools included Seumas MacNeill and a host of other top competitive pipers from Scotland.

What better way is there to promote the Scottish tourist trade internationally and ensure further musical standardization than with regular summer visits from some of Scotland's top and most influential performers?

> The most prominent members of the piping establishment in Scotland were not only frequently ignorant of Gaelic culture but also tended to be intolerant of the challenge its aesthetic presented to their own brand of traditionalism. Proponents of the modern style in Scotland claimed ultimate and indisputable authority over the tradition and sought to legitimize their stylistic innovations through reference to an almost apostolic line of pipers, which they claimed represented the only true link to the past. Quite simply, in that sort of intellectual environment, there was no room for such radically differing traditional styles, and the piping establishment vigorously dismissed the Gaelic style as inferior to its own, in order to establish and protect its authority. Most of what followed in Nova Scotia was purely momentum and, more often than not, well intentioned.[53]

In this environment of narrow-mindedness the Gaelic-flavoured piping traditions of Scotland had been largely eliminated by the mid-20th century. In the first few decades of the 20th century, musically literate competitive pipers were sent by the Piobaireachd Society to such piping "hotbeds" as South Uist to "improve" the playing standards of the island's inhabitants.[54] The improvements introduced by well-known pipers such as John MacDonald, Inverness, and Pipe Major Willie Ross, among others, included musical literacy and technical standardization. In South Uist these "improvements" eventually displaced the older aural form of learning.

This is not to say that the tradition of ear-learned dance piping in Nova Scotia was in a healthy state at this time—it wasn't. Piping had been in decline in most areas of the province after about 1930. In the cities fewer musicians were being trained, and changing fashions in entertainment brought on by the shift from rural to urban life, as well as improvements in communication and transportation limited the need for community pipers and severely curtailed opportunities to perform. The culture of the Gael in the new world has always had its ups and down. Early local historians mention a "Gaelic Revival" as early as 1917.[55] This unfortunately did not materialize. Perceptions among many native speakers, especially in the towns and villages, that their language and culture were inferior continued largely unabated among their descendants. Gradual erosion of Gaelic-speaking areas, and with it many of its traditional arts, has persisted despite several attempts to save it. Gaelic culture, and with it traditional-style piping, weakened first in Colchester and Pictou counties in the late 19th century. By the 1930s and 40s it was in retreat in Antigonish and Richmond counties and parts of Inverness, Victoria, and Cape Breton counties. It declined first in those regions which bordered mainly English-speaking communities and industrialized centres, but eventually affected all areas of the Nova Scotia *Gaidhealtachd*. For many Gaels in Nova

Scotia it became easier to display one's Scottish heritage by wearing a tartan tie, or wearing a kilt on special occasions, rather than maintaining a second language and its cultural adjuncts.

Conclusion

New pipers were still being trained in Nova Scotia, and in significant numbers, but their roles in society had changed. Many of these pipers were amateur players and a large percentage of them moved away or gave up piping after reaching adulthood. The growth of pipe bands, with their limited repertoire and performance requirements, severed links with the ear-trained community piper. Traditional piping was seen by young pipers as an historical anomaly, and by the 1970s and 80s there were only a handful of these ear-trained musicians left in Nova Scotia. The tradition at this time consisted of a few elderly men and women who had learned their piping skills in early 20th-century rural Nova Scotia and who had been marginalized by new attitudes towards Scottish culture and music in the province and by overall trends in leisure and recreation in a broader North American context.

By the 1970s the transformation of the bagpiper in Nova Scotia society from a Gaelic-influenced community musician to a literate competitive piper was complete. The number of active pipe bands in Nova Scotia had increased considerably from two decades earlier, and almost every weekend in the summer was taken up by Highland games and Scottish concerts. The mandatory wearing of a kilt during competitions and for presentation of awards, and the exhibition of kilted pipe bands marching in numerous parades assured at least the visual presence of Scottish culture. Instructors were still being brought over from Scotland to teach piping and drumming at the Gaelic College and pipers in Nova Scotia continued to be exposed to the very latest developments in repertoire and pipe band performance in Scotland. The links with traditional piping had finally been severed. The reality is that, while commercially successful and important to the tourist industry of the province, none of this reflects the actual traditional piping culture of Nova Scotia.

Chapter Seven
In Conclusion

The Scots carried the pipes to the new land and there have always
been those willing to retain the music and associated traditions. The
proper setting for the pipes is a band parade: there, in the expanse
of outdoors, in the required regalia and ritual, pipers produce their
greatest effect. Participation in such activities has become almost a
full-time occupation for some during the summer months in eastern
Nova Scotia. During that time thousands of "diaspora" return home to
participate in the leisure culture on an ethnic or regional basis. Though
the bands are composed largely of young girls who eventually lose interest or move away, there are always those willing to replace them
and the pipers may therefore witness the demise of the fiddlers.*

It has been a long journey for one of the most recognizable icons in Scottish
music in Nova Scotia, and the above quotation from two well-respected
historians, D. Campbell and Ray MacLean, illustrates just how complete
the transformation from community dance piper to band enthusiast has been.
The image of the kilted piper playing alone, or en masse with a pipe band, has
become synonymous with both Scotland and Nova Scotia. This colourful depiction illustrates how the great Highland bagpipe in Nova Scotia has managed
to secure a niche in present-day society. From the bagpipe's permanent arrival
in Nova Scotia around 1773 to its present use in countless tourism brochures
and advertising, street parades and Highland games, the bagpipe has managed to survive changing trends in entertainment and leisure and a collapsing
cultural base which once supported it. In order to make this transformation

---

* Campbell and MacLean, Beyond the Atlantic Roar, 190.

a success the Nova Scotia piper has had to adapt to changing times and both external and internal pressures.

The Scottish Gaels who immigrated to Nova Scotia more than two hundred years ago succeeded in buying time for a culture and language already in decline; relative isolation allowed them to continue their traditional lifestyle for much of the 19th century. The Gaelic language and the music of the pipes were intertwined for much of the bagpipe's presence in Nova Scotia and in many ways traditional piping in Nova Scotia mirrored the fate of the Gaelic language. The relative isolation of many Gaelic communities in Nova Scotia was a period of growth both in population, economic stability and the number of people who could perform and be entertained by the music of the bagpipe. Outward migration and industrialization in the province during the late 19th century destabilized many of these smaller communities and contributed to a decline in the number of Gaelic speakers and traditional musicians. During the 19th century Nova Scotia became a stepping stone for many ethnic groups, as well as those of Highland descent, to other more prosperous destinations in North America. Industrialization attracted Gaels from rural areas of the province, but also provided opportunities for a much smaller population to remain on the farm. The need for foodstuffs such as meat, fish and fresh produce and for timber for building supplies and pit-props used in the expanding coal-mining industry allowed a portion of the rural population to remain engaged in farming and lumbering. The arrival of Lowland Scottish pipers to Nova Scotia's growing industrial base (part of a much larger European workforce) throughout much of the first half of the 20th century and two world wars, afforded Nova Scotia pipers an opportunity to observe, and be influenced by, changes in Scotland in the hundred years since major immigration to Nova Scotia had ceased. Gradually the regional fingering styles, technique and tune repertoire brought to Nova Scotia with the original Highland settlers were replaced with a homogeneous form of bagpipe playing developed in Scotland in the first half of the 20th century. During the last quarter of the 20th century Nova Scotian pipers and pipe bands have successfully adopted modern playing styles, and a few have won awards in international competitions. Meanwhile, the musicians who clung to the older styles were criticized as being backward and incorrect and, as Gaelic culture eventually slipped away, many of these pipers died without passing on their knowledge to anyone. There was little interest in preserving or perpetuating this particular aspect of Gaelic culture.

This transformation has been so effective that most pipers today refuse to entertain the idea that there was any other way to play the bagpipe, let alone acknowledge that the older, and probably more authentic, style continued in some areas of Nova Scotia until well into the 20th century.

Similarly the language and culture of the Gael in Nova Scotia has been gradually replaced with the Victorian/Lowland Scottish stereotype of a kilted, Haggis-eating, Burns-quoting Scot, festooned in a costume of dubious authenticity. This "Cult of Clanship"[1] did little to preserve and promote either Gaelic or traditional piping. In the 19th century, Scottish writers such as

James MacPherson, Sir Walter Scot and James Logan succeeded in redefining the culture of Scottish Gael. In Nova Scotia a similar metamorphosis occurred during the mid-20th century, spearheaded by organizations such as the Gaelic College and supported by the media and an emerging tourist industry.[2]

As a result traditional piping withered and died in many areas of the province; the English language and customs gradually replaced Gaelic. During the 20th century the bagpipe was further displaced as a social instrument by more modern forms of entertainment and more versatile musical instruments, such as the violin. The community pipers of the 19th and early 20th century were gradually replaced with musicians who represented standards of the modern Scottish style, and who were increasingly restricted in their function. The descendants of many of the older, established piping families in Nova Scotia either abandoned traditional music or sought other means of musical expression. It is perhaps no coincidence that several of today's fiddlers have prominent pipers or piper/fiddlers in their extended family trees. During the mid-20th century there was renewed interest in bagpipe playing, but this occurred outside the Gaelic cultural community and did not reflect traditional or regional styles. Once the connection to this cultural community was severed, the role of the Highland piper in Nova Scotia society changed from one of community musician to not much more than a tourist "prop."

By the 1970s Gaelic instrumental music performed on the bagpipe and violin was at an all-time low. In 1971 a film documentary by Ron MacInnis entitled "The Vanishing Cape Breton Fiddler" appeared on television warning its viewers of an impending crisis in the Gaelic cultural community. This documentary prompted several local clergy and fiddlers to rally in support of the music and arrange concerts, fiddle classes and eventually an organization known The Cape Breton Fiddlers Association.[3] The story of the rejuvenation of the Cape Breton fiddling tradition is well-known and it need not be discussed in detail here. No such effort was made to capture what little remained of the Cape Breton piping tradition despite its precarious state.

Traditional piping in Nova Scotia had all but disappeared by the 1980s. The last few decades of the 20th century witnessed a slight interest in the older playing styles, but this interest was restricted to a few cultural anthropologists and pipers from abroad who were initially attracted by the drive and lift of the now well-known Cape Breton fiddle tradition. Unfortunately, this international interest has led to a whole new set of misconceptions arising from a lack of knowledge and understanding of the cultural history of the Gaels in Nova Scotia. Despite a certain "international" appeal in the 1990s, most pipers in Nova Scotia showed little interest in their musical heritage; at times, many viewed any attempts at saving what little remained of the tradition with suspicion.

There is some hope on the horizon—it's coming from a handful of younger Nova Scotia-born pipers who are experimenting with dance music and playing alongside other musical instruments such as the fiddle, guitar and piano.

Although they have not had the opportunity to sit down with the old-style pipers and learn directly from them, they have been attempting to imitate the rhythmic structure and tempo of a rejuvenated Cape Breton fiddle tradition on the bagpipe. These musical experiments have been met with cautious optimism from a musically astute population and time alone will tell if this proves a success or not.

Barry W. Shears

Notes to Introduction

1. Neil MacNeil, *The Highland Heart*, 155.
2. Collinson, *The Bagpipe*.
3. Cannon, *The Highland Bagpipe and its Music*.
4. Donaldson, *The Highland Bagpipe and Scottish Society*.
5. Malcolm, *The Piper in Peace and War*.
6. Orme, *The Piobaireachd of Simon Fraser*.
7. Gibson, *Traditional Gaelic Bagpiping*.
8. Gibson, *Old and New World*.
9. Donaldson, 3.
10. Originally formed in 1969 as the Nova Scotia Pipers and Pipe Band Association, the organization changed its name to reflect increased membership by bands in New Brunswick and Prince Edward Island.
11. A notable exception to this was the newspaper *Mac-Talla* which was published in Cape Breton by Jonathon G. MacKinnon between 1892 and 1904. The newspaper was published entirely in Gaelic and was the longest running publication of its type in the world.
12. Malcolm, *The Piper in Peace and War*, 225.
13. Kirincich, *A Centennial History of Stellarton*, 54.
14. Davey and MacKinnon, "Nicknaming Patterns and Traditions Among Cape Breton Coal Miners," *Acadiensis*, 71-83.
15. Campbell and MacLean, *Beyond the Atlantic Roar*, 285.
16. MacNutt, *The Atlantic Province*, 95.
17. This was particularly evident in my hometown of Glace Bay. My grandmother, Maggie (MacLean) Shears was one of many Gaelic-speakers who migrated to industrial Cape Breton and who consciously did not to teach their children Gaelic. She felt that Canada was an English country and two languages would only hinder social acceptance and advancement.
18. This sentiment was confirmed by several of the attendees at the Gaelic College in the early 1960s.
19. Over the past three decades the use of synthetic materials in bagpipe manufacture has increased substantially. Some bagpipes are now made almost entirely of plastic. The pipe bag, once made of tanned animal hide, is now being produced from synthetic materials like Gortex. The drone reeds are made from Spanish or French cane known as Arundo Donax, but these too are now being made of molded plastics and carbon fibre.
20. See Bennett, *The Last Stronghold*; Shears, *The Gathering of the Clans Collection* Vol. One and Vol. Two; and Gibson, *Old and New World*.
21. MacLean, *Highlanders*, 135.
22. Cheape, "The Piper to the Laird of Grant," *Proceedings of the Society of Antiquaries*, 4-10.
23. Ibid.
24. Donaldson, 177-78.
25. Cannon, 54.
26. Donaldson, 124.
27. Gibson, *Old and New World*, 69.
28. MacKay, *A Collection of Ancient Piobaireachd*, 7.
29. Gibson, *Traditional Gaelic Bagpiping*, 161-62.

30. Gibson, *Old and New World*, 13-14
31. Cannon, *The Highland Bagpipe*, 52-53.
32. MacKay, *Collection*, 6.
33. Ibid., 1. See also Donaldson, 401-403 for a reappraisal of the importance of this family to piping.
34. MacNeill, *Piobaireachd*, 36.
35. Gibson, *Traditional Gaelic Bagpiping*, 98.
36. Robertson, *The Kings Bounty*, 78, 168.
37. Donaldson, 64.
38. Cannon, *A Bibliography of Bagpipe Music*, 31.
39. Angus MacKay, *A Collection of Ancient Piobaireachd* and *The Piper's Assistant*; William MacKay, *The Complete Tutor*; Gunn, *The Caledonian Repository*; Ross, *Ross's Collection*; Glen, *David Glen's Collection*.
40. Cannon, *A Bibliography of Bagpipe Music*, 41.
41. MacNeill, *Piobaireachd*, 18.
42. Cannon, *The Highland Bagpipe*, 46.
43. Ibid., 81.
44. MacNeill, *Piobaireachd: Classical Music*, 17.

Notes to Chapter One

1. Necker, *Voyage to the Hebrides*, 232.
2. See Cheape, "The Piper to the Laird of Grant," 4-10, for a more detailed description of the role of piper in 18th-century Scotland.
3. There is no official date for the combination of pipers and drummers in a pipe band format.
4. These include: Manson, *The Highland Bagpipe*; Flood, *The Story of the Bagpipe*; Cannon, *The Highland Bagpipe*; Gibson, *Traditional Gaelic Bagpiping* and *Old and New World*; Donaldson, *The Highland Pipe*.
5. Cheape, *The Book of the Bagpipe*, 18.
6. Baines, *Bagpipes*, 63.
7. Cannon, *The Highland Bagpipe*, 8.
8. Ibid. "The Highlanders employed pipers at the battle of Pinkie in 1549 and in 1544, pipers accompanied Irish soldiers marching in London. ...with it they accompany their dead to the grave, making such sorrowful sounds as to invite, nay compel, the bystanders to weep."
9. Cheape, *The Book of the Bagpipe*, 35.
10. Adam, *Clans, Septs and Regiments*, 13.
11. Grant, *The Clan Donald*, 9. The Lordship of the Isles (Dominus Insularum) lasted from 1354 until 1493.
12. MacLean, *Highlanders*, 175. According to MacLean, MacDonald of Clanranald sentenced a woman, found guilty of stealing his money; to have her long hair tied to the seaweed growing on the rocks. She was to be left there for the incoming tide to drown her.
13. Adam, *Clans, Septs and Regiments*, 108.
14. Ibid.
15. The practice of a clan chief retaining a piper enjoyed a dramatic increase during the Victorian revision of popular Scottish culture in the mid-1800s.
16. Cannon, *The Highland Bagpipe*, 52.
17. Bumsted, *The People's Clearance*, 34.
18. Ibid., 36.
19. Cannon, *The Highland Bagpipe*, 54.

20. Dorian, *Language Death*, 17.
21. Cox, "Gaelic," *Nova Scotia Historical Review*, 21-22.
22. In Adam, *The Clans, Septs, and Regiments*, 440.
23. Ibid.
24. Gibson, *Old and New World*, 104-105.
25. Cannon, *The Highland Bagpipe*, 119.
26. Henderson, *Highland Soldier*, 246-47.
27. Ibid., 44.
28. Gibson, *Old and New World*. Gibson has listed numerous family pipers and their employers in the first two sections of his book.
29. Henderson, *Highland Soldier*, 33.
30. Donaldson, *The Highland Pipe*, 10.
31. Ibid., 5-19.
32. Cannon, *The Highland Bagpipe and its Music*, 81.
33. Donaldson, *The Highland Bagpipe*, 101.
34. Ibid., 150.
35. Ibid.
36. Ibid., 152.
37. It is only recently that James Logan has been verified as the author of these sections of MacKay's book. MacKay's collection was the piper's "bible" for much of the 19th century and the information supplied by Logan was used extensively by early 20th-century writers of Scottish history.
38. Donaldson, *The Highland Bagpipe*, 153-54.
39. Thomas Rawlinson, a Lancashire industrialist who founded an iron-making facility near Inverness, is credited with making the first changes to accommodate several Highlanders who were working at his plant around 1725.
40. Prebble, *The Highland Clearances*, 146.
41. Ibid.
42. Ibid.
43. Donaldson, *The Highland Pipe*, 153.
44. Prebble, *The Highland Clearances*, 139.
45. On June 29, 1821, the *Inverness Journal* in Scotland reported the departure of the emigrant ship *Ossian* from Cromarty on June 25 bound for Pictou. Included in the passenger manifest is a list which includes many necessities of life for the new emigrant, including the number of hatchets, spades, axes, saws and nails, Bibles (Gaelic and English), barrels of pork and yards of tartan. Five families listed a mere three yards of tartan and others, such as seventy-year-old John Sutherland and widow Margaret MacDonald, left Scotland with thirty-six yards of tartan each. For a more comprehensive breakdown of the passenger list, see Campey, 216.
46. Hornby, *Celts and Ceilidhs*, 39. Rule 8 of the Constitution of the Caledonian Club of Prince Edward Island, approved in 1864, stipulates that among other prizes "A prize will be awarded to the wearer of the best Highland Costume—P. E. Island manufacture Tartan to be preferred."

Notes to Chapter Two

1. Rogers, ed., *Johnson and Boswell in Scotland*, 195.
2. See Reid, *Sir William Alexander*; and *Acadia, Maine and New Scotland*, 7, 14, 23-33. Shortly after the Treaty of Utrecht (1713), the French, seeking to reinforce their claims to North America, built the fortified town of Louisbourg not far from the settlement at Baleine.
3. Kennedy, *Gaelic Nova Scotia*, 21.

4. Bumsted, *The People's Clearance*. Bumsted's book makes a good case for middle-class immigration, but he does not mention the Strathglas clearances of almost five thousand people to Antigonish County between 1801-1803, mentioned both by Prebble, *The Highland Clearances* and Fergusson, *Beyond the Hebrides*.

5. Kennedy, *Gaelic Nova Scotia*, 18. See also Prebble, *The Highland Clearances*, 63-65, 248-52, for a more detailed examination of the hardship endured by people as a result of the economic restructuring which occurred after the introduction of the Cheviot sheep to the Highlands and Islands.

6. Kennedy, *Gaelic Nova Scotia*, 18. See also Bumsted, *The People's Clearance*, 55-80.

7. See Adams and Somerville, *Cargoes of Despair and Hope*, for a detailed analysis of many of the causes of Scottish emigration to North America between the years 1603-1803 and the decline of immigration to the United States after the American Revolution.

8. Bumsted, *The People's Clearance*, 57. Other sources claim it was Alexander MacDonald of Boisdale and not Colin MacDonald of Boisdale.

9. Ibid., 116. Another successfully transplanted group of four hundred Protestant settlers, stewarded by Lord Selkirk, settled at Belfast, Prince Edward Island in 1803.

10. Morrison. *History of the Morison or Morrison Family*, 431. A copy of this book, minus the publishing information and a few other pages, is on Microfilm at the Nova Scotia Archives and Records Management (NSARM), Halifax, NS. Micro, M-879.

11. Ibid.

12. Ibid.

13. Fergusson, *Beyond the Hebrides*, 31.

14. The *New Illustrated Webster's Dictionary* describes Kelp as: 1. any large coarse seaweed (family Laminariaceae). 2. the ashes of seaweeds: formerly the source of soda as used in glass-making and soap-making, now a source chiefly of iodine.

15. Stanley, *The Well-Watered Garden*, 9.

16. Quoted in Campbell, *Songs Remembered in Exile*, 59.

17. Bumsted, *The People's Clearance*, 104.

18. Hornsby, "Scottish Emigration and Settlement," in *The Island*, 54.

19. Nova Scotia Archives and Records Management (hereafter NSARM). Cape Breton Land Petitions and Other Material 1787-1843. http://www.gov.ns.ca/nsarm/gene/cb.htm. According to this website Captain Hector MacKenzie boasted in 1825 that over the last eighteen years he alone had "brought 1500 hundred immigrants from Scotland." Cape Breton No.: 3064, NSARM microfilm 15799.

20. Prebble, *The Highland Clearances*, 140.

21. PANS, Vol. 307, Doc. 126, John Whyte, Surgeon, to R. D. George, Sydney, 19 December 1827.

22. *Acadian Recorder*, 12 July 1828.

23. NSARM C.O. 217/146, Sir James Kempt to Wilmot Horton, 14 September 1826.

24. Kennedy, *Gaelic Nova Scotia*, 27.

25. See Campbell and MacLean, *Beyond the Atlantic Roar*, 35-75, for settlement patterns and early economic development in the counties of northeastern Nova Scotia and Cape Breton.

26. Dunn, *Highland Settler*, 21.

27. Campey, *After the Hector*, 23, 134-37.

28. Fergusson, *Beyond the Hebrides*, 30.

29. Ibid., 31-34.
30. MacMillan, *A West Wind to East Bay*, 622.
31. Campey, *After the Hector*, 13.
32. Fergusson, *From the Farthest Hebrides*, 246.
33. Ibid., 236.
34. Prebble, *The Highland Clearances*, 131.
35. MacKay, *A Collection of Ancient Piobaireachd*, 7.
36. Hornsby, "Scottish Immigration," 57.
37. Ibid.
38. MacMillan, *A West Wind to East Bay*, 623.
39. Stanley, *The Well-Watered Garden*, 23. This was not true of all areas of Cape Breton. Some Scottish Gaels became very successful farmers. See Bitterman, "The Hierarchy of the Soil," *Acadiensis*, 33-55.
40. Campbell and MacLean, *Beyond the Atlantic Roar*, 285.
41. Ibid., 93-100.
42. Frank, *J. B. McLachlan*, 46-49, 201-202; see also Martell, "Early Coal Mining in Nova Scotia"; and D. Frank, "The Cape Breton Coal Industry," MacGillivray and Tennyson, eds., *Cape Breton Historical Essays*, 41-53, 110-32.
43. See Appendix B for a partial list of piper/fiddler/bards among the second- and third-generation Gaels. Other sources such as MacGillivray's *The Cape Breton Fiddler*, and *A Cape Breton Ceilidh*, contain lists of traditional musicians.
44. Kennedy, *Gaelic Nova Scotia*, 26.
45. Ibid.
46. Muise, "The Making of an Industrial Community," in MacGillivray and Tennyson, eds., *Cape Breton Historical Essays*, 83.
47. Campbell and MacLean, *Beyond the Atlantic Roar*, 108-109; Brookes, "Out-migration," *The Acadiensis Reader*, 34-63.
48. Dunn, *Highland Settler*, 134.
49. See Appendix A for a partial list of immigrant pipers to Nova Scotia, 1773-1848.
50. MacKay, *A Collection of Ancient Piobaireachd*, 1-8.
51. Cannon, *Joseph MacDonald's Compleat Theory*, 1r.
52. MacKenzie, *One Hundred Years in the Highlands*, 192. One tale relates how some of his fellow students became envious of MacKay's superior piping skills and, even though he was blind, threw him down a 24-foot precipice, only to have him land on his feet and survive unharmed. This spot became known in Gaelic as Leum an Doill or The Blind's Leap.
53. Ibid., 194.
54. MacKenzie, *Piping Traditions of the North of Scotland*, 152.
55. MacKenzie, "The Editor in Canada," *Celtic Magazine*, 71.
56. Gibson, *Traditional Gaelic Piping*, 128.
57. An interesting relic carried to Nova Scotia by the Gairloch MacKays, which is currently held privately in Halifax, is a pipe chanter said to have belonged to the Blind Piper and which dates to the late 17th century.
58. MacKenzie, *Piping Traditions of the North of Scotland*, 143.
59. MacKay, J. P., *Reminiscences of Long a Life*, NSARM, MG20674 7.
60. Campbell, *Songs Remembered in Exile*, 60.
61. Walker, *Pioneer Pipers of British Columbia*, 28.
62. In 2000, bagpipe maker Julian Goodacre of Peebles, Scotland, spent a few days measuring the chanter which is now located in Halifax, Nova Scotia. Julian specializes in reproductions of antique instruments and after years of research he now makes reproductions of Iain Dall's pipe chanter.
63. Hawkins, MacKenzie and MacQuarrie, *Gairloch, Pictou County*, 20-21.

64. MacLean, ed., *A History of Antigonish*, 55.
65. Ibid., 55.
66. "Makers of Gaelic Poetry," *Celtic Heritage*, 35.
67. Dunn, *Highland Settler*, 75.
68. For a more detailed account of Robert MacIntyre, see Shears, "The Fate of Clanranald Piper Robert MacIntyre." *Piping Today*, 36-38.
69. Alexander MacDonald (Dall Mor), *The Uist Collection*.
70. Collinson, *The Great Highland Bagpipe*, 134.
71. James McGregor Collection.
72. MacLellan, *Failte Cheap Breatuinn*, 42.
73. Another family tradition has the family leaving Cape Breton and possibly returning to Scotland, only to re-emigrate to what later became the province of Ontario, Canada. Both traditions have the family resettling in Saskatchewan and this has been borne out by census records for the area.
74. The MacIntyre family of Perthshire was one of the prominent piping families in the late 17th and 18th centuries beginning with Donald Roy, born ca. 1644, died ca. 1722. The MacIntyre "piping" family tree presented here is still very much a work in progress. I am indebted to Keith Sanger of Edinburgh for allowing me to publish some of the results of his ongoing research into the family. Keith generously supplied the names of several additional MacIntyre pipers in Scotland and several dates. These names are marked with an asterisk.
75. Gibson, *Old and New World Highland Bagpiping*, 73.
76. Morrison, "Clann Duiligh-Pipers to the MacLeans," *Transactions of the Gaelic Society of Inverness*, 79. Gaelic translation of this article generously supplied by Effie Rankin, Mabou.
77. Ibid., 81. Gibson states that Condullie Rankin received a commission in the New Brunswick Fencibles in 1804, but this date seems to be contradicted by Neil Rankin Morrison's account of Rankin's military involvement.
78. Morrison, "Pipers to the Clan MacLean," 75-76.
79. Hornby, *Celts and Ceilidhs*, 77.
80. Morrison, "Pipers to the Clan MacLean," 77.
81. Gibson, *Traditional Gaelic Bagpiping*, 278.
82. Ibid.
83. Morrison, 69.
84. Of the more than 260 second- and third-generation pipers listed in Appendix B, more than twenty left Nova Scotia for places as far away as California, Boston, Montana and the western provinces of Canada.

Notes to Chapter Three

1. "The Community as Object," *American Anthropologist* 63, 241-64.
2. Shaw, trans. and ed., *Tales Until Dawn*, xv.
3. Campbell, *Songs Remembered in Exile*, 219. Campbell's informant was Angus MacIsaac, Giant's Lake, Guysborough County, NS. Fenian tales, while more often associated with Ireland, were well known and recited in both Ireland and Scotland.
4. Some of the early works of these bards can be found in the following collections: John MacGillivray; *Brigh an Oran* by John Shaw; John MacLean; *Clarsach na Coille* and *The Glenbard Collection*, edited by A. Maclean Sinclair; Allan MacDonald (Bohuntin); *As A' Bhraighe - Beyond the Braes,* by Effie Rankin. Some of Angus Campbell's songs have been published in *Gaelic Songs of Nova Scotia*, edited by Helen Creighton and Calum MacLeod. Genealogical information on the

descendants of Neil Currie in Cape Breton can be found in *A West Wind from East Bay*, by Father Allan MacMillan.

5. He was a son of Allan MacDonald, Bohuntin, later Mabou Ridge, Cape Breton.
6. Fergusson, *Beyond the Hebrides*, 34.
7. Keith N. MacDonald, *MacDonald Bards*.
8. Kennedy, *Gaelic Nova Scotia*, 133.
9. "Gaelic in Nova Scotia," *The Dalhousie Review*, 254. D. MacLean Sinclair quoting Dr. P. J. Nicholson, president of Saint Francis Xavier University, an avid collector of Gaelic songs and material.
10. During this period some tunes composed by Cape Breton pipers like Archie A. Beaton, Malcolm Gillis and Ranald Gillis were published by David Glen, Edinburgh, and James Logan, Inverness.
11. The late Joe Hughie MacIntyre played settings of tunes like "The Sheepwife" and "The Smiths of Chilliechassie," which extended to ten or twelve parts.
12. Gibson, *Old and New World*, 197.
13. Appendix A lists the names of more than sixty immigrant pipers (including several of the hereditary pipers) to present-day Nova Scotia. To date there has been little research into the numbers of pipers among Highland settlers to New Brunswick and Prince Edward Island.
14. Gibson, *Old and New World*, 218.
15. MacMillan, *To the Hill of Boisdale*, 130.
16. Ibid.
17. Translation kindly supplied by Brian Stinson, Bellevue, WA.
18. Personal interview, Alex Currie.
19. Ibid., 73.
20. Cannon, *The Highland Bagpipe*, 119-24.
21. Ross, *Ross's Collection*, vi.
22. Emmerson, *Rantin' Pipe*, 200.
23. See Farnham, "Cape Breton Folk," *Harper's*, 610, 618. http://cdl.library.cornell.edu. also Gibson, Old and New World.
24. Emmerson, *Rantin' Pipe*, 108.
25. MacKenzie, *Piping Traditions*, 80.
26. Ibid.
27. MacGillivray, *A Cape Breton Ceilidh*, 61.
28. Dunlay and Greenberg, *Traditional Celtic Violin*, 5.
29. Emmerson, *Rantin' Pipe*, 49.
30. Statistical Account, 209.
31. Rhodes, 272.
32. MacGillivray, *A Cape Breton Ceilidh*, 24.
33. Ibid.
34. Gibson, *Old and New World*, 236.
35. James D. Gillis and Thomas Raddall, CBC interview, 1945, NSARM, AR 2693.
36. MacInnes, "Cape Breton Dance-An Irish or Scottish Tradition?" Http://www.siliconglen.com/celtfaq/3_2.html. See also Bennett, "Step-dancing: Why we must learn from past mistakes." http://www.siliconglen.com/scotfaq/10_3.html and also Haurin and Richens, "Irish Step Dancing: A Brief History." http://www.indyirishdancers.org/irhist.htm
37. Personal interview, Alex Currie, Frenchvale.
38. Fergusson, ed. *The Hebridean Connection*, 514.
39. Kennedy, *Gaelic Nova Scotia*, 215.
40. Strathspey is the name given to that musical form developed for the violin in the Strathspey region of Scotland.

41. Emmerson, *Rantin' Pipe*, 109. In 1760, Joseph MacDonald wrote a treatise on the Highland bagpipe which was later published by his brother in 1803.
42. Fergusson, *The Hebridean Connection.*
43. Dunlay and Greenberg, *Traditional Celtic Violin*, 3. See also Hunter, *The Fiddle Music of Scotland*, x-xiv.
44. For an assessment of Cape Breton fiddling styles and technique see Dunlay and Greenberg, *Traditional Celtic Violin*; and Graham, *The Cape Breton Fiddle.*
45. Stanley, *The Well-Watered Garden*, 5.
46. Cannon, *The Highland Bagpipe*, 89.
47. MacKenzie, *Piping Traditions of the North of Scotland*, 152.
48. Dunn, *Highland Settler*, 55.
49. Farnham, "Cape Breton Folk," 618.
50. MacDonald, *MacDonald and MacKinnon Families*, 18-26.
51. Farnham, "Cape Breton Folk," 610.
52. Gibson, *Old and New World*, 281.
53. Ibid., 288.
54. Telephone interview, Florence Bonner, Bay St. Lawrence.
55. Ibid.
56. Personal interview, Alex Currie, Frenchvale.
57. Ibid.
58. MacKenzie, *History of Christmas Island*, 185.
59. Personal correspondence, Duncan MacDougall, Sydney.
60. MacDonald, "Piping in Cape Breton," 10.
61. I am indebted to Allan Gillis, Ottawa, for this historical reference taken from Lawson, *Croft History*, 13. Unfortunately no description of the type of dance is given.
62. *Statistical Accounts of Scotland*, 181, Vol 14, account of 1834-45
63. *Smeorach nan Cnoc's nan Gleann*, 198.
64. Farnham, "Cape Breton Folk," 618.
65. Personal interview, Paddy and Gussie MacIntyre, Grand Mira.
66. MacDonald, "Piping in Cape Breton," 8-9.
67. MacDonald, *MacDonald and MacKinnon Families*,19.
68. Ibid.
69. Ibid.
70. Ibid., 25.
71. MacLean, "The Pioneers of Washabuckt," 17.
72. See Appendix C for a list of known bagpipe makers in Nova Scotia.
73. Cannon, *The Highland Bagpipe*, 19-20.
74. Cheape, "The Making of Bagpipes in Scotland," 600.
75. Campbell, *Highland Bagpipe Makers*, 1-4.
76. Henderson, *Highland Soldier*, 38. Henderson, quoting a recruiting memorandum, states: "in 1825 upwards of 15,000 men were recruited in the districts."
77. Ibid., 44.
78. Cheape, "The Making of Bagpipes in Scotland," 605.
79. Ibid.
80. Ibid., 606.
81. Ibid., 608.
82. Dunn, *Highland Settler*, 55.
83. Cheape, "The Making of Bagpipes in Scotland," 605.
84. Ibid., 608. Wood turning is a very old profession which was first developed by the Greeks after the 7th century BCE.

85. This is borne out by comparisons with several immigrant and modern bagpipes held in private collections throughout Nova Scotia.
86. Cheape, "The Making of Bagpipes in Scotland," 613.
87. Campbell, *Highland Bagpipe Makers*, 39-42.
88. See Appendix C for a comprehensive list of bagpipe makers in Nova Scotia, 1817-1940.
89. See Appendix C.
90. MacDonald, *Sketches of Highlanders*, Appendix, viii.
91. Cannon, *The Highland Bagpipe*, 16. Two-droned bagpipes are easier to tune than three-droned instruments.
92. MacDonald, "Piping in Cape Breton," *Piping Times*, 9.
93. Personal interview, Alex Matheson.
94. Ibid.
95. Personal interview, Alex Currie.
96. Personal correspondence, Jean Ross, 26 May 2003.
97. Adam, *The Clans, Septs and Regiments of the Scottish*, 465.
98. Campbell, *Highland Bagpipe Makers*, 16.
99. Personal Correspondence, Jean Ross, 26 May 2003.
100. MacGillivray, *The Cape Breton Fiddler*, 29.
101. This song was published in Hector MacDougall's *The Songster of the Hills and Glens* in 1939, a translation of which was kindly sent to me by Effie Rankin, Mabou, NS. A complete version of the song in English can be found in Appendix D.
102. Jim MacDonald also refers to a set of Duncan Gillis bagpipes on display in a museum in Sydney, Australia, in "Piping in Cape Breton," 9.
103. Personal interview, Arthur Severence, Fourchu, Cape Breton.
104. Personal interview, Dave MacKinnon, Bay St. Lawrence.
105. Ibid.
106. MacKenzie, *History of Christmas Island*, 116.
107. Personal interview, Archie A. MacKenzie, Halifax, NS.
108. *Sydney Post*, 23 March 1905.
109. Ross, *The Pioneers and Churches*, 146.
110. See Appendix C. As recently as 1999, Albert MacDonald of Melfort, Inverness County was still making sets of bagpipes for musical enthusiasts patterned after a set made at River Denys Mountain around 1895. Personal interview, Albert MacDonald.
111. Personal interview, Archie MacDonald, Grand River. It was Archie's opinion that the period leading up to about 1930 was the heyday of the dance piper in Cape Breton. Archie grew up in West Bay, Cape Breton, but spent much of his life living in Boston. He remembered several gatherings of Cape Bretoners in Boston which often included a dance piper.

Notes to Chapter Four
1. Kennedy, *Gaelic Nova Scotia*, 70-76.
2. Adams and Somerville, *Cargoes of Despair*, 122-23.
3. Creighton and MacLeod, eds., *Gaelic Songs in Nova Scotia*, 76-89.
4. Gillis, *Stray Leaves From Highland History*, 36.
5. These were pipers Robert Ross and John MacDonald, Pictou County, and Donald Stewart, Mira.
6. The 1838 census for Pictou County is available on line: http://www.rootsweb.com/~nspictou/
7. This is borne out by my own interviews with Alex Currie and those of several other researchers such as John Shaw and John Gibson.

8. Shaw, *Tales Until Dawn*; *Brigh an Orain*.
9. Shaw, *Brigh an Orain*, 52.
10. Personal interviews, Alex Currie, Frenchvale, and Joe Neil MacNeil, Sydney.
11. Shaw, *Brigh an Orain*, 36.
12. In MacGillivray, *Cape Breton Ceilidh*, 208.
13. Caplan, *Talking Cape Breton Music*, 184.
14. Pearson, "At the White Millers—A Visit To Glencoe Mills In 1929." Originally published in the *Toronto Star Weekly*, reprinted in *The Clansman*, 9, 43, 44. Thanks to Kate Dunlay for supplying this reference.
15. Personal interview, Paddy MacIntyre.
16. Personal interview, Gussie MacIntyre.
17. Telephone interview, Mac Campbell.
18. Personal correspondence, John Pearson.
19. Personal interview, Allan Cameron.
20. Obituary, David Walter Beaton, *Pictou Advocate*, 1.
21. *The Pictou Book*, 262.
22. *Eastern Chronicle*, September 1866.
23. *The Caledonian Club*, n.p.
24. Ibid.
25. Ibid.
26. Obituary, David Walter Beaton, *Pictou Advocate*, 1.
27. Personal correspondence, Lawrence Campbell.
28. *Annals of the North British Society*, 613.
29. Personal correspondence, Lawrence Campbell. Lawrence was told this story by Dan Angus Beaton, Blackstone, Inverness County.
30. Personal interview, Arthur Severence.
31. Unpublished MS, n.d., n.p., Gorry's Mountain is located just behind the present town of Inverness and at present it is largely uninhabited.
32. Handwritten MS generously provided by Roddy MacLennan, Halifax, NS.
33. Bridget MacKenzie, *Piping Traditions of Argyll*, 202-10.
34. The story was conveyed to me by the late Archie MacDonald, Grand River, Richmond County.
35. Personal interview, Arthur Severence. Arthur remembered seeing John MacKinnon play for the Scotch fours, solo step dancers and the more modern square sets at an afternoon "picnic" at Inverness Town in the early 1920s.
36. Old 78 rpm records from the 1920s of Scottish pipers playing strathspeys and reels further illustrate how unsuitable this type of music had become for step-dancing.
37. Malcolm, *A Piper in Peace and War*.
38. Personal interview, Archie MacDonald.
39. Ibid.
40. Ibid.
41. Ibid.
42. Brookes, "Out-Migration from the Maritime Provinces," 34-63.
43. MacFarlane and MacLean, eds., *Drummer on Foot,* 52.
44. MacMillan, *A West Wind to East Bay*, 632.
45. Personal interview, Archie MacKenzie, Halifax, NS.
46. Donaldson, *The Highland Pipe and Scottish Society*, 319. Donaldson claims this figure only reflects Scottish piping casualties and there is currently no accurate figure for Commonwealth pipers.

47. Personal interview, Sandy MacBeth, Riverton, and Peter Morrison, Sydney. Two of the most influential "homegrown" pipers influenced in this manner were Fraser Holmes, New Glasgow, and Roddy Nicholson, Sydney. Both men went on to instruct dozens of pipers in Nova Scotia.

48. MacKenzie, "The Editor in Canada," *Celtic Magazine*, 110. Pipe Major Ronald MacKenzie, 79th Highlanders, is known to have instructed at least one pupil while serving with his regiment in Halifax in 1879.

49. O'Shea, *The Louisburg Brass Bands*, 3.

50. Scobie, *Pipers and Pipe Music*, 20, 24; see also MacLauchlan, *A History of the Scottish Highland*, 357-58.

51. Other early pipe bands included the Pictou County Pipe Band, ca. 1906, the Inverness Pipe Band, ca. 1908, and the Clan Thompson Pipe Band of Halifax, ca. 1909.

52. The four brothers were all sons of "Big" Jim MacIntyre and included: Dan, Joe, Archie and Michael. The Pipe Major of the band was their first cousin, "Long" Joe MacIntyre.

53. Dickson, "The Piping Tradition of South Uist," 86.

54. Angus MacKay states in his notes that the Rannoch MacIntyres originally came from the Western Isles. Keith Sanger has discovered a Duncan MacIntyre, piper, who was born in 1691 in Perthshire and there is a possibility that he was another son of Donald Roy MacIntyre. See *The MacIntyres of Perthshire Family Tree*; Chapter three.

55. Dickson, "The Piping Tradition of South Uist," 21-30, 70-71. Dickson gleaned his information on the musical abilities of the MacIntyres from nine different sources, including personal interviews and existing material held at the School of Scottish Studies, Edinburgh, Scotland.

56. I had often heard my first tutor, Angus MacIntyre, mention during my weekly lessons that he was descended from Clanranald's piper. A published interview with Angus MacIntyre repeating this claim appeared in a Toronto area newspaper in 1975. Unfortunately, I only have a photocopy of the article and not the name of the actual publication.

57. Personal interview, Danny MacIntye, Sydney, NS, 1988.

58. Shears, "Two of the Extraordinary Piping Families," 26-27.

59. Dunn, *Highland Settler*, 130-31.

60. MacGillivray, *Cape Breton Ceilidh*, 210.

61. Personal correspondence, Randy Smith. Randy received this information from Ian Blue, one of George Dey's former pupils.

62. Ibid.

63. Personal interview, Peter Morrison.

64. Sutherland, *The Rise and Decline of the Community of Earltown*, 96.

65. Ibid.

66. *The Evening News*. This information is from a photocopied article which was sent to me several years ago. Unfortunately, I do not have the date or page number.

67. Cameron, *Pictonians*, 212.

68. Newspaper interview, New York. The name of the paper is unknown, but an excerpt from the article was reprinted in the *Pictou Advocate*, 1916.

69. Ibid.

70. Ibid.

71. Cameron, *Pictonians*, 212.

72. http://college.hmco.com/history/readerscomp/ships/html/sh_016300_hmscalliope.htm

73. Ibid.

74. Ibid.
75. Cameron, *Pictonians*, 212.
76. Mackenzie, *Piping Traditions of the North of Scotland*, 78-79.
77. Personal interview, Alex Sutherland.
78. Ibid.
79. "Death Claims Pipe Major," *Pictou Advocate*, 18 April 1924, 9.
80. Cameron, *Pictonians*, 209-11.
81. Personal interview, Peter Morrison.
82. Cameron, *Pictonians*, 212.
83. Personal interview, Alex Sutherland.
84. Personal interview, Billy Matheson. Billy is a fiddler from River Denys and his father, Kenny, learned several tunes on the pipes and violin from Pipe Major Baillie.
85. Telephone interview, Hector MacNeil, Sydney.
86. Kennedy, *Gaelic Nova Scotia*, 39-91; Cox. "Gaelic and the Schools in Cape Breton," 21-22.
87. Personal interview, Peter Morrison, Sydney.
88. Dickson, "The Piping Tradition of South Uist," 119-38. The phenomenon of tradition abandonment has also been observed among pipers in early 20th-century South Uist. Improvers were sent to the island from the Scottish mainland to bring the local musicians up to modern standards as early as 1907. Traditional Gaelic-flavoured piping continued longest in Cape Breton and the west coast of Newfoundland. The transition was so complete that by the late 1980s, there were only a handful of people in Cape Breton and Newfoundland who could be classified as traditional pipers.

Notes to Chapter Five

1. MacLean, *Highlanders*, 243. MacLean quotes General Stewart of Garth.
2. Harper, *A Short History of the Old 78th Regiment*, 41, 43. This book also includes several eyewitness accounts of both the siege of Louisbourg and the fall of Quebec.
3. MacKenzie, *The History of Christmas Island Parish*, 141.
4. Two other veterans of the taking of Louisbourg who returned to Barra with gloing reports of the land potential in Cape Breton were Finlay "Glas" MacKenzie (grey) and Donald MacNeil, former bodyguard to Captain Donald MacDonald. MacKenzie, *The History of Christmas Island Parish*, 167.
5. MacLeod, *Stories from Nova Scotia*, 28.
6. For a more detailed account of veterans of the Seven Years war and the Napoleonic wars who settled in Pictou County see Cameron, *Pictonians in Arms*, 19-36.
7. Allan MacLean was the son of MacLean of Torloisk. In 1757 he had been a captain in Montgomery's Highlanders.
8. Stacey, *A Short History of the 84th Regiment*.
9. Personal correspondence, Keith Sanger. Sanger is preparing an article on Neil Maclean entitled "One Piper or Two, Neil Maclean of the 84th Highlanders." Note the various spellings: MacLaine, MacLain, MacLean. Neil himself was illiterate. As late as 1811 they spelled it MacLaine.
10. Ibid.
11. Ibid. Neil MacLean of the 84th may have been the same Neil MacLean, who was later piper to the Highland Society of London.
12. Poulter, *History of the Clan MacCrimmon,*
13. Duncanson, *Rawdon and Douglas*, 166.
14. Bryant, *Years of Victory*, 233.

15. Ibid.
16. Ibid., 234-36.
17. Ibid., 286-95.
18. *Pictonians in Arms*, 33-34.
19. MacQuarrie, *Lansdowne Sketches*, 35.
20. Unpublished genealogical information compiled by Allan Fergusson, formerly of Cape Breton.
21. National Archives of Canada, RG 8, C Series, Vol. 1908.
22. Fergusson, *Beyond the Hebrides*, 94-96.
23. Ibid.
24. MacMillan, *A West Wind to East Bay*, 133.
25. "Bagpipes were an early part of Pictou County's History," *Evening News*, New Glasgow.
26. *The Story of Dartmouth*, 366-67.
27. Alexander MacKenzie, *Celtic Magazine*. This quote indicates MacLauchlan was proficient at playing *ceòl mór* or big music.
28. Personal interview, Dan Fortune.
29. Morrison and Slaney, *The Breed of Manly Men*, 52-53.
30. Hunt, ed., *Nova Scotia's Part in the Great War*, 263.
31. Malcolm, *The Piper in Peace and War*, 217-18.
32. MacDonald and Gardiner, *The Twenty-Fifth Battalion*, 10.
33. Ibid., 205-206. In the closing months of the war the officers and men of the 25th battalion voted overwhelmingly in a plebiscite to have the battalion designated as a Highland unit (25th Canadian Highland Battalion, Nova Scotia), but the war ended before any action towards that end could be completed.
34. Personal interview, Archie MacDonald.
35. MacDonald and Gardiner, *The Twenty-Fifth Battalion*, 205.
36. For many years this instrument, a beautiful set of full silver-mounted Henderson bagpipes, lay in a display box at the Public Archives Building at Dalhousie University. The bagpipe has been since been gifted to the Nova Scotia Museum.
37. This figure probably represents those pipers who were used as musicians and attached to their companies and battalion pipe bands. Pipers who served other functions and lost their lives were most likely not counted in this figure. Rory MacIsaac's son, John R., lost his life while performing his duties as a gunner in the artillery and not in any capacity as a piper.
38. Nova Scotian pipers received instruction in Canada from Kenneth MacKenzie Baillie and Sandy Bowes. While the pipers were overseas, Pipe Major Harry McCulloch, Dundee, and a Pipe Major W. Hosie, Aberdeen, provided additional instruction.
39. *The Breed of Manly Men*. This motto is currently used by the two battalions of the Nova Scotia Highlanders, (Reserve).
40. *Cape Breton's Deserted Mining Town, Broughton*.
41. Anderson, *Broughton, Cape Breton Ghost Town*, 9.
42. "A Short History and Photographic Record of the 185th Battalion," *Cape Breton Highlanders Overseas*, CEF, 3.
43. Malcolm, *The Piper in Peace and War*, 264.
44. Ibid., 225.
45. Unnamed newspaper article dated April 13, 1921, kindly forwarded by John Gillies, Port Hood.
46. MacDonald and Gardiner, *The Twenty-Fifth Battalion*, 211.
47. Malcolm, *A Piper in Peace and War*. Leonard Planner is credited with being the last piper to fall in action in the First World War. A piper in the Argyll and

Sutherland Highlanders of Scotland, he was killed two days before the end of the war on November 9, 1918.

48. MacGillivray, *The Cape Breton Song Collection*, 37.
49. Walsh, *Cape Breton's Lillian Crewe Walsh*, 1.
50. Personal interview, Sandy MacBeth.
51. Personal interview, Ben MacIntyre.
52. Personal interview, Gussie MacIntyre.
53. Morrison and Slaney, *The Breed of Manly Men*, 31.
54. Ibid., 138.
55. *Canadian-American Gael.*
56. Personal interview, Alex Currie.

Notes to Chapter Six

1. Beaton, "The Canso Causeway," 95-112.
2. MacKay, "Tartanism Triumphant," 5-47.
3. *National Geographic Magazine* had a Cape Breton connection in the person of Gilbert Grosvenor. Grosvenor, who served as editor of the magazine from 1899 until 1954, was married to Alexander Graham Bell's daughter, Elsie. The Grosvenor's spent a great deal of time at Bell's summer home at Beinn Bhreagh (Beautiful Montain), overlooking Baddeck Bay, Cape Breton.
4. Brown, "Salty Nova Scotia," *National Geographic*, 574-624.
5. New Glasgow *Evening News*, 4 February 1971, 9.
6. The *Chronicle Herald*, 18 April 1973.
7. The Queen could not attend but instead sent her cousin, Princess Alexandra, and her husband, the Honourable Angus Ogilvy, in her place.
8. New Glasgow *Evening News*, 4 January 1973. n.p.
9. MacKay, "Tartanism Triumphant,"5-47.
10. The Gaelic College of Celtic Arts and Crafts, St. Ann's, NS.
11. These included the 25th Battalion, Canadian Expeditionary Force, the 85th-Battalion, Nova Scotia Highlanders and the 185th Battalion, Cape Breton Highlanders.
12. MacGillivray, *Cape Breton Ceilidh,* 213.
13. Personal interview, John Willie Macleod, Dartmouth. Another Nova Scotia piper who attended the Army School of Piping during the Second World War was Duncan MacIntyre. After the war Duncan taught piping in the Amherst area.
14. Shears, *Cape Breton Collection of Bagpipe Music*, ii.
15. Gibson, *Traditional Gaelic Bagpiping*, 1745-1945, 206-207.
16. Personal interview, Alex Sutherland, Dartmouth.
17. It was during one of these visits to Ontario that Sandy was presented with a silver- and ivory-mounted set of Henderson bagpipes, an instrument he carried with him wherever he went.
18. Some of his host families included the MacDonnell family of Deepdale, the MacKenzies of St. Peter's, the MacNeils of Barra Glen and the Beatons of Antigonish.
19. Marches rose to prominence during the late 19th century as pipers, who had recently been recognized by the military establishment as musicians, were required to march soldiers from place to place. As previously mentioned, the original dance forms associated with tune types such as strathspeys and reels had been replaced with a handful of display dances relegated now to competitions and Highland games. Dances, such as seann triubhas and others, incorporated European ballet technique and the musical form associated with these non-traditional dances changed to accommodate external influences.

20. Immigration to Ontario, and later Alberta, began to replace the Boston States as a preferred destination in the 1950s.

21. Personal interview, Frank Carey, Halifax, 1974. This information was kindly forwarded to me in 1991 by the interviewer, Ken Grant, Halifax.

22. These included: the Heatherbell Girls Pipe Band, Pictou; Dunvegan Girls Pipe Band, Westville; Ceilidh Girls Pipe Band, New Glasgow; and the Balmoral Girls Pipe Band, Stellarton.

23. Campbell and MacLean, *Beyond the Atlantic Roar*, 190. Campbell and MacLean denote very little space in their study of Nova Scotia Scots to the cultural importance of the bagpipe (or the violin) among the new world Gaels. Their comments on piping are both condescending and inaccurate.

24. Kennedy, *Gaelic Nova Scotia*, 181.

25. Alyce Taylor Cheska, "The Antigonish Highland Games," *Nova Scotia Historical Review*, Vol 13, No 1, 1983, 55-56.

26. One exception was the Gaelic Society of Inverness, Cape Breton, which met in March, 1924 to celebrate the bicentenary of the birth of the famous Gaelic bard, Duncan Ban MacIntyre. *The Collected Works of Malcolm Gillis*, 109.

27. MacDonald, *Sketches of Highlanders*, 43.

28. Ibid., 56.

29. *Eastern Chronicle*, September, 1866.

30. *Cape Breton News*, 17 September 1870, n.p.

31. MacLaren, *The Pictou Book*, 261-62.

32. Foster, *Language and Poverty*, 93.

33. Ibid., 83.

34. Ibid., 85.

35. Kennedy, *Gaelic Nova Scotia*, 181.

36. Ibid., 181. MacLeod did collect and publish two books on Gaelic culture in Nova Scotia, *Sgialachdan a Albainn Nuaidh* and *Bardachd a Albainn Nuaidh*, and he worked jointly with Helen Creighton on *Gaelic Songs in Nova Scotia*.

37. Lamb, *Celtic Crusader*, 48.

38. Ibid., 42.

39. *Silver Jubilee Souvenir Mod* booklet, 39.

40. Ibid., 40.

41. Kennedy, *Gaelic Nova Scotia*, 247.

42. Ibid.

43. MacNeill, Editorial, *Piping Times*, January 1995, 16.

44. Kennedy, *Gaelic Nova Scotia*, 245.

45. Personal interview, Fred MacPherson, Marion Bridge.

46. Personal interview, Danny MacIntyre, Sydney.

47. Lamb, *Celtic Crusader*, 41.

48. Kennedy, *Gaelic Nova Scotia*, 182.

49. Ibid.

50. Personal Interview, Danny MacIntyre.

51. Kennedy, *Gaelic Nova Scotia*, 182.

52. Ibid., 179.

53. Ibid.

54. Dickson, "The Piping Tradition of South Uist." This paper was recently updated as "When Piping Was Strong." Dickson found that by the mid-20th century, orally taught piping was deemed inferior to the modern competitive model.

55. Gillis, *Stray Leaves from Highland History*, 36.

Notes to Chapter Seven

1. Kennedy, *Gaelic Nova Scotia,* 247.
2. Ibid., 247. See also MacKay, "Tartanism Triumphant."
3. Graham, *Cape Breton Fiddle,* 100-107.

APPENDIX A

A partial list of early immigrant pipers from Scotland to Nova Scotia, 1773-1848, gleaned from sources cited in the bibliography, land grants applications and family lore.

Abbreviations: s/o- son of, d/o- daughter of, s/o-sister of, b/o- brother of, n/o-nephew of.

Name	Native of	Year	Settled	Comments
Campbell, Angus	Benbecula	ca. 1840	Salmon River	piper, fiddler, bard
Campbell, Neil	Mull		Alba Station	piper
Campbell, Roderick d. 1826	Scotland		Carleton County, NB	piper, 74th Regiment
Carmichael, John	Lewis	ca. 1848	Tarbotvale	piper
Chisholm, Kenneth	Strathglas	ca. 1801	Antigonish	piper to Chisholm of Strathglas, killed by a falling tree, ca. 1833
Ferguson, Robert	North Uist	ca. 1829	Catalone	Black Watch, veteran piper of Waterloo
Gillis, John	Morar	ca. 1816	Ben Eoin	piper/fiddler
Johnson, Hector	Coll	ca. 1818	River John	piper, later moved to PEI
MacAulay, Donald	Barra?	ca. 1817	Washabuck	piper
McCarle, Donald	?	1814	Middle River	piper
MacCormack, Allan	South Uist		West Lake Ainslie	piper
MacCrimmon, Donald	Skye	ca. 1778	Shelburne	Via North Carolina. Hereditary piper to MacLeod of Dunvegan
MacDonald, Alexander	?		Antigonish	piper. known as "The Big Piper"
MacDonald, Alexander 1820-1904	Glenuig	1830	Keppoch, NS	piper, fiddler, bard, known as Keppoch Bard
MacDonald, Alexander	Moidart		West Lake Ainslie	via PEI, piper.
MacDonald, Archibald	Lochaber	1831	Mount Young	piper/fiddler
MacDonald, Donald	?		Halifax	piper, North British Society
MacDonald, Donald	Glen Urquhart		Thorburn	piper
MacDonald, Finlay	Glen Urquhart	1801	MacLellan's Mtn	piper
MacDonald	?		Sunnybrae	piper and pipe maker
MacDonald, Big Ronald	?		River Denys Mtn	piper
MacDonnell, Donald	Glengarry		Inverness	piper
MacDonnell, John			Inverness	piper
MacDougall, Angus Ban	?		West Lake Ainslie	piper
MacDougall, Donald	Arisaig	ca. 1818	Inverness	piper
MacDougall, Duncan	?		Halifax	piper

Name	Origin	Location	Date	Notes
MacDougall, John 1744-1826	Scotland	Carleton Co., NB		piper
MacGillivray, Hugh	?	Glenmorrison		piper
MacGillivray, John	Moidart	Malignant Cove		piper and bard to MacDonald of Glenaladale
MacGregor, Alexander	?	Nine Mile River	1818	piper, 84th Royal Highland Emigrants
MacGregor, Alexander	?	Halifax		piper, North British Society
MacInnis, John	North Uist	Kennington Cove		piper
MacIntosh, Kenneth	?	Halifax		piper, North British Society
MacIntyre, Duncan	South Uist	North Side East	ca. 1844	piper, s/o Lauchlin
MacIntyre, Lauchlin	South Uist	Beechmont	ca. 1844	piper, bard
MacIntyre, Donald . 1748	South Uist	Boisdale	ca. 1820	piper
MacIntyre, Robert	Rannoch	Port Hood	ca. 1813	Clanranald's piper
MacIsaac, Alexander "Ban"	Moidart	Giants Lake	ca. 1843	piper, pipe maker
MacKay, Angus	Gairloch	Pictou	1805	piper, s/o John Roy
MacKay, John	Gairloch	Pictou	1805	piper, s/o John Roy
MacKay, John Roy	Gairloch	Pictou	1805	hereditary piper to MacKenzie of Gairloch
MacKenzie, John	?	Halifax	ca. 1846	piper
MacKinnon, Archibald 1784-1818	Muck	East Lake Ainslie	1820	piper/fiddler
MacKinnon, Hugh b. 1818	Barra	Woodbine		piper
MacKinnon, John A.	Skye	Meat Cove		piper
MacLean, "Father" Allan	Morar	Judique	1857	piper/fiddler/step dancer
MacLean, Duncan	?	Shelburne		piper, via North Carolina, 76th MacDonald Highlanders
MacLean, John	Barra	Big Pond	1831	piper
MacLean, Murdock	?	Halifax		piper, North British Society
MacLean, Neil d. 1820	?	McNab's Island		piper, 84th Royal Highland Emigrants
MacLean, Peter	Barra	Washabuck	1817	piper, b/o Roderick
MacLean, Roderick	Barra	Washabuck	1817	piper
MacLeod, Donald 1791-1875	Skye	Landsowne	ca. 1817	Black Watch, veteran piper of Quatre Bras
Macleod, Alexander	South Uist	French Road	1841	piper
Macleod, John	?	Glenmorrison	1841	piper
MacMillan, Donald "Mor" b. ca. 1811	South Uist	Glenmorrison	1841	piper, b/o Donald "Mor"
MacMillan, James b. ca 1822	South Uist	Glenmorrison	1841	piper, b/o Donald "Mor," returned to Scotland
MacMillan, Neil	North Uist	Red Islands		piper/fiddler
MacMullin, Neil	?			piper
MacNeil, Donald b. ca. 1758	Barra	Rua Dileas	1818	piper
MacNeil, John	?	Big Bras d'Or		piper
MacNeil, Hector	Barra	Pipers Cove	1805	piper

Name	Origin	Place	Year	Description
MacNeil, Rory	Barra	Pipers Cove	1805	Piper
MacNeil, ?	?	Cape North		piper
MacPhee, John	South Uist	French Road	ca. 1828	piper
MacPhee, Jonathon b. 1835	Barra	East Bay		piper
MacPherson, Alexander	North Uist	New Boston		piper
MacPherson, Hector	?	Halifax		piper, North British Society
MacQuarrie, Archibald	Eigg	Antigonish	1852	piper, first settled at River Denys, moved to Antigonish
MacQuarrie, John	Eigg	Antigonish	1852	piper, b/o Archibald
MacVicar, Neil 1779-1861	North Uist	Catalone	1829	Black Watch, veteran piper of Waterloo
Matheson, Dougald	Localsh	River Denys		piper
Morrison, Angus 1792-1878	Harris	St. Ann's	ca. 1826	piper
Ross, Alexander	Dornoch	Pictou	ca. 1817	piper s/o Robert Ross
Ross, Robert 1769-1843	Dornoch	Pictou	ca. 1817	piper, pipe maker
Ross, William	Dornoch	Pictou	ca. 1817	piper, s/o Robert Ross
Steele, Donald	South Uist	Boisdale		piper, later moved to Glace Bay
Stewart, Donald	?	Mira		piper

A partial list of second, third, and fourth generation pipers in Nova Scotia gleaned from sources quoted in the bibliography, newspaper clippings and personal interviews. This list does not include pipers born after 1910.

Abbreviations: s/o- son of, d/o- daughter of, s/o-sister of, b/o- brother of, n/o-nephew of.

Name	Birth/Death	Locality	Comments
Beaton, Ambrose	b. 1889	Black River	piper/ fiddler, moved to Detroit
Beaton, Angus Ranald	1866-1933	Mabou	piper/fiddler
Beaton, Archie A.	1840-1923	Mabou	described as a "professor of pipe music"
Beaton, "Old" Donald	b. ca. 1855	Mabou	piper/fiddler
Beaton, "Young" Donald	b. ca. 1860	Mabou	piper/fiddler, b/o "Old" Donald
Beaton, Norman	ca. 1847-1891	Middle River	piper/dancer, moved to San Francisco
Beaton, Ranald	1858-1960	Mabou	piper/fiddler/bard, known as Rannuill Mairi Bhan
Beaton, Walter	ca. 1855-1922	Middle River	piper/fiddler, b/o of Norman
Briand, George		L'ardoise	piper/fiddler, Acadian descent
Brown, John		Bay St. Lawrence	piper, moved to Washabuck
Buchanan, W. J.		Ingonish	piper, 185th Battalion, WWI, moved to British Columbia
Calder, Fred	1868-1955	West Bay	piper, moved to Dawson City, settled in Cache Creek, BC
Cameron, John W. H.	1839-1925	Springville	piper, moved to Dartmouth, later returned to New Glasgow
Campbell, Hector		Judique	piper/ bard
Campbell, Fred		Judique	piper and pipe maker
Campbell, Michael	1876-1962	Boisdale	piper, later moved to Sydney
Campbell, Michael		Rear Hay Cove	piper/fiddler
Campbell, Neil	b. ca. 1847	Judique	piper
Campbell, Peter	b. ca. 1845	Hay Cove	piper/fiddler, moved to Bangor, Maine
Campbell, Robert		Scotsville	piper, moved to Boston ca. 1914
Campbell, Roderick		North side East Bay	piper
Carmichael, John	1872-1964	Tarbotvale	piper, s/oJohn Carmichael, immigrant piper
Chisholm, "Big" Colin	1845-1928	Marydale	piper
Chisholm, Duncan	1887-1947	Marydale	piper, s/o "Big" Colin
Chisholm, John		Marydale	piper
Chisholm, John J.	d. 1935	MacAdams Lake	piper/historian, later moved to Pictou
Currie, Peter		MacAdams Lake	piper/ step-dancer
Currie, Lauchie		Old Barns	piper, s/o Peter
Forbes, Charles	1855-1935	Pleasant Valley	piper, later moved to Milford, NS
Gillis, Dougald		Margaree	piper, lived for awhile in Montana, ca. 1905
Gillis, Alex			piper, s/o Hugh, moved to Winnipeg

Name	Dates	Location	Notes
MacCuish, ?		Glendale	piper, possibly moved to Pictou County
MacDonald, Alex		Lakevale	piper
MacDonald, Alex	ca. 1850	Sunnybrae	Piper
MacDonald, Alexander		Springfield	piper
MacDonald, Alex S.	1893-1966	South West Margaree	piper/fiddler
MacDonald, Allan B.		Kenloch	piper
MacDonald, Allan C.		East Bay	piper, settled at New Waterford
MacDonald, "Big" Angus		Little Mabou/ Colindale	piper, 185th Battalion, moved to Ontario
Macdonald, Angus L.		Dunvegan	piper, Premier of Nova Scotia
MacDonald, Angus D. F.	1893-1978		piper, 85th Battalion, moved to Kingston, ON
MacDonald, Angus "The Ridge"		Lower South River	piper/ fiddler/bard
MacDonald, "Black" Angus	1849-1939	Mount Young	piper/fiddler
MacDonald, Archie		Grand River	piper
MacDonald, Augustus "Gusty"		Springfield	piper, b/o Dave
MacDonald, Dannie "Donald Big Ranald"		River Denys Mtn	piper
MacDonald, Dan "Uisdean"		Soldiers Cove	piper
MacDonald, Dan A		French Road	piper, moved to Bridgeport
MacDonald, Dan C.		East Bay	piper, b/o Allan C. MacDonald
MacDonald, Dave		Springfield	piper, b/o John
MacDonald, Donald "Grace"	d. ca. 1917	Glencoe	piper
MacDonald, Duncan		Glace Bay	piper/fiddler
MacDonald, Rev. Duncan 1848-1930		River Denys Mountain	piper
MacDonald, Elizabeth		Lower River Inhabitants	piper
MacDonald, Frederick "D. F."	1891-1973	West Lake Ainslie	piper, 85th Battalion
MacDonald, Hector		Antigonish	piper
MacDonald, Hugh		Soldiers Cove	piper, b/o Black Jack
MacDonald, "Black" Jack		Soldiers Cove	piper, 185th Battalion, WWI
MacDonald, James		French Road	piper, s/o Mary MacDonald
MacDonald, John		Big Glace Bay	piper, won 'Best Piper' in 1876, Glace Bay
MacDonald, John		Boisdale	piper
MacDonald, John Alex		River Denys Mtn	piper/ fiddler, b/o Dannie "Donald Big Ranald"
MacDonald, John Francis 'Jack'		Big Bras d'Or	piper/fiddler
MacDonald, John 'Jack'	1885-1971	Springfield	piper, n/o Alexander
MacDonald, Joseph		French Road	piper, s/o Mary MacDonald
MacDonald, Mary		French Road	chanter player, (nee' MacIntyre)
MacDonald, Michael (Mike)		Macleod's Hill, Whitney Pier	piper
MacDonald, "Red" Mick		Morien Hil	piper/fiddler
MacDonald, Rannie Dan		North Side East Bay	Piper
MacDonald, Sandy Malcolm	1860-1947	River Denys Mtn	piper

Name	Dates	Place	Description
MacDonald, William		Antigonish	piper, s/o Hector
MacDonnell, Angus Hughie		River Denys Road	piper/fiddler
MacDonnell, Alexander 'Mor'	1835–1922	*Gleann Mor* / Kiltarlity	piper/step-dancer
MacDonnell, Archie		Kiltarlity	piper, s/o Alexander "Mor"
MacDonnell, Hughie		Kiltarlity	piper, s/o Alexander "Mor"
MacDonnell, James John		Inverness	piper, s/o Alexander "Mor"
MacDonnell, John Angus		Kiltarlity	piper, s/o Alexander "Mor"
MacDonnell, Neil		Gorry's Mountain	piper
MacDonnell, Sandy		Inverness	piper
MacDougall, Angus		Judique	piper
MacDougall, Catherine	ca. 1835–ca. 1905	Rear Christmas Island	piper
MacDougall, Dan Rory	1885–1957	Ingonish	piper/fiddler
MacDougall, 'Old' Mike		Sugar Loaf	piper/fiddler
MacDougall, Rory		Bay St Lawrence	piper/fiddler
MacEachen, Fadrick	1848–1936	River Denys Mtn.	piper and pipe maker
MacEachern, Allan R	b. ca. 1847	North Side East Bay	piper
MacEachern, Angus		MacEachern Road	piper
MacEachern, Dan		Grand Mira North	piper
MacEachern, Hugh		MacEachern Road	piper, cousin of Angus
MacEachern, John		Grand Mira North	piper
MacEachern, Sarah		MacEachern Road	piper, s/o Angus
MacFarlane, 'Little' Allan	1880–1938	South West Margaree	piper/fiddler
MacFarlane, Angus 'Ban'	1843–1931	Egypt	piper/bard
MacFarlane, John		South West Margaree	piper
MacFarlane, Malcolm D.		South West Margaree	piper
MacFarlane, Patrick		South West Margaree	piper
MacGillivray, Dan C.		Truro	piper
MacGillivray, Hugh		Glen Morrison	piper
MacGillivray, Hugh		Gulf Shore, Ant. Co.	piper, 3rd prize winner, Antigonish Highland games, 1863
MacGillivray, John		Lismore	Piper
MacGillivray, John		Maryvale	piper
MacGillivray, Joseph	d. 1901	Maryvale	piper, bard, s/o John MacGillivray, immigrant piper, bard.
MacGillivray, Steve	1885–1934	Glen Morrison	piper, s/o Hugh, died in motorcycle accident
MacIntyre, Angus	d. 1916	Glen Morrison	piper, s/o Hugh, killed overseas with the 13th Battalion
MacIntyre, Angus		Rear Boisdale	piper, moved to Gannon Road, North Sydney
MacIntyre, Archie		Glace Bay	s/o Joe MacIntyre
MacIntyre, Archie	1861–1953	Caledonia Mines	piper, s/o James

Name	Dates	Place	Notes
MacIntyre, Archie		Canoe Lake	piper
MacIntyre, Dan	b. 1869	Caledonia Mines	piper, s/o James
MacIntyre, Donald "Beag"	b. ca. 1890	Boisdale	piper, s/o Donald Mor
MacIntyre, Donald John	1838-1906	Louisbourg	piper
MacIntyre, Donald 'Mor'		Boisdale	piper
MacIntyre, Hugh		Boisdale	piper, served in the North Nova Scotia Highlanders, WWII
MacIntyre, James	1833-1916	French Road	piper/step-dancer, moved to Glace Bay
MacIntyre, Joe	1872-1948	Caledonia Mines	piper, s/o James
MacIntyre, 'Long' Joe	b. 1857	French Road	piper, moved to Glace Bay
MacIntyre, John		Lakevale	piper
MacIntyre, Capt. John		Gabarus	piper, Great Lakes sea Captain
MacIntyre, Kate		MacAdam's Lake	piper, married Dougald Currie
MacIntyre, Lauchie		Canoe Lake	piper, b/o Archie
MacIntyre, Michael 'Mickey'	b. 1875	Caledonia Mines	piper, 185th Battalion, WWI, s/o James
MacIntyre, Sandy		Lakevale	piper
MacIntyre, William		Gabarus	Gabarus piper/ fiddler worked as a lighthouse keeper
MacInnis, Dan S	b. ca. 1840	Morley Road	piper, 94th Regiment, lived at Glace Bay
MacInnis, Donald		Glendale	piper, with Nova Scotia Militia
MacInnis, Steve		Morley Road	piper, 94th Regiment, b/o Dan S.
MacIsaac, Alex Angus		Broad Cove	piper/fiddler/step-dancer, b/o Donald Angus
MacIsaac, Catherine		Dunvegan	piper, s/o Dan Alex, moved to Washington State
MacIsaac, Dan Alex	d. 1971	Dunvegan	piper and pipe maker, moved to Vancouver, BC
MacIsaac, Donald Angus		Broad Cove Banks	piper/ fiddler moved to Amherst, NS, b/o Alex Angus
MacIsaac, 'Red' Dougald		Antigonish County	piper/fiddler/step-dancer, moved to west coast of Newfoundland, ca. 1860.
MacIsaac, Hughie		South West Margaree	piper
MacIsaac, 'Red' Jimmy		Margaree	piper
MacIsaac, John		Judique	piper/fiddler
MacIsaac, John R.	1896-1915	Ben Eoin	piper, s/o Rory 'Shim', killed overseas
MacIsaac, Neil R.	d. 1971	Ben Eoin	piper, s/o Rory 'Shim'
MacKay, Kenneth		Scotsville	piper
MacIsaac Rory 'Shim'	b.1855	Ben Eoin	piper/fiddler
MacKenzie, Hughie		Rear Christmas Island	piper/fiddler/bard
MacKenzie, William		Centreville	piper
MacKinnon, Little Angus		Woodbine	piper
MacKinnon, Annie		East Lake Ainslie	piper/ fiddler, s/o Big Farquhar

Name	Dates	Place	Description
MacKinnon, David		Meat Cove	piper/fiddler
MacKinnon, Duncan		Meat Cove	piper, b/o Dave
MacKinnon, Big Farquhar	1834-1923	East Lake Ainslie	East Lake Ainslie
MacKinnon, 'Little Farquhar	1868-1941	East Lake Ainslie	piper
MacKinnon, Hector	1857-1943	Framboise	piper
MacKinnon, Hugh Fred		East Lake Ainslie	piper, b/o Little Farquhar
MacKinnon, Jimmy Alex		Framboise	piper/ step-dancer, moved to Boston
MacKinnon, J.J.		Lewis Bay West	piper/fiddler/Gaelic playwright
MacKinnon, Joe	1878-1963	Inverness	piper
MacKinnon, John	1869-1936	Inverness	piper, known as the "Burnt Piper," b/o Joe.
MacKinnon, John		East Lake Ainslie	piper/fiddler
MacKinnon, John	1894-1975	Framboise	piper, 185th Battalion
MacKinnon, John	b. 1808	Williams Point	piper
MacKinnon, "Red" John		Meat Cove	piper/fiddler, b/o Dave
MacKinnon, Jimmy Alex		Framboise	piper/ step-dancer, moved to Boston
MacKinnon, Michael		Woodbine	piper
MacKinnon, Peter	b. ca. 1897	Meat Cove	piper, b/o Michael
MacKinnon, Rory	1898-1968	Halifax	piper/story-teller
MacLachlan, John		Judique	piper
MacLean, (Father) Allan		Mull Cove	piper/fiddler/step-dancer
MacLean, Angus Hector		Orangedale	piper
MacLean, Hector	1874-1950	Boisdale	piper/fiddler
MacLean, John		Malagawatch	piper, known as Seanaidh Chaluim Ruaidh
MacLean, John Eddie	1878-1950	Scotsville	piper/fiddler
MacLean, John M.		Scotsville	piper/fiddler
MacLean, Murdoch		Stillwater	piper, drowned at sea
MacLean, Ronald		Foot Cape	piper and pipe maker, moved to Boston c. 1890
MacLean, Sandy		Salmon River	piper/fiddler
MacLean, Stephen		Egypt	piper
MacLellan, Angus		Egypt	piper
MacLellan, Archie A.	ca. 1834-1912	Judique	piper, 185th, killed by German sniper, November 11, 1918
MacLellan, Donald		Meat Cove	piper
MacLellan, Johnnie Archie		Egypt	piper and bagpipe maker
MacLellan, John H.		Upper Margaree	piper/fiddler
MacLellan, Neil		Meat Cove	piper
MacLellan, Sandy			piper

Name	Dates	Place	Notes
MacLellan, Vincent	1865-1935	Grand Mira	piper/fiddler/bard
MacLennan, James		Old Town	piper
Macleod, Daniel		Grand River	piper/fiddler moved to Bridgewater
MacLeod, Danny		Inverness County	piper, moved to New Waterford
MacLeod, Murdoch	1888-1931	Trenton	piper
MacLeod, Philip	1883-1968	Gabarus Lake	piper
MacMaster, Hector		Judique	piper/step- dancer
MacMaster, Hughie		Judique	piper
MacMillan, Andrew	b. ca. 1856	Glenmorrison	piper, s/o John, moved to Glace Bay
MacMillan, Angus	born 1865	Glenmorrison	piper, s/o John, moved to Reserve Mines
MacMillan, Annie		Grand Mira	piper, married John MacMillan, at Glen Morrison
MacMillan, Anthony		Glenmorrison	piper, s/o John, moved to Boston
MacMillan, J.J.	1876-1953	North Side Mira	piper, s/o John
MacMillan, John		East Bay	Marquis of Lorne's piper, 1878
MacMillan, Michael		Glenmorrison	piper, s/o John, died young
MacMillan, Murdoch	d. ca. 1940	Johnstown	piper/fiddler, grandson of Neil MacMillan, immigrant piper
MacMillan, Murdoch	1861	Glenmorrison	piper, s/o John, moved to New Glasgow
MacMillan, Patrick		East Bay	piper, died young
MacMullin, Alexander		Coxheath	piper
MacMullin, Annie	1843-1919	Boisdale	chanter player, (nee MacIntyre)
MacNeil, Alex Dan		St. Rose	piper/step-dancer
MacNeil, Capt. Angus J.		Gillis Point	piper, 94th Regiment
MacNeil, George	b. ca. 1818	Cape North area	piper, s/o pioneer MacNeil
MacNeil, Malcolm		Piper's Cove	piper
MacNeil, "Black" Peter		Piper's Cove	piper and pipe maker
MacNeil, Stephen B.	1851-1940	Gillis Point	moved to Port Hawkesbury
MacNeil, Tom P.	1877-1975	Piper's Cove	piper, moved to Glace Bay, s/o Peter
MacPhee, Dan Ranald		Cape North area	piper
MacPhee, E.		Nine Mile River	piper
MacPhee, Archie		French Road	piper
MacPhee, John Peter	b. 1886	Glen Morrison	piper, moved to Bridgeport ca. 1919
MacPhee, Norman		French Road	piper
MacPherson, Daniel		Louisbourg	piper
MacPherson, Hector		New Boston	piper/fiddler

Name	Location	Dates	Description
MacQuarrie, Angus Hector	Antigonish		piper
MacQuarrie, Dan	Antigonish		piper
MacQuarrie, "Red" Gordon	Dunakin	1897–1965	piper/fiddler, served with the Cape Breton Highlanders, WWII
MacQuarrie, Hector	Kenloch		piper, n/o "Big" Farquhar MacKinnon
MacQuarrie, Kenneth	Rear Port Hastings	1857–1902	piper, decapitated by a passing locomotive
Matheson, Daniel	River Denys		piper
Matheson, Dougal	River Denys		piper, went out west
Matheson, John Duncan		d. 1923	piper, died in Utah from pneumonia
Matheson, Kenneth	River Denys		piper/fiddler, played in Militia, 94th Regiment
Matheson Pipers	Spittle Hill	ca. 1900	A family of pipers Colchester County
Morrison, Dan	Blues Mills		piper, 25th Battalion, WWI, moved to Boston
Morrison, Jessie	Point Aconi	d. 1915	piper
Murray, Donald	Rogers Hill	1830–1899	piper
Nicholson, Angus	Skye Mountain	1911–1943	piper, s/o Sam Nicholson, 48th Highlanders, killed in England
Nicholson, Archie	Skye Mountain		piper, s/o Sam Nicholson
Nicholson, Donald "D.J."	Coire Mor,	1894–1917	piper, 185th Battalion, died from wounds
Nicholson, John	Boisdale		piper
Nicholson, Patrick			piper
Nicholson, Roddy	Gillanders Mountain	b. 1891	piper, b/o DJ , 185th, moved to Sydney
Nicholson, Samuel	Skye Mountain	1857–1936	piper/fiddler
Ross, Colin	Lime Hill		piper
Ross, Norman	Peter's Brook	1886–1940	piper, 48th Highlanders, WWI, moved to Whitney Pier
Ross, William	Cummings Mountain	1826–1915	piper, involved in local militia
Rumley, P.	Truro		piper 85th Battalion
Stewart, Daniel	Blue Mountain		piper
Stewart, Robert			piper
Sutherland, Alex	Earltown	1903–2001	piper, moved to Dartmouth
Sutherland, John	Earltown		piper/fiddler
Walker, Lauchie	Grand Mira		piper
Whyte, William	Canoe Lake	1891–1950	piper

APPENDIX C

The following is a list of known bagpipe makers in Nova Scotia from 1807-1940. * indicates the individual(s) made only one set of bagpipes. The information has been collected from personal interviews, newspaper articles and books mentioned in the bibliography.

Name	Years of Prodcution	Locality	Comments
Cameron, Dan	ca. 1900	Centreville	Turner Repaired bagpipes
Campbell, "Old" Fred	ca. 1900	Judique	Cabinet Maker, repaired bagpipes
Fraser, Thomas	ca. 1930	New Glasgow	Bagpipe Maker
Gillis, Allan "Turner"	ca. 1850	Grand Mira	Turner, Bagpipe Maker
Gillis, Duncan "Tailor"	ca. 1885-1920	Grand Mira	
Henderson, John R. H. *	ca. 1940	Camden/Truro	Worked with brother, John
Henderson, Roy *	ca. 1940	Camden/Truro	Made bagpipes and Violins, moved to Boston
MacDonald, John	ca. 1890	Centreville	
MacDonnell, Alexander "Mor"*	ca. 1860	Gleann Mor/ Big Glen	Made several sets of bagpipes
MacEachern, Fred	ca. 1890-1900	River Denys Mtn.	
MacIsaac, Alexander "Ban"*	ca. 1870	Giants Lake	Moved to British Columbia
MacIsaac, Dan Alex*	ca. 1930	Dunvegan	
MacKinnon, Rory	ca. 1920	Meat Cove	
MacKinnon, "Red" John *	ca. 1920	Meat Cove	
MacLean, Murdock *	ca. 1925	Trenton	Wood-carver, Moved to Boston
MacLean, Ronald *	ca. 1890	Stillwater/Louisburg	Carved bagpipes by hand
MacLellan, Johnnie Archie	ca. 1920	Meat Cove	
MacLeod, ?*	ca. 1910	Six Mile Brook/Pictou	Wood Turner
MacNeil, "Black" Peter	ca. 1890	Christmas Island	Wood Turner
Ross, Alexander	ca. 1840-1880	West Bay	Bagpipe Maker
Ross, Robert	ca. 1817-1843	Bayview/Pictou	Architect
West, W. H. *	ca. 1935	Hopewell/New Glasgow	

APPENDIX D

SONG TO DUNCAN GILLIS OF MIRA, A MAKER OF BAGPIPES

We received news a year ago
News which pleased and cheered me
News delightful to every Gael;
Who was brought up in this area:
Duncan Tailor of Upper Margaree
My dear handsome man
Is now making pipes in Mira-
Blessings on his bountiful hand!

In his youth he was brought up
In Upper Margaree
Among the kind and friendly Gaels
His relations there are many;
He loved that place well
He said to me this very Thursday,
"There is not a hill or dale or cairn there
Which is not dear to my heart today"

Said he to me; 'In my youth
In every group that congregated
Our custom was always
To sing songs with gusto;
Passing time cheerfully and happily
Dancing awhile on the chamber floor
While a toast went around
Which would banish sorrow from our minds.

And though I visit there today
I will be sad when I come over,
As I think on happy times
I once spent there;
Among the noble and kind people
Some of whom are now lost to the grave
While those few who survive
Have become slow of movement"

Blessings on his skilful hand
Noted for every task,
And on his intellect which produced
Much artistic beauty:
There will be no defect in his work
It will be shapely, firm and secure,
Small wonder as his people were
Adept and talented long ago!

Often was heard in battles
That noble music of the grandest tone,
To incite the kilted ones
When fighting grimly against an army;

In the castle, the chiefs would be
Cheerful and affectionate with their clansmen,
Invigorated by the chanter's music
Dancing close and nimble on the floor.

Many a very knowledgeable man
Praised your pipes in Mabou,
At the Exhibition where you earned
Much fame, so I heard;
Your musical instruments were so splendid
That as a result, before you parted
You sold one to Honourable Sam
And a couple in Margaree.

There is not a Gael in this place
But will gladly welcome you,
Dear, kindly, gracious man
You are renowned right now overseas;
Duncan Tailor I declare
I regard him as a courteous man,
Sensible of speech
Never inviting anger or reproach.

All those who made your acquaintance
Will desire your company,
You are learned but without arrogance,
Boastfulness or conceit of disposition;
Though I did not know you when I was young
I heard much from others,
And all I was told of your merits
I will never forget.

Many a tale of your fine qualities
I listened to in my day,
Which made me eager to meet you
Long before the time arrived;
You came over across the Narrows
I can attest to that,
Many a man in Upper Margaree
Praised your warm humanity.

Well does a suit of elegant cloth
Become your shapely, solid frame,
You who are truly without fault
Maker of most melodious pipes;
Listening to the skirl of one
Has inspired my mind to song;
You who set the mountings tightly on it
I wish you continued health.

APPENDIX E

A partial list of late nineteenth and early 20th-century immigrant Scottish pipers. The list has been compiled from local histories and personal interviews and does not include the names of piping instructors who taught on a weekly basis during the summer schools at the Gaelic College, St. Ann's.

Name	Year of immigration	Place of origin	Comments
Baillie, Catherine (MacLennan)	1901	Inverness	Loganville
Bowes, Alexander "Sandy"	ca. 1900		Glace Bay/ Louisburg
Boyd, Alexander Ross "Sandy"	ca. 1940	Ayrshire	itinerant piper / piping teacher
Cant, James	ca. 1901	Broughty Ferry	Boston/ Halifax
Carson, John "Jock"	ca. 1920	Greenock	Boston/ Cape Breton
Cooper, George	ca. 1914	?	Halifax/ Truro
George Dey	1906	Bonniebridge,	Halifax
Gillies, Alex	1905	Moidart	Port Hood, b/o Allan
Gillies, Allan	1905	Moidart	Port Hood, b/o Alex
Jamieson, John "Jock"	1926	Musselburgh	Glace Bay/ Donkin
Lavery, Arthur	ca. 1910	Scotland	Sydney Mines
Manson, David	1895	Ross-shire	Halifax
MacKay, P/M James	1923	Tongue	Annapolis Valley
MacLeod, Major Calum I.N.	1949		Cape Breton/ Antigonish
John Muir	1928		Glace Bay/ Valley Mills
Patterson, John "Jock"	1856		Dartmouth
Russell, Alexander "Sandy"	ca. 1910	Dundee	Inverness Town
Thomson, Duncan	1896	Jedburgh	Halifax, s/o Robert, Sr.
Thomson, James	1896	Jedburgh	Halifax, s/o Robert, Sr.
Thomson, Robert, Junior	1896	Jedburgh	Halifax, s/o Robert, Sr.
Thomson, Robert, Senior	1896	Galashields	Halifax
White, Alexander	ca. 1900	Scotland	New Glasgow, s/o John
White, John	ca. 1900	Scotland	New Glasgow
Wilson, P/M William Leaske "Tug"	ca. 1910		New Glasgow

APPENDIX F

A Guide to Dance Music for the Great Highland Bagpipe

Tune Type	Time Signature	Metric Accent	Phrase pattern	Tempo (BPM)
Slow Strathspey	4/4 or C Simple Time	4 beats to the bar: Strong/ Weak/ Weak/medium	Usually one bar phrases	108–120
Competition Strathspey	Written as 4/4 Simple Time, but played closer to a 12/8 or Compound Rhythm	4 beats to the bar: Strong/ Weak/ Medium/ Weak	Usually two bar phrases	104
Dance Strathspey	4/4 or C played with a bouncy, song-like Rhythm Simple Time	4 beats to the bar: Strong/ Strong Equal weight to the off-beat	Usually one bar phrases	140–164
Competition Reel	2/2 or Split Common C Simple Time	2 beats to the bar Strong/ Weak	Usually two bar phrases	108–112
Step-dance Reel	2/2 or Split Common C Simple Time	2 beats to the bar Strong/Weak	Usually one bar phrases	116–120
Competition Jig	6/8, 9/8, 12/8 Compound Time	2 beats to the bar: Strong/Weak	Usually two bar phrases	120
Dance Jig	6/8, 9/8, 12/8 Compound Time	2 beats to the bar: Strong/Weak	Usually one bar phrases	118–120

Fingering styles

Many of the pipers featured on this featured in the recordings accompanying this book (see appendix G, page 218), used a fairly standard fingering style but pipers such as Rory MacKinnon, Jimmy MacArthur and Alex Currie played in what can best be described as a free style. This free style consists of some notes played with a single finger and notes on the top hand of the chanter played with two or more fingers of the bottom hand off the chanter entirely. There is historical evidence to support this style of piping in 19th-century Scotland. In William Donaldson's book *The Bagpipe and Highland Society, 1750-1950* there is a reference to a competitive piper being penalized by a local piping judge for keeping several fingers off the chanter while playing particular notes.

Pipers such as Joe Hughie MacIntyre played a bagpipe scale similar to the one described by Joseph MacDonald in his treatise on bagpipe music compiled in 1760. Perhaps the differences in fingering technique between these players highlights the differences between those unschooled pipers and those who attended one of the piping colleges before their demise in the late 18th century. In Scotland the free-handed style of playing was frowned upon and any one who played in this fashion, despite his or her musicality, was often referred to by the derogatory term "Tinker Piper."

Gracenotes and Embellishments

There was a wide range of gracenotes and embellishments or doublings (sometimes called cuttings) used by Cape Breton pipers. These included doublings on B and C melody notes performed with two D gracenotes instead of the modern doublings which require a G and D gracenote to obtain the doubling effect. Many of the old style players could not play the embellishment known as the birl, to perfection. Sandy Boyd said that his instructor, John MacColl, often referred to this embellishment as "a nasty Glasgow habit." The birl is performed by sliding the bottom finger of the bottom hand back and forth across the Low A hole of the chanter, in effect playing two Low A notes separated by two Low G gracenotes. Fiddlers also use this form of embellishment or cutting, but by using the bow they can perform this on any note of the violin. Pipers such as Rory MacKinnon and Alex Currie didn't play the 20th-century birl, but separated Low A notes by a series of G, D and E gracenotes to match the rhythmic structure of the tune.

Another embellishment used by pipers and also by fiddlers is the slur. It is produced by playing a quick note just below the melody note, usually ornamenting this movement with a single gracenote of higher pitch. Pipers in Cape Breton used this embellishment on the following notes: D, High G and High A.

During the 20th century the performance of two of these slurs were altered. The High A slur became a High A doubling and the D slur had Low G gracenotes added and this change transformed the embellishment to a grip (*leumluath*) or heavy throw on D.

Tunes

The tunes on the accompanying recordings represent a cross section of the piper's repertoire from marches to reels with particular emphasis on dance music. Marches such as "Leaving Glenurquhart" and "Millbank Cottage" were composed in the later half of the 19th century, while "Donald MacLean's Farewell to Oban" is a much more recent composition. As the recordings indicate, marches were played much rounder and faster in the first half of the 20th century and in the 19th century may have been used as dance music. The old "dance" tunes include classic melodies such as the strathspeys "Tulloch Gorum" and "Monymusk," which began as violin strathspeys and were adopted by pipers; and reels with a very old history such as "Lord MacDonald's," "The Reel of Tulloch," "Miss Proud," "The Night We had the Goats" and "The Black Mill." The various settings of the tune known as "The Reel of Tulloch," which survived in Maritime Canada, attest to popularity of the tune and provide further evidence of regional settings and performance styles.

The variations in individual tunes and reel settings played by the ear-learned pipers on the recordings are connected by the common threads of dance rhythm and tempo. It is interesting to compare the different settings of the strathspey "Tulloch Gorum" performed by both Jimmy MacArthur and Sandy Boyd. MacArthur's rounder interpretation is meant for step-dancing while Boyd's more pointed version is better suited for the competition platform.

Sources

Nova Scotia has produced dozens of bagpipe recordings in the past ninety years including solo pipers, pipe bands and folk groups. The sound samples featured on the accompanying recordings were taken from both professionally produced recordings prior to 1960 and amateur recordings so the sound quality is not of the standard capable from a modern recording studio. With the exception of Peter Morrison, all of the pipers featured on the Compact Disk were over the age of fifty when they were recorded and several of the pipers were in their sixties, seventies and eighties.

In addition to the bagpipe selections on the recordings are examples of three notable Cape Breton fiddlers: the late Donald MacLellan (1918-2003), the late John Willie Campbell (1928-ca. 1986) and Buddy MacMaster; and piano accompanists the late Marie MacLellan (d. 2006), Kevin MacCormack and Joan MacDonald Boes.

Bagpipe music has had a major influence on the fiddling traditions of Cape Breton. As the late Cape Breton fiddler Bill Lamey once noted

> It (the drone) helps, especially in Scottish music. We only have four strings anyway, so we've got to make the best of them. Of course what I try to do is emulate or imitate the pipes, especially in the reels when you have the chanter and you can hear the birls [cuttings] coming out. You don't have a chanter in this case: you have a bow and a fiddle. Without them (the embellishments or birls) the tune wouldn't sound like much.[1]

What better way to illustrate these close musical influences than by featuring a few examples of fiddlers playing tunes which are suitable for both instruments.

Note

1. The Music of Cape Breton: Cape Breton Scottish Fiddle. Topic Records. London; 1976. Accompanying Booklet p. 3.

APPENDIX G

Dance to the Piper: A Musical Anthology

Editor's note: Readers may access a free download of bagpipe tunes selected to accompany this book. The selections featured on the recordings have been collected as part of the author's research. We are grateful to the performers, composers and their heirs, and to those who hold the original recordings, for allowing their inclusion here. The recordings are included with the book for the purposes expressed and not for commercial use—it is not to be sold or copied. All rights reserved. U.S. and U.K. purchasers may download the recordings from: www.cbupress.ca/piper.

1. **Pipe Major Kenneth MacKenzie Baillie**, Marches: "PM George Ross' Farewell to the Black Watch" (Wm. Lawrie), "Miss Elspeth Campbell" (T. Douglas). Pictou County. Studio recording 1923, Victor 19107.

Baillie was a multi-instrumentalist who played violin, Highland bagpipes and *uillean* pipes. He learned to play the bagpipes while serving with the Royal Marine Artillery and while stationed in Glasgow during the 1880s. The major influence on his piping was his wife, Catherine and father-in-law, Pipe Major Sandy MacLennan, Inverness, Scotland. Features of his playing include a much rounder presentation of two classic bagpipe marches, modern playing of the birl at the end of each eight-bar measure of the tune. Baillie had lung cancer when this recording was made and was prevented from playing a full set of bagpipes opting instead for a set of bellow-blown pipes. He died the following year.

2. **Pipe Major Fraser Holmes**, Highland bagpipes. March, Strathspey, Reel: "Miss Elspeth Campbell" (T. Douglas), "Money Musk," "Lord MacDonald." New Glasgow. Studio recording ca. 1956, courtesy of the Holmes family.

Fraser Holmes and his father learned to play the bagpipes at the same time. They were inspired to learn to pipe from a relative, James Holmes Cameron. Fraser Holmes had some instruction from MacKenzie Baillie and over his lifetime he taught hundreds of pipers in the Pictou County area. What is presented here is the classic "March, Strathspey, Reel" (MSR) format.

3. **Pipe Major Roderick Nicholson** (1891-1979), Highland bagpipes. March: "Millbank Cottage" (W.D. Dumbreck). Sydney. Studio recording ca. 1949, courtesy of the Patterson family.

Roddie was originally from Gillander's Mountain, Victoria County. He learned to play the bagpipes as a youth, receiving instruction from MacKenzie Baillie and several army pipers in Scotland during the First World War. He was the first piping instructor at the Gaelic College in St. Ann's, Victoria County, and taught several pipers in the Sydney area. This recording was one of several made for a short film on Scottish culture in Nova Scotia by the National Film Board of Canada in 1949 and presented to Pipe Major Nicholson.

4. **Alex Sutherland**, Highland bagpipes. March: "Leaving Glenurquhart" (Wm. MacDonald). Dartmouth. Home recording ca. 1980, courtesy of the late Alex Sutherland.

Alex Sutherland was inspired to learn the bagpipes as a boy after hearing a local piper, John Sutherland, playing the bagpipes in the back of a wagon in Earltown, Colchester County, just before the First World War. In order to learn the bagpipe Alex Sutherland moved in with the Baillie's over the winter months and performed farm chores in exchange for piping lessons. Alex's son, Gordon, was the founder of the Dartmouth Boy's Pipe Band.

5. **Peter Morrison**, Highland bagpipes. Slow March and March: "Loch Rannoch" (John Wilson), "The Day We Crossed the Ferry" (A. Cameron). Sydney. Recording courtesy of Theresa Morrison.

Peter Morrison was a fluent Gaelic-speaker whose ancestors came from South Uist in the 1830s and settled at an area known as Glen Morrison. Peter was a piping student of PM Roddie Nicholson and several of Peter's relatives played the bagpipe.

6. **Sandy Boyd** (1907-1982), Highland bagpipes. March, Strathspey, Reels: "Colonel Stockwell," "*Tulloch Gorum*," "The Grey Bob" (trad.), "Malcolm the Tailor" (trad.), "Mrs. Macleod of Raasay" (trad.). Sydney. Home recording 1972.

Sandy was piping student of John MaColl and Duncan Grant and he had additional lessons in piobaireachd from Robert Reid. He left an indelible mark on Nova Scotia's piping traditions in the second half of the 20th century and a few of his students went on to teach piping and adjudicate competitions across the province.

7. **Duncan MacIntyre**. March and Strathspey: "The 71st Highlanders Quickstep" (H. MacKay), "The Pipers Bonnet" (trad.). Sydney. Home recording ca. 1970.

Duncan MacIntyre was Joe Hughie MacIntyre's younger brother but, as can be heard, his playing is quite different. This recording shows significant 20th-century influences represented by a competition style march and strathspey. Duncan was a member of the North Nova Scotia Highlanders during the Second World War and attended piping courses in Scotland with Pipe Major Willie Ross, one of the most influential Scottish pipers of the 20th century.

8. **Duncan MacIntyre**. Strathspey and Reels: Unknown strathspey, "Reel of Tulloch," "Bessie MacIntyre" (W. MacLean), "The Bridge of Bogie" (R. Meldrum). Home recording ca. 1972.

On this track Duncan plays a strathspey and group of lively reels. Notice the use of the Crunluath movement in the "Reel of Tulloch."

9. **Joe Hughie MacIntyre**, Highland bagpipes, Marie MacLellan, piano. March: "Donald MacLean's Farewell to Oban (A. MacNeill)." Recording courtesy of the MacIntyre family.

10. **"Big" Donald MacLellan**, violin, Marie MacLellan piano. March: "Donald MacLean's Farewell to Oban" (A. MacNeill). Recording courtesy of Theresa MacLellan and Dave MacIsaac.

Donald and Marie MacLellan belonged to a family of musicians which included their father Ranald MacLellan, and sister and brother, Theresa and Joe MacLellan.

11. **John Willie Campbell**, violin, Kevin MacCormack, piano. March: "Donald MacLean's Farewell to Oban" (A. MacNeill). Recording courtesy of Tony Engle, Topic Records, U.K.

Campbell was from Glencoe, Inverness County and he had a large repertoire of tunes played in a style known as "High Bass". The 'High Bass' or *Scordatura* tuning of a violin (which normally tunes G/D/A/E) is achieved by tuning the G string to A and the D string to E resulting in A/E/A/E configuration. This tuning technique allows the player to use open strings to produce a "droning" sound on tunes played in the key of A. The effect, as can be heard on Track 10, is quite dramatic and the overall sound is reminiscent of a set of bagpipes.

12. **Alex Currie** (1910-1997), A visit with Alex Currie, 1996: Discussing the tune "*Sid Mar Chaidh an Càl a Dholaid*" (That's How the Cabbage was Boiled). Frenchvale.

Alex's forbears were from South Uist. Alex learned to play the bagpipe as a youth from his father and mother. Alex Currie had a very unique style of playing and sadly no one today plays this particular style. He didn't play grips or *leumluaths* and sometimes substituted G,D,E gracenotes on three Low A notes in succession by playing a very open birl or double strike with the bottom finger of the bottom hand. He, like several other pipers in Cape Breton, did play the *piobaireachd* embellishment known as the 'Dre' in his light music. My visits with Alex usually started with me playing one or two tunes on the chanter and this would stimulate his memory and result in a cascade of tunes and stories.

13. **Alex Currie**, Highland bagpipes. Reels: "*Am Muilean Dubh*" (The Black Mill), "*Buntata Charach*" (The Gnarly Potato), "*An Oidche bha na Gobhair Again*" (The Night We had the Goats). Home recording 1973, courtesy of Alex Currie.

14. **Jimmy MacArthur**, Highland bagpipes. (home recording c. 1971). "*Tulloch Gorum*," "Reel of Tulloch." Cornerbrook, Newfoundland. Recording courtesy of Margaret Bennett and the MacArthur family.

This selection was originally collected by Scottish folklorist, Margaret Bennett, during her field work on the west coast of Newfoundland in the 1970s. Jimmy learned piping from his father, Allan MacArthur, who in turn learned from his uncle Dan MacIsaac. Both of these families were late immigrants from Scotland, the MacArthurs coming from the isle of Canna and the MacIsaacs from Moidart. These families left Cape Breton in the 1860s and settled in the Codroy River area of Newfoundland. "*Tulloch Gorum*" and the "Reel of Tulloch" are both very old tunes. Notice the use of gracenotes and the absence of taorluaths or grips.

15. **Joe Hughie MacIntyre**, Highland bagpipes, Marie MacLellan, piano. Reel: "Miss Proud." Grand Mira. Recording courtesy of the MacIntyre family.

Joe Hughie MacIntyre was descended from Scottish immigrants from South Uist who settled at French Road around 1828.

16. **Buddy MacMaster**, violin, Joan MacDonald Boes, piano. Toronto. Reel: "Miss Proud." Recording courtesy of Buddy MacMaster and Dave MacIsaac.

Buddy MacMaster is one of the most respected violinists in the Cape Breton fiddling tradition. This short recording is presented with the performance of the same tune played by Joe Hughie MacIntyre to illustrate the close relationship between Gaelic-influenced bagpipe and violin dance music.

17. **Rory MacKinnon**, Highland bagpipes. Reels: "A Cape North Reel," "The Reel of Tulloch." Sugarloaf, Cape Breton, ca. 1959.Recording courtesy of Helen Creighton.

Rory was descended from Skye pioneers who settled first at Inverness but later moved to the Meat Cove / Bay St. Lawrence area of Cape Breton. His father, Sandy, and three brothers were pipers and another brother, Angus "Mossy" MacKinnon, was an exceptional step-dancer.

18. **Barry Shears**, Highland bagpipes, Tracey Dares-MacNeil, piano, Patrick Gillis, guitar, The Young Mabou Dancers. Scotch Four Dance, Strathpey and Reels: "Devil in the Kitchen" (trad.), "*Am Muilean Dubh*" (The Black Mill. Trad. Arr. B. Shears), "*Ruidhle Nan Innseanach*" (The Mi'kmaq Reel. Trad. Arr. B. Shears). Recorded live, Strathspey Place, Mabou, Cape Breton, October 7, 2007. Recording courtesy of Linda Rankin, Strathspey Place, Mabou.

One of the many immigrant dances brought from Scotland to Nova Scotia was the "Scotch four." It is performed by two couples, dancing to a strathspey and several reels, and was often used as a wedding dance. During the early 20th century the performance of this dance declined in many areas of Cape Breton but in the last few decades it has seen a revival.

Unpublished Sources

Dalhousie University Archives, Halifax, Nova Scotia

MS2/82-T-I-A-I, Archibald MecMechan Papers. Anonymous article, "John MacKay ... The Blind Piper of Gairloch."

National Archives of Scotland

MacLaine of Lochbuy papers. (NAS)GD174/2106/2.

MacLean, Dr. John. Letter to Captain John Grant regarding the Gairloch MacKays. Online. Available: http://195.153/dservea/cgi-bin/cidletcl.exe.

National Archives of Canada

RG 80, C Series, Vol. 1908.

Nova Scotia Archives and Records Management (NSARM)

NSARM, microfilm, reel# 1344. Information on Ronald MacLean, bagpipe maker. *Sydney Post.* March 23, 1905.

NSARM, AR, 2693. Thomas Raddall and James D. Gillis. CBC interview, 1945.

NSARM, MG 01, vol. 2016, # 35.

NSARM, MG 20674 7. Squire John MacKay, J. P. *Reminiscences of a Long Life.*

NSARM, microfilm, reel# 4628. "Death Claims Pipe Major Who Won World Fame." *Pictou Advocate*, 18 April 1924, 9.

NSARM, C.O. 217/146. Sir James Kempt to Wilmot Horton, 14 September 1826.

Public Archives of Nova Scotia (PANS)

John Wyte, Surgeon, to R. D. George, Sydney, 19 December 1827.

Interviews

Bonnar, Florence, Bay St. Lawrence, Victoria County, telephone interview, 24 October 1998.
Cameron, Allan, Antigonish, NS, personal interview, November 1986.
Campbell, Mac., Port Hawkesbury, NS, telephone interview, May 2001.
Carey, Frank. Interview by Ken Grant, Halifax, NS. 1974.
Currie, Alex, Frenchvale, Cape Breton County, personal interview, 1995.
Fortune, Dan, Glendale, NS, personal interview, April 1999.
Grant, Ken, Halifax, NS, telephone interview, 11 October 2004.
MacBeth, Sandy, Riverton, Pictou County, personal interview, 2000.
MacDonald, Albert, Melfort, Inverness County, telephone interview, 1998.
MacDonald, Archie, Grand River, Richmond County, personal interview, 1997.
MacKenzie, Archie, Halifax, NS, personal interview, 27 May 1987.
MacKinnon, Dave, Bay St. Lawrence, Victoria County, personal interview, 10 July 1992.
MacIntyre, Danny, Sydney, Cape Breton County, personal interview, 1988.

MacIntyre, Gussie, Grand Mira, Cape Breton County, personal interview, 15 March 2002.
MacIntyre, Paddy, Grand Mira South, Cape Breton County, personal interview, 15 March 2002.
MacLeod, John Willie. Dartmouth, NS, personal interview, February 2000.
MacNeil, Hector, Sydney River, Cape Breton County, telephone interview, 6 December 2004.
MacPherson, Fred, Marion Bridge, Cape Breton County, telephone interview, 9 August 2002.
Matheson, Alex, River Denys, Inverness County, personal interview, July, 2001.
Matheson, Billy, River Denys, Inverness County, personal interview, July, 2001.
Morrison, Peter, Sydney, Cape Breton County, personal interview,1986.
Severence, Arthur, Fourchu, Richmond County, 1989.
Sutherland, Alex, Dartmouth, NS, personal interview, 1987.

Personal Correspondence

MacDonald, Archie. Grand River, Cape Breton
MacDougall, Duncan. Sydney, Cape Breton
Sanger, Keith, Edinburgh, Scotland
Smith, Randy, Halifax, NS

Published Sources

Discography

The Music of Cape Breton, Volume 2, Cape Breton Scottish Fiddle. Topic Records, London: 1976

Ross Farewell to the Black Watch March. Elspeth Campbell, et al. Pipe Major Kenneth McKenzie Baillie. 1923. Victor 19107.

Internet Sources

Haurin and Richens. "Irish Step Dancing: A Brief History." http://www.indyirishdancers.org/irhist.htm.

"The Making of America." Cornell University. http://cdl.library.cornell.edu

Pictou County Census, 1838, Online. Available: http://www.rootsweb.com/~nspictou/.

Traditional Scottish songs. «Wi a Hundred Pipers an a', an' a'.» http://www.rampantscotland.com/songs/blsongs_100.htm

Newspapers and Journals

Acadian Recorder 12 July 1828.
American Anthropologist 63. Conrad Arensburg "The Community as Object and as a Sample," April 1961, 241-64.
"Bagpipes were an early part of Pictou County's History." *New Glasgow Evening News.* N.d., n.p.
"A Short History and Photographic Record of the 185th Battalion," *Cape Breton Highlanders Overseas, CEF.* Mortimer, 1916, 3. (NSARM F105,N85).
Celtic Heritage 9, no. 5, 1995, "Makers of Gaelic Poetry."
The Chronicle Herald. 18 April 1973, n.p. (NSARM MG 01, Vol. 2016, # 35).
Eastern Chronicle. 13 September 1866, 2.
The National Geographic Magazine, 77, no. 5, 1940, 575-624.
New Glasgow Evening News. 4 February 1971, 9.
New Glasgow Evening News. 4 January 1973, n.p. (NSARM MG 01, Vol. 2016, # 35).
Pictou Advocate, 3 March 1922, 1; 18 April 1924, 9.
Piping Times, January, 1995, 15-17.

Sydney Post. 23 March 1905.

Toronto Star Weekly. 12 January 1929. Reprinted in *The Clansman*. June/July 1991, 9, 43, 44.

Books

Adam, Frank. *Clans, Septs and Regiments of the Scottish Highlands*. London: Johnstone and Bacon, 1908. Reprint, New York: Cassell & Collier Macmillan, 1975.

Adams, Ian, and Meredith Somerville. *Cargoes of Despair and Hope: Scottish Emigration to North America, 1603-1803*. Edinburgh: John Donald, 1993.

Anderson, Eleanor L. *Broughton: Cape Breton's Ghost Town*. Sydney: Nova Scotia, n.d.

Annals of the North British Society: Halifax, Nova Scotia, with Portraits and Geographical Notes: 1924-1949. Halifax: Imperial Press, 1949.

Baines, Anthony. *Bagpipes*. Oxford: Oxford University Press, 1960.

Beaton, Meaghan. "The Canso Causeway: Regionalism, Reconstruction, Representations, and Results." MA thesis, Saint Mary's University, 2001.

Bennett, Margaret. *The Last Stronghold*. St. Johns: Breakwater Books Ltd., 1989. Online as "Step-dancing: Why we must learn from past mistakes." http://www.siliconglen.com/ scotfaq/10_3.html

Bitterman, Rusty. "The Hierarchy of the Soil: Land and Labour in a Nineteenth Century Cape Breton Community." *Acadiensis* 18 (Fall 1988): 33-55.

Brander, M. *The Emigrant Scots*. London: Constable, 1982.

––––––. *The Scottish Highlanders and Their Regiments*. London: Seeley, Service and Company, 1971.

Brookes, Alan A. "Out-migration from the Atlantic Provinces 1880-1900." In *Acadiensis Reader: Volume Two*, 34-63. Fredericton, NB: Acadiensis, 1985.

Bruford, Alan. "The Rise of the Highland Piper." Unpublished expanded version of a talk given to the International Celtic Congress, Oxford, 1983.

Bumsted, J. M. *The People's Clearance: Highland Emigration to British North America*. Winnipeg: University of Manitoba Press, 1982.

The Caleodnian Club of San Fransico: The First Hundred Years, n.p., 1966. N.p.

Cameron, James M. *Pictonians in Arms, A Military History of Pictou County*. Published by the author through arrangement with the University of New Brunswick, Fredericton, 1969.

––––––. *More About New Glasgow*. Kentville: Kentville Publishing, 1974.

Campbell, Alexander. *Albyn's Anthology or a Select Collection of the Melodies & Vocal Poetry Peculiar to Scotland & The Isles Hitherto Unpublished*. Edinburgh: Oliver and Boyd, 1816. Reprint, Norwood, PA: 1976.

Campbell, Archibald. "The Highland Bagpipe." *Piping Times* 14, no. 11 (August 1962), 6-9.

––––––. "The History and Art of Angus MacKay" in *Piping Times*, 2, no. 5 (February 1950), 8-9.

––––––. "The History and Art of Angus MacKay" in *Piping Times*, 2, no. 6 (March 1950), 8-10.

––––––. *The Kilberry Book of Ceòl Mór*, 3rd edition. Glasgow: John Smith & Son, on behalf of the Piobaireachd Society, 1969.

––––––. "The MacGregor Pipers of the Clann an Sgeulaiche." *Piping Times* 2, nos. 10-12 (July 1950), 5-6.

––––––. "The MacGregor Pipers of the Clann an Sgeulaiche." *Piping Times* 2, nos. 10-12 August 1950), 12-13.

––––––. "The MacGregor Pipers of the Clann an Sgeulaiche." *Piping Times* 2, nos. 10-12 (September 1950), 5-6.

Campbell, D., and R. A. MacLean. *Beyond the Atlantic Roar: A Study of the Nova Scotia Scots*. Toronto: McClelland and Stewart, 1974.

Campbell, Jeannie. *Highland Bagpipe Makers*. Glasgow: Magnus Orr Publishing, 2001.

Campbell, John Francis. *Popular Tales of the West Highlands Orally Collected with a Translation*, 4 vols. Edinburgh, 1860, 1862.

––––––. *Canntaireachd: Articulate Music, dedicated to the Islay Association, by J.F. Campbell, Iain Ileach. 14th August, 1880*. Glasgow: Archibald Sinclair, 1880. Facsimile edition. Edinburgh, 1989.

Campbell, John Gregorson. *Witchcraft and Second Sight in the Highlands and Islands of Scotland*. Glasgow: James MacLehose and Sons, 1902.

Campbell, John Lorne, ed. and trans. *Hebridean Folksong: A Collection of Waulking Songs by David MacCormick*. Tunes transcribed by Francis Collinson. Oxford and Toronto: Clarendon Press, 1969.

———. *Hebridean Folksong, 2, Waulking Songs from Barra, South Uist, Eriskay and Benbecula*. Tunes transcribed by Francis Collinson. Oxford and Toronto: Clarendon Press, 1969.

———, ed. *Songs Remembered in Exile - Traditional Gaelic Songs from Nova Scotia Recorded in Cape Breton and Antigonish County in 1937 with an Account of the Causes of Hebridean Emigration, 1970-1835*. Most tunes transcribed by Seamus Ennis. Aberdeen: Aberdeen University Press, 1990.

Campey, Lucille H. *"A Very Fine Class of Immigrants", Prince Edward Island's Scottish Pioneers, 1770-1850*. Toronto: Natural Heritage/ Natural History, 2001.

———. *After the Hector*. Toronto: Natural Heritage/ Natural History, 2004.

Campsie, Alistair Keith. *The MacCrimmon Legend - The Madness of Angus MacKay*. Edinburgh: Canongate Publishing, 1980.

Cannon, Roderick. *Joseph MacDonald's Compleat Theory of the Scots Highland Bagpipe*. N.p.: The Piobaireachd Society, 1994.

———. *The Highland Bagpipe and its Music*. Edinburgh: John Donald Publishers Ltd., 1995.

———. *A Bibliography of Bagpipe Music*. Edinburgh: John Donald Publishers Ltd., 1980.

Caplan, Ron. *Talking Cape Breton Music: Conversations with People Who Love and Make the Music*. Halifax, NS: Nimbus, 2006.

———, ed. *Cape Breton's Lillian Crewe Walsh: A Treasury of Ballads and Poems*. Sydney, NS: Breton Books, 2006.

Cheape, Hugh. "The Piper to the Laird of Grant." *Proceedings of the Society of Antiquaries of Scotland* 125, (1995): 4-10.

———. "Portraiture in Piping." *Scottish Pipe Band Monthly*, no. 6 (January 1988): 1163-73.

———. *The Book of the Bagpipe*. Chicago: Contemporary Books, 2000.

———. "The Making of Bagpipes in Scotland." *From the Stone Age to the Forty-Five*, edited by Anne O'Connor and D. V. Clark, 596-615. Edinburgh: John Donald, 1983.

Cheska, Alyce Taylor. "The Antigonish Highland Games: A Community's Involvement in the Scottish Festival of Eastern Canada." *Nova Scotia Historical Review* 3, no. 1 (1983): 51-63.

Collinson, Francis. *The Bagpipe: The History of a Musical Instrument*. London and Boston: Routledge & Kegan Paul, 1975.

———. *The Great Highland Bagpipe*. N.p., n.d.

Cooke, Peter. "Text, Transcriptions and Notes." In *George Moss, Scottish Tradition*, with accompanying cassette, *"Scottish Tradition Cassette Series 6, Piobroch."* Edinburgh: School of Scottish, University of Edinburgh, 1982.

Cox, Lori Vitale. "Gaelic and the Schools in Cape Breton." *Nova Scotia Historical Review* 14, part 2 (1994): 21-22.

Creighton, Helen, and Calum MacLeod, eds. *Gaelic Songs in Nova Scotia*. Reprint, Ottawa: National Museums of Canada, 1979.

Cromb, James. *The Highland Brigade: Its Battles and Its Heroes*. Edited and brought down to the end of the Boer War, 1902, by David L. Cromb. Stirling: Eneas MacKay, 1902.

Dalyell, Sir John Graham. *Musical Memoirs of Scotland, with Historical Annotations*. Edinburgh, 1849.

Davey, William, and Richard MacKinnon. "Nicknaming Patterns and Traditions Among Cape Breton Coal Miners," *Acadiensis* 30, (Spring 2001): 71-83.

Dickson, Joshua. "The Piping Tradition of South Uist." PhD thesis, Edinburgh University, 2001.

Dorian, Nancy. *Language Death, The Life Cycle of a Scottish Gaelic Dialect*. Philadelphia: University of Pennsylvania Press, 1981.

Donaldson, William. *The Highland Pipe and Scottish Society, 1750-1950*. East Lothian, Scotland: Tuckwell Press, 2000.

Donovan, Ken. ed. *The Island: New Perspectives on Cape Breton History, 1713-1990*. Sydney, NS: University College of Cape Breton Press, 1990.

Duncanson, John Victor. *Rawdon and Douglas: Two Loyalist Townships in Nova Scotia.* Belleville, ON: Mika Publishing, 1989.

Dunlay, Kate, and David Greenberg. *Traditional Celtic Violin Music of Cape Breton.* Published privately by Kate Dunlay and David Greenberg, 1996.

Dunn, Charles. *Highland Settler, A Portrait of the Scottish Gael in Nova Scotia.* Reprint, Toronto: University of Toronto Press, 1971.

Dwelly, Edward. *The Illustrated Gaelic-English Dictionary.* 7th ed. Glasgow: Gairm Publications, 1971.

Emmerson, George S. *Rantin' Pipe and Tremblin' String, a History of Scottish Dance Music.* Montreal: McGill-Queen's University Press, 1972.

Farnham, C. H. "Cape Breton Folk," *Harper's New Monthly Magazine,* vol. 72, no. 427 (December 1885), 607-622.

Fergusson, Donald A., ed. *Fad air falbh as Innse Gall leis comh chruinneachadh Cheap Breatunn (Beyond the Hebrides).* Halifax, NS: Printers Lawson Graphics Atlantic, 1977.

———. *From the Farthest Hebrides.* Toronto: MacMillan of Canada, 1978.

———. *The Hebridean Connection.* Halifax: Donald Fergusson, 1984.

Flett, J. F., and T. M. Flett. *Traditional Dancing in Scotland.* London: Routledge and Kegan Paul, 1964.

Flood, William Gratton. *The Story of the Bagpipe.* London: n.p., 1911.

Forbes, E. R., and D. A. Muise, eds. *The Atlantic Provinces in Confederation.* Toronto: University of Toronto Press, 1993.

Foster, Gilbert, *Language and Poverty: The Persistence of Scottish Gaelic in Eastern Nova Scotia.* St John's: Memorial University of Newfoundland, 1988.

Frank, D. "The Cape Breton Coal Industry and the Rise and Fall of the British Empire Steel Corporation." In *Cape Breton Historical Essays,* edited by Don MacGillivray and Brian Tennyson, 110-32. Sydney, NS: College of Cape Breton Press, 1980.

Frank, David. *J.B. McLachlan: A Biography.* Toronto: James Lorimer & Company Ltd., 1999.

"Gaelic in Nova Scotia." *The Dalhousie Review* 30, no. 3 (October 1950): 252-260.

Gibson, John G. "Genealogical and Piping Notes from 'Squire' John MacKay's 'Reminiscences of a Long Life (ca. 1794-1884)." *The Scottish Genealogist Quarterly Journal of the Scottish Genealogy Society* 30, no. 3 (September 1983): 94-98.

———. "Piper John MacKay and Roderick McLennan: A Tale of Two Immigrants." *Nova Scotia Historical Review* 2, no. 2 (December 1892): 69-82.

———. "Mabou in Its Halcyon Days." "Sunflower" (insert of the *Scotia Sun* weekly newspaper), Port Hawkesbury, NS, 19 May 1982.

———. *Traditional Highland Bagpiping, 1745-1945.* Montreal: McGill-Queen's University Press, 1998.

———. *Traditional Gaelic Bagpiping, 1745-1945.* Montreal: McGill-Queens University Press, 2000.

———. *Old and New World Highland Bagpiping.* Montreal: McGill-Queen's University Press, 2002

Gillis, Allan. "From Kitchens to Pipebands Alex 'the piper' MacDonald - piper of transition." *Am Braighe* (Summer 1993): 20-2.

Gillis, James D. *A Little Sketch of My Life.* Halifax, NS: N.p., n.d.

Gillis, Malcolm Hugh. *Smeorach nan Cnoc's nan Gleann: The Songster pf the Hills and the Glens: The Collected Works of Malcolm H. Gillis.* Compiled by Bernard Gillis, et al. N.p., 1939. Reprinted with foreword by Rannie Gillis. North Sydney, NS: n.p., 2004.

Gillis, R. *Stray Leaves from Highland History.* Sydney: Published privately, 1918.

Glen, David. *The Music of the Clan MacLean Compiled and Arranged under the Auspices of the Clan MacLean Association and Dedicated to Colonel Sir Fitzroy Donald MacLean, Bart. C.B. Chief of the Clan.* Edinburgh: David Glen, 1900.

———. *David Glen's Collection of Highland Bagpipe Music.* Edinburgh: David Glen, 1876.

Gordon, Seton Paul. *Hebridean Memories.* London: Cassell and Co., 1923.

———. *Highland Summer.* London: Cassell and Co., 1971.

Grant, I. F. *The Clan Donald.* Reprint, Edinburgh: Johnston and Bacon Publishers, 1979.

Graham, Glenn. *The Cape Breton Fiddle: Making and Maintaining Tradition.* Sydney: Cape Breton University Press, 2006.

Gunn, William. *The Caledonian Repository of Music.* Glasgow: William Gunn, 1848.

Harper, J. Ralph. *The 78th Fighting Frasers, A Short History of the Old 78th Regiment of Fraser's Highlanders 1757-1763.* Chomedey, PQ: Devsco Publishing, 1966.

Hawkins, Marjorie (MacKenzie), Hector L. MacKenzie and John R. MacQuarrie. *Gairloch, Pictou County, Nova Scotia.* N.p.: N.p., 1977.

Henderson, Diana M. *Highland Soldier: A Social Study of Highland Regiments, 1820-1920.* Edinburgh: John Donald Publishers Ltd, 1989.

Hornsby, Stephen. :Scottish Emigration and Settlement in Nineteenth Century Cape Breton." In *The Island: New Perspectives on Cape Breton History 1713-1990,* edited by Kenneth Donovan, 49-49. Sydney, NS: University College of Cape Breton Press, 1990.

Hornby, Susan. *Celts and Ceilidhs,* n.p. Prince Edward Island: n.p., n.d.

Hunt, M. S. 1920. *Nova Scotia's Part in the Great War.* Halifax, NS: The Nova Scotia Veteran Publishing Company.

Hunter, James. *A Dance Called America.* Edinburgh: Mainstream Publishing, 1998.

Hunter, J. *The Fiddle Music of Scotland,* Edinburgh: W&R Chambers Ltd., 1979.

Hutchison, Col. Paul. *Canada's Black Watch: The First Hundred Years, 1862-1962.* Montreal: Black Watch (RHR) of Canada, 1962. Reprint, 1987.

Johnson, Samuel. *A Journey to the Western Islands of Scotland.* Introduction and notes by J. D. Fleeman. Oxford: Clarendon Press, 1985.

Johnston, Reverend A. A. *A History of the Catholic Church in Eastern Nova Scotia,* 2 vols. Antigonish, NS: Saint Francis Xavier University Press, 1960, 1971.

Kirincich, Stephen M.. *A Centennial History of Stellarton.* Antigonish, NS: Scotia Design Publications, 1990.

Kennedy, Michael. *Gaelic Nova Scotia: An Economic, Cultural, and Social Impact Study.* Halifax: Nova Scotia Museum, 2002.

Lamb, James. *The Celtic Crusader: The Story of A.W.R. MacKenzie and the Gaelic College.* Hantsport, NS: Lancelot Press Limited, 1992.

Logan, James. *The Scottish Gael; or, Celtic Manners, as Preserved among the Highlanders.* 2 vols. London: N.p., 1831.

MacDonald, Alexander (Dall Mor). *The Uist Collection: The Poems and Songs of John MacCodrum, Archibald MacDonald and some of the Minor Uist Bards.* Glasgow: Archibald Sinclair, 1894.

MacDonald, Clyde F. *Sunny Brae: A Village since 1802.* Pictou: Advocate Printing and Publishing, 2002.

MacDonald, Reverend D. *Cape North and Vicinity: Pioneer Families History and Chronicles including Pleasant Bay, Bay St. Lawrence, Aspy Bay, White Point, New Haven and Neil's Harbour.* N.p., N.p., 1933.

MacDonald, Hugh N. *MacDonald and MacKinnon Families (A Biographical Sketch).* Handwritten manuscript, dated 21 August 1937. Privately held, East Lake Ainslie, Nova Scotia.

MacDonald, Hugh N. *MacDonald and MacKinnon Families (A Biographical Sketch).* 2nd ed. Truro, NS: N.p., 1937.

MacDonald, J. M. "Piping in Cape Breton." *Piping Times* 21, no. 2 (November 1968), 8-12.

MacDonald, Keith N. *MacDonald Bards from Medieval Times.* Glasgow: Alex MacFarlane and Sons, 1900.

MacDonald, Patrick. *A Collection of Highland Vocal Airs Never hitherto published. To which are added a few of the most lively Country Dances or Reels of the North Highlands & Western Isles. And some Specimens of Bagpipe Music.* Edinburgh, 1784.

MacDonald, R.bC. *Sketches of Highlanders.* Saint John, NB: N.p.,1843.

MacDonnell, Margaret. *The Emigrant Experience: Songs of the Highland Emigrants in North America.* Toronto: University of Toronto Press, 1982.

MacDougall, Hector, ed. *The Songster of the Hills and Glens.* Glasgow: Alexander MacLaren & Sons, 1939. Reprint, North Sydney, NS: Northside Printers Ltd., 2004.

MacDougall, J. L. *History of Inverness County.* Belleville, ON: Mika Publishing, Canadiana Reprint Series, no. 43, 1922, 1976.

MacFarlane, D. and R.A. MacLean, eds. *Drummer on Foot.* N.p. N.d.

MacGillivray, Allister. *The Cape Breton Fiddler.* Sydney: College of Cape Breton Press, 1981.

————. *Cape Breton Ceilidh*. Sydney: Sea-cape Music Ltd., 1988.

MacGillivray, Don, and Brian Tennyson, eds. *Cape Breton Historical Essays*. Sydney: College of Cape Breton Press, 1980.

MacGillivary, Rev. Ronald (Sagairt Arasaig). "History of the County of Antigonish, Nova Scotia." Published serially in Casket, 1890-92. Reprint, *History of Antigonish*, edited by R. A. MacLean. Antigonish, NS: Casket printing and Publishing Company, 1976.

MacInnes, Sheldon. "Cape Breton Dance-An Irish or Scottish Tradition?" http://www.siliconglen.com/celtfaq/3_2.html.

MacIntyre, Duncan Ban. " Ode to Gaelic and the Great Pipe in the year 1783." In *Orain Dhonnchaidh Bhain - The Songs of Duncan Ban MacIntyre*, edited and translated by Angus MacLeod, 285-95. Edinburgh: Scottish Gaelic Texts Society (vol. 4), 1952.

MacKay, Angus. *A Collection of Ancient Piobaireachd or Highland Pipe Music, many of the pieces being adapted to the piano forte with full instructions for those desirous of qualifying themselves in performing on the National Instrument. To which are prefixed some sketches of the principal HEREDITARY PIPERS and their ESTABLISHMENTS with historical & traditional notes respecting the origin of the various pieces. Dedicated by permission to the Highland Society of London.* Includes n.d. "A Circumstantial Account of the Competitions for the Prizes given by the Highland Society in London, to the best Performers on the Great Highland Bagpipe, from the year 1781," 15-20; N.d. "Account of the Hereditary Pipers," 7-14; and N.d. "Historical and Traditional Notes on Piobaireachds," 1-14. Wakefield, UK: EP Publishing, 1972.

————. *The Piper's Assistant*. Edinburgh: Alexander Glen, 1843.

MacKay, Donald. *Scotland Farewell: The People of the Hector*. Toronto and Edinburgh: McGraw-Hill Ryerson/ Paul Harris Publishing, 1980.

Mackay, William. *The Complete Tutor for the Great Highland Bagpipe*. Edinburgh: Alexander Glen, 1840.

MacKenzie, Alexander. "The Editor in Canada." *Celtic Magazine* 5, no. 49 (November 1879), 79, 110.

MacKenzie, Archibald A. *The MacKenzies' History of Christmas Island Parish*. Sudbury: Mackenzie Roth Publishing, 1984.

MacKenzie, Bridget. *Piping Traditions of the North of Scotland*. Edinburgh: John Donald Publishers Ltd., 1998.

————. *Piping Traditions of Argyll*. Glasgow: The College of Piping, 2004.

MacKenzie, Osgood. *One Hundred Years in the Highlands*. Reprint, London: Butler and Tanner, 1960.

MacKinnon, P. M. Stephen. "The Bagpipe in Canada." *Canadian Geographical Journal* (April 1932), vol. 4, no. 4: 232-41.

MacLaren, George. *The Pictou Book*. New Glasgow: The Hector Publishing Company, 1954.

MacLauchlan, Rev. Thomas. *A History of the Scottish Highlands, Highland Clans and Highland Regiments*. 2 vols. Edinburgh: A. Fullerton & Co., 1875. Ed. John S. Keltie.

MacLean, Fitzroy. *Highlanders*. Reprint, London: Penguin, 1997.

MacLean, John. "Am Piobaire Dall." *Transactions of the Gaelic Society of Inverness 41* (1951-52): 283-306.

MacLean, R. A., ed. *A History of Antigonish*, vol. 2. Antigonish, NS: Casket Printing and Publishing, 1976.MacLellan, Vincent. *Failte Cheap Breatainn (Cape Breton Salute)*. N.p.: n.p., 1891.

MacLeod, Calum Iain Norman, ed. *Bardachd A Albainn Nuaidh*. Glaschu: Gairm, 1970. Reprinted as *Stories from Nova Scotia*. Antigonish, NS: Formac Limited, 1974.

MacMillan, Rev. Allan J. *To the Hill of Boisdale, A Short History and a Genealogical Tracing of the Pioneer Families of Boisdale, Cape Breton, and the Surrounding Areas*. Sydney, NS: City Printers, 1986.

————. *A West Wind to East Bay*. Antigonish: The Casket Printing and Publishing Co., 2001.

MacNeil, Neil. *The Highland Heart in Nova Scotia*. Reprint, Toronto: Saunders, 1969.

MacNeil, Stephen R. *All Call Iona Home*. Antigonish, NS: Formac Publishing, 1979.

MacNeill, Seumas. *Piobaireachd*. Glasgow: College of Piping, 1968.

MacNutt, W. S. *The Atlantic Provinces*. Toronto: McClelland and Stewart Ltd., 1968.

MacQuarrie, Gordon F., compiler and arranger. *The Cape Breton Collection of Scottish Melodies for the Violin Consisting of Marches, Slow Airs, Strathspey, Reels, Jigs, Hornpipes, Etc.*

Mostly Original, and Containing 152 Selections, edited by J. Beaton. Medford, MA: J. Beaton, 1975. First printed in 1940.

MacQuarrie, John R. *Lansdowne Sketches: Battery Hill, Wilkins Grant, Upper New Lairg*, 2nd ed. Pugwash, NS: Privately published, 1975.

Malcolm, C. A. *The Piper in Peace and War*. London: Harwick Press, 1975. First published 1927 by John Murray.

Manson, W. L. *The Highland Bagpipe: Its History, Literature and Music*. Paisley, UK: A. Gardner, 1901.

Martell, J. S. "Early Coal Mining in Nova Scotia." In *Cape Breton Historical Essays*, edited by Don MacGillivray and Brian Tennyson, 41-53. Sydney, NS: College of Cape Breton Press, 1980.

McGregor James Collection. National Archives of Scotland. GD 50/225/5/27.

McKay, Ian. "Tartanism Triumphant: The Construction of Scottishness in Nova Scotia, 1933-1954." *Acadiensis* 22, no. 2 (1993): 105-38.

———. *The Quest of the Folk: Anti-modernism and Cultural Selection in Twentieth Century Nova Scotia*. Montreal: McGill-Queen's University Press, 1994.

McLachlan, John, ed. *The Piper's Assistant: A new Collection of Marches, Quick-Steps, Strathspeys, Reels and Jigs*. Edinburgh, May, 1854.

Menzies, D. P. "The Bannockburn Bagpipes of Menzies." Proceedings of the Society of Antiquaries Scotland, vol. 29 (1894-95): 231-34.

Meyer, Duane. *The Highland Scots of North Carolina, 1732-1776*. Chapel Hill, NC: University of North Carolina Press, 1957. Reprint, 1987.

Morgan, R. J., ed. *More Essays in Cape Breton History*. Windsor, NS: Lancelot Press, 1977.

Morrison, Alex, and Ted Slaney. *The Breed of the Manly Men: The History of Cape Breton Highlanders*. Sydney, NS: N.p., 1994.

Morrison, L. A. *History of the Morison or Morrison Family*. Np.p., 1890.

Morrison, Neil Rankin. "Clann Duiligh: Pipers to the Clan MacLean." *Transactions of the Gaelic Society of Inverness, Vol. 37, 1934-36*, 59-78.

Moss, George. "*An Da Phiobair*" ("The Two Pipers"). Translated by George Moss. *Tocher, 26*, (Autumn 1977): 114-19.

Muise, Del. "The Making of an Industrial Community, Cape Breton Coal Towns, 1867-1900. In *Cape Breton Historical Essays*, edited by Don MacGillivray and Brian Tennyson, 76-94. Sydney, NS: College of Cape Breton Press, 1980.

Murray, Logan, G. *Scottish Highlanders and the American Revolution*. Halifax, NS: McCurdy Printing Cp., 1976.

Necker, L. A. *Voyage to the Hebrides, or Western Isles of Scotland*. London: Sir Richard Phillips, 1822.

Orme, Dr. Barry Maclachlan. *The Piobaireachd of Simon Fraser With Canntaireachd*, 2nd ed. Victoria, Australia.: Privately published, 1985.

O'Shea, William A. *The Louisburg Brass Bands*. Louisburg,NS: Louisbourg Historical Society, 1991.

Patterson, Rev. George. *A History of the County of Pictou, Nova Scotia. Montreal, 1877*. Reprint, Toronto: James Campbell and Son, 1977.

Patterson, George Geddie. *The History of Victoria County (Nova Scotia)*. N.p., 1885.

Pennant, Thomas. *A Tour of Scotland and Voyage to the Hebrides, 1772*. Chester, UK, 1774.

Pìobaireachd Society. *Pìobaireachd*. Books 1-13. Glasgow: Aird and Coghill. Book 2, 1963; book 9, n.d.; Bell, Aird and Coghill, books 1, 3-8, 1968, book 11, n.d.; London: Lowe and Bryden Printers, book 10, 12, n.d.; West Central Printing Co., book 13, 1970.

Prebble, John. *The Highland Clearances*, Markham, ON: Penguin, 1969. Reprint, 1974.

Rankin, Reginald, ed. *Mabou Pioneer II*. Port Hawkesbury, NS: N.p., 1977.

Rhodes, Frank. "Dancing in Cape Breton Island Nova Scotia." Appendix In J.F. Fletts and T.M. Flett. *Traditional Dancing in Scotland*. London: Routledge and Kegan Paul, 1964.

Reid, John G. *Acadia, Maine and New Scotland*. Toronto: University of Toronto Press, 1981.

———. *Sir William Alexander and North American Colonization*. Edinburgh: University of Edinburgh, 1990.

Reid, W. Stanford. *The Scottish Tradition in Canada*. Toronto: McClelland and Stewart, 1977.

Robertson, Marion. *The King's Bounty: A History of Early Shelburne, Nova Scotia.* Halifax, NS: Nova Scotia Museum, 1983.

Rogers, Pat, editor. *Johnson and Boswell in Scotland.* New Haven and London :Yale University Press, 1993.

Ross, Rev. D. K. *The Pioneers and Churches.* New Glasgow: Hector Publishing Co., 1956.

Ross, Donald. "A Sutherland Highlander's Welcome to the Governor General of Canada." *Celtic Magazine* 5, no. 49 (November 1879): 39-40.

Ross, William. *Ross's Collection of Pipe Music.* West Yorkshire, England: EP Publishing, 1976.

Scobie, I. H. MacKay. "Highland Military Dress: A Short Historical Review." *Transactions of the Gaelic Society of Inverness 30* (1921): 223-39.

———. *An Old Highland Fencible Corps.* Edinburgh and London: Blackwood and Sons, 1914.

———. *Pipers and Pipe Music in a Highland Regiment - A record of Piping in the 1st Seaforth Highlanders, originally the Earl of Seaforth's or 78th (Highland) regiment, afterwards the 72nd or Duke of Albany's Own Highlanders.* Dingwall: Ross-shire Printing and Publishing Company, 1924.

Scots Guards Standard Settings of Pipe Music. London: Paterson's Publications, 1954.

Shaw, John. *Tales Until Dawn.* Montreal: McGill-Queen's University press, 1987.

———. *Brigh an Orain.* Montreal: McGill-Queen's University Press, 2000.

Shaw, Margaret Fay. *Folksongs and Folklore of South Uist.* London: Routledge and Kegan Paul, 1955.

Shears, Barry. *The Gathering of the Clans Collection,* Vol. 1. Halifax, NS: Privately published. Bounty Press, 1991.

———. *The Gathering of the Clans Collection,* Vol. 2. Halifax, NS: Privately published. Bounty Press, 2001.

———. *The Cape Breton Collection of Bagpipe Music.* Halifax, NS; Privately published, 1995.

———. "Two Extraordinary Piping families in Cape Breton: The MacIntyres and Jamiesons." *Mac-Talla,* Spring, 2003, 26-27.

———. "The Fate of Clanranald Piper Robert MacIntyre." *Piping Today,* 11 (2004): 36-38.

Silver Jubilee Booklet. Sydney, NS: n.p., 1964.

Spedan, A. H. *Rambles Among the Bluenoses.* Montreal: John Lovell, 1863.

Stanley, Laurie. *The Well-Watered Garden: The Presbyterian Church in Cape Breton 1798-1860.* Sydney, NS: University College of Cape Breton Press, 1983.

Sutherland, G. R. *The Rise and Decline of the Earltown Community, 1813-1970.* Truro: Colchester Historical Society, 1980.

Thomason, Charles S. *Ceòl Mór: written in a new and abbreviated system of musical notation for the piobaireachd as played on the Highland bagpipe.* Part III. Glasgow: John MacKay, 1897.

Walker, Carl Ian. *Pioneer Pipers of British Columbia: Biographical Directory of Pipers Active in BC by the 1950s.* Squamish, BC: Western Academy of Pipe Music, 1987.

Walsh, Lillan Crew. 2006. *Cape Breton's Lillian Crew Walsh: A Treasury of Ballads and Poems.* Sydney, NS: Breton Books.

Young, Reverend Walter Erskine. "Preface." In Patrick MacDonald, *A Collection of the Highland Vocal Airs,* 1-22. Edinburgh: n.p., 1784.

Webster's New Illustrated Dictionary. New York: Pamco Publishing Company Inc.,1992.

Baleshare, Scotland, 64, 77

Balmoral Girls Pipe Band (Stellarton), 171, 199n22

Barclay, Adam (ca.1740), 88

Barisdale, Scotland, 135

Barr, Billie, 122 fig.42

Barra (Barray), Isle of, Scotland, 17, 27, 47, 51, 56, 65, 75, 80, 97, 135-37

Battle of Corunna (1809), 139, 141, 142

Battle of Culloden (1746), 26, 35, 36, 66, 68, 128, 129

Battle of Lens (1648), 155

Battle of Loos (1915), 152

Battle of Louisbourg (1758), 134, 136-37

Battle of Paschendaele (1917), 154

Battle of Pinkie (1549), 186n8

Battle of Sheriffmuir (1715), 77

Battle of Waterloo (1815), 62, 91, 128, 140, 141

Bay St. George, NL, 105

Bay St. Lawrence, NS, 80, 166

Bayview, NS, 92

Beaton, Angus Campbell, 78 fig.18

Beaton, Archie A. "Professor" (ca.1840-ca.1923), 73, 107, 109

Beaton, David Walter (1855-1922), 106-07, 108, 121

Beaton, Mary MacDonald (1795-1880), 76

Beaton, Norman (d.1891), 106

Ben Eoin, NS, 104, 155

Benbecula, Isle of, Scotland, 51, 60, 70, 72, 100

Black Watch, 10, 35, 44, 127, 139-43, 150, 152, 173

Blue Feather Society, 151

Blues Mills, NS, 111

Boer War, 156, 157

Boisdale, NS, 4, 102, 103

Boisdale, Scotland, 46, 102, 117, 135

Bonnie Prince Charlie. *See* Stewart, Charles Edward

Boreraig, Scotland, 25, 34, 56, 78

Boston, MA, 97, 112, 126, 148

Boston States, 54, 165, 199n20

Bowes, Alexander "Sandy," 120, 122, 132, 197n38

Boyd, Sandy, 109, 168-69, 177 fig.73, 198n17, n18

Brand, W., 149

Bras d'Or Lake, NS, 51, 115, 136-37, 156

brass bands, 116, 151, 154, 156. *See also under individual names*

Breed of the Manly Men, 150, 197n39

British Square, 127

Broad Cove, NS, 85, 101, 102

Broughton, NS, 151

Brudenell River, PEI, 67

Calder, Fred (b.1868), 59

Caledonia Club: of New Glasgow, 171-72; of PEI, 107, 171, 187n46; of Glace Bay, 172

Caledonian Society of Cape Breton, 171

Calliope, HMS, 127

Cameron, Donald, 128

Cameron, John "Old," 112

Cameron, William D., 114

Cameron Highlanders, 112

Campbell, Angus, 70, 100

Campbell, Archie "Giad," 83

Campbell, Charles (1819-1906), 145

Campbell, D., 181

Campbell, George I., 59

Campbell, Hector, 82 fig.22

Campbell, John, 140

Campbell, John Lorne, 70: *Songs Remembered in Exile*, 58

Canadian Women's Army Corps pipe band, 170

Canna, Isle of, Scotland, 76, 119

Cannon, Roderick: *The Bagpipe and its Music*, 14; *The Literature of the Bagpipe*, 28

Canso Causeway, NS, 21, 166, 176

Cant, Allan, 162

Cant, Jim, 162

Cantly, Thomas, 151

Cape Breton County, NS, 10, 19, 43, 51, 54, 72, 80, 91, 92, 93, 97, 99, 100, 101, 104, 115, 117, 135, 155, 176, 179

Cape Breton Fiddlers Association, 183

Cape Breton step-dancing, 173; origins of, 76-77. *See also* dancing styles: step-dancing

Carson, John "Jock," 111, 149

Catalone , NS, 52, 142

Catholic Ladies Patriotic Front, 151

Centredale, NS, 97

Ceilidh Girls Pipe Band (New Glasgow), 171, 199n22

Celtic Society of Scotland, The, 39

ceòl beag, 28-30, 78

ceòl meadhonach, 28-29

MacDonald, Donald (Captain), 196n4

MacDonald, Elizabeth, 101

MacDonald, Gordon, 161

MacDonald, Hector, 135

MacDonald, Hugh, 160

MacDoanld, Jack "Black," 160, 161 fig.68

MacDonald, James, 77

MacDonald, Jim, 83, 84-85

MacDonald, John, 46

MacDonald, John (d.1792), 27, 62, 64-65, 77, 117, 186n12

MacDonald, John (soldier), 164

MacDonald, John "Wild," 140

MacDonald, Joseph, 77

MacDonald, Keith N., 71

MacDonald, Margaritta, 65

MacDonald, Patrick, 27, 77

MacDonald, Robertson. See Robertson, David

MacDonald, Ronald, 79, 160

MacDonald of Centredale, John, 97

MacDonald of Egerton, John, 92

MacDonald of Glace Bay, John, 172

MacDonald of Inverness, John, 179

MacDonald of Pictou County, John, 193n5

MacDonald of the Strand, 62

MacDonnell, Alexander "Mor," 95

MacDonnell, Jim, 108

MacDonnell, Neil, 108-09

MacDonnell, Sandy, 21 fig. 6, 96 fig29, 109

MacDougall, Allan, 88

MacDougall, Angus Ban, 76; bagpipes of, 24 fig.8

MacDougall, Dan Rory (1885-1957), 80-81, 80 fig.19

MacDougall, Donald (ca.b1802), 80

MacDougall, Gabriel (1925-1986), 81

MacDougall, Mike (1928-1981), 81, 111, 170

MacDougall, Rory, 131

MacDougall, Rory (Roderick, 1848-1936), 80

MacDougall Girls Pipe Band, 170

MacEachern, Fred, 95

MacFarlane, Allan "Little," 78 fig.18, 84

MacFarlane, Angus "Ban," 120

MacGillivray, Alexander, 62

MacGillivray, Steve, 152, 155

MacGillivray, John (1774-1862), 27, 56, 60-62, 67, 70MacGregor, Alexander, 137

MacIain, Margaret, 62

MacInnis, Dan S., 147

MacInnis, Donald, 145

MacInnis, John, 83

MacInnis, Ron, 183

MacInnis, Steve, 147

MacIntosh, Robbie, 126

MacIntyre, Andrew, 66

MacIntyre, Angus, 195n56

MacIntyre, Archie, 118, 121 fig.40

MacIntyre, Ben, 159

MacIntyre, Charlie, 66

MacIntyre, Dan, 118, 121 fig.40, 176

MacIntyre, Davie Jr., 66

MacIntyre, David, 65

MacIntyre, Donald, 117

MacIntyre, Duncan, 159, 159 fig.67, 163, 198n13

MacIntyre, Duncan (b.1691), 195n54

MacIntyre, Duncan "Ban," 199n26

MacIntyre, Hugh, 66

MacIntyre, Jean, 66

MacIntyre, James "Big Jim" (b.1833), 118, 118 fig.36

MacIntyre, Joe, 118, 121 fig.40

MacIntyre, Joe Hughie, 71, 105, 176, 191n11

MacIntyre, Joe "Long," 121 fig.40

MacIntyre, John, 66

MacIntyre, John, 65

MacIntyre, Katherine, 118 fig.37

MacIntyre, Maggie, 66

MacIntyre, Mickey, 118, 121 fig.40

MacIntyre, Peter, 121 fig.40, 176

MacIntyre, Robert (1769-1833), 62, 64-65, 117

MacIntyre of Clanranald, Duncan, 27

MacIntyre of Perthshire: family tree, 66, 195n54

MacIntyre Pipe Band, 116-18, 120-21, 121 fig.40, 147, 195n52

MacIssac, Alex John, 82 fig.22

MacIsaac, Angus, 190n3

MacIsaac, Dan, 105

MacIsaac, Dougald "Red," 105

MacIssac, John R., 155, 155 fig.61

MacIsaac, Rory "Shim," 104, 155, 155 fig.62

MacKay (Lord), 91

MacKay, Alexander, 137

MacKay, Angus (b.1725), 28, 38, 55, 56-57, 58, 59, 60, 62, 71

MacKay, Donald Doughal, 56

MacKay, George, 91

MacKay, Ian, 167

MacKay, Isabel, 91

MacKay, John, 142

Second World War, 21, 102, 113, 121, 157-63, 176

Seven Years War, 21, 36, 44, 88, 137

Shaw, John, 70, 101, 102

Shelburne County, NS, 26, 44

Shears, Maggie (MacLean), 185n17

Ships Passenger Act (1803), 48, 49

Sinclair, Archibald, 62

Sinclair, Clarence, 122 fig.42

Sinclair, Robert Bligh, 143

Sir Sidney Smith (vessel), 57, 60

Skye, Isle of, Scotland, 25, 26, 34, 47, 51, 56, 95, 145, 173

Small, John, 137

Sobieski, Charles Edward and John, 39

Soldiers Cove, NS, 160

South Uist, Scotland, 47, 51, 65, 70, 72, 83, 100, 102, 115, 117, 134, 179

South West Margaree, NS, 94

Southerland, Alexander, 130

spinning wheel, 92 fig.26

St. Ann's, NS, 15, 22, 44, 46, 171, 172, 176

Statutes of Iona, 34-35. *See also* Gaelic language: loss of

Stellarton, NS, 16, 53, 171

Stephen Wright (vessel), 49

Stevenson, Robert Louis, 127

Stewart, Charles Edward, 35, 36

Stewart, Donald, 92, 193n5

Stillwater, NS, 97

Stone, Ross, 170

Strathglas, Scotland, 27, 50, 52, 188n4

Sutherland, Alex, 131 fig.49

Sutherland, Bill, 176

Sutherland, George, 160, 161 fig.68

Sutherlandshire, Scotland, 27, 50

Sydney, NS, 16-17, 47, 52, 53, 54, 112, 119, 148, 167, 172, 176

Sydney Mines, NS, 53, 102

tacksman. *See* Highland Scots: and clan system

Tarelton's British Legion, 26

tartanism, 166

tartans, 38-39, 40, 167; 187n45; and Black Watch, 140, 150. *See also* tourist industry

Taylor, George Douglas, 152, 152 fig.58

Teachdaire Nan Gaidheal, 115

Telfer, Walter, 149

Temeraire, HMS, 126

Thompson, W.S., 151

Thompson, Annie, 125 fig.45

Thompson, Robert, 123, 124

Tiree Isle of, Scotland, 51, 70

tourist industry, 15, 17, 22, 36-39, 165-68. *See also* Gaelic College; Highland games: and tourism; tartans

traditional piper: defined as, 16. *See also* pipers: functions of

Truro, NS, 130, 148; Girls Pipe Band, 170

Universe (vessel), 49

Upper Margaree, NS, 93

Vallay Island, Scotland, 52

Vancouver Ladies Pipe Band, 170

Vancouver Pipers Society Pipe Band, 124

Victoria County, NS, 43, 47, 88, 95, 179

Victoria, Queen of Great Britain, 28, 39, 61, 127

Vimy Ridge, 149, 153

violin, 77-78

Volunteer Battalion of the Highland Light Infantry, 123

Walpole, Robert, Earl of Oxford, 35

Walsh, Merriam Crewe, 156

Washabuck, NS, 51, 88, 137

West Bay, NS, 59, 92, 111, 112

West Nova Scotia Regiment, 157, 168; and Pipe Band, 158 fig.65

Westville, NS, 53, 60, 108

Whyte, John, 49

Wilson, William "Tug," 156

York and Lancaster Regimental Museum, 137

CPSIA information can be obtained at www.ICGtesting.com
Printed in the USA
BVOW04s0311070115

382208BV00001B/126/P